*To
the memory
of
my mother
and
to my students
past
and present*

ISBN 0-8294-0504-6
Printed in the United States of America
Loyola Press
3441 North Ashland Avenue
Chicago, Illinois 60657

Library of Congress Cataloging in Publication Data
Reichmann, James B., 1923-
    Philosophy of the human person.

    Bibliography: p. 303
    Includes index.
    1. Philosophical anthropology. 2. Persons. 3. Ex-
    perience. 4. Knowledge, Theory of. 5. Life. I.
    Title.
BD450.R367   1985   128   85-139
ISBN 0-8294-0504-6

02 03 04 05 M-V   15 14 13 12 11 10 9

Philosophy of the Human Person

James B. Reichmann, S.J.

 Loyola Press
Chicago

Contents

ix   Contents

Preface

This text is the result of many years of teaching a course on the philosophy of the human person. It seeks to provide the undergraduate student of philosophy with a fairly comprehensive, albeit introductory, discussion of the entire field of human experience with the single aim of uncovering the meaning of being a human person. The order and development of the topics treated grew out of the everyday classroom encounter where this or that fact of the human experience spontaneously surfaced as a meaningful subject for philosophic discussion and reflection. Thus it is literally true that the comments and questions of students have played an active and formative role in shaping the development and the organization of the text.

It has not been the intent of the author that the present book be used as an introduction to philosophy itself; its primal focus is, as the title makes clear, the human person. Accordingly there is a presumption that the reader has some acquaintance with the nature of logic and philosophic inquiry and with the early developments of Greek philosophy. Though written primarily with the college student in mind, it should prove of interest to any graduate with an inclination to further pursue his or her quest for an understanding of the human person.

The reader's attention is drawn to several features of this text which, I believe, are unique to an introductory work of this kind. For instance, the second chapter contains a detailed discussion of the fundamental phenomenon of human questioning; the third chapter contains a brief historical overview of human knowing from Plato to the contemporary era; the fifth chapter contrasts mere imagining with remembering and explores the creative, fictionalizing dimension of the former; chapter eight, in discussing the phenomenon of language, lays special emphasis on the plurality of language and the philosophic significance of written language; chapter eleven treats of habits, viewing them as acquired operational structures and correlating them with learning, the arts, and the technological world of the human; chapter twelve addresses the question of personhood and personality and contains a reflective description of intersubjective communication; it also inquires into the grounding of the social dimension of human behavior; the concluding chapter discusses the difficult problem of human origin, specifically addressing the classical evolutionary theory of Darwin and its related contemporary adaptations. Finally, a conscious attempt has been made throughout to situate each topic within the context of our contemporary world and to use language familiar to the non-professional philosopher.

For the student's convenience a brief summary of each of the chapters is provided together with a listing of the more significant conclusions reached within each of the chapters. In addition, study-aid questions for each chapter are provided in an appendix.

I wish to express my gratitude to my colleagues and to my students who over the years, consciously or unconsciously, contributed in some positive way to the text in its final form by their questions, comments, and suggestions. In particular my thanks are due Father Henry H. Kohls, S.J. who has utilized this text in its preliminary form in the classroom and who was thus able to point out many of its deficiencies both from a philosophical and pedigogical standpoint and to suggest numerous improvements, many of which have been implemented. I am also much in the debt of Father Leo B. Kaufmann, S.J. who has long been supportive of this project with his interest and incisive, constructive criticisms. I am also much indebted to my chairman, Fr. J. Patrick Burke, for his continued encouragement and support in this undertaking. None of the above can be held accountable for the defects which still remain, but the text is certainly less defective than it would have been without their interest and assistance. Lastly, I must express my special thanks and acknowledge my indebtedness to my editor, Jeanette Ertel of Loyola University Press who, through her probing questions, helpful suggestions, and deftness at disassembling and then reconstituting defective sentences, has contributed so much to improving both the quality and the readability of this book.

I also acknowledge my indebtedness to my former teachers and particularly to my students over the years who in ways they would certainly never suspect, have contributed to this undertaking. It is my earnest wish that this book may assist those who read it to come to an ever fuller appreciation of the wonder of being human.

Seattle University   J. B. R.

1 Introduction

Philosophy is essentially a disinterested activity, directed toward truth loved for its own sake, not utilitarian activity for the sake of power over things.

Jacques Maritain

The Nature of Philosophic Inquiry

Philosophy is a love of wisdom. That is what the word itself means. Hence, the philosopher is one who seeks wisdom, which is knowledge of the underlying first causes of things. By its nature, philosophic knowledge is general rather than specific. Rather than searching out a detailed understanding of the various things that make up our world of experience, the philosopher focuses on the basic questions arising out of human experience by seeking its underlying first causes. Philosophical knowledge is by nature encompassing and integrative because it extends to the outermost reaches of human awareness and seeks to connect and interrelate all aspects of the human experience. The philosopher's quest for underlying causes is likewise a quest for the unity and inner meaning of the ultimate nature of the whole range of human experience.

Understandably, then, the philosophic enterprise tends by its very essence to be somewhat intangible; hence, it is comparatively elusive. This helps to explain the critical eye with which it is often viewed by those whose primary vision and interest look to the pragmatic and to the immediately given. For such people, philosophy signifies little more than a superficial, even fanciful, reflection on the world, rather than a serious inquiry into the ultimate nature and underlying causes of existing things.

There are others for whom philosophy is hardly distinguishable from a religious attitude that is thought to depend primarily, if not exclusively, on cultural conditioning and personal preference. According to these people, philosophy is pretty much a matter of personal taste. One philosophy, they would be likely to assume, is as good as another. At best, they would admit only that any philosophy serves to provide some sort of mental pastime; that "philosophizing" may provide a kind of whetstone by which the mind is "sharpened," but beyond this admittedly useful function, which it shares with jigsaw and crossword puzzles, it has little else to recommend it.

It may be granted that a sizeable portion of what has gone under the guise of philosophy has been unworthy of the name. In plain truth, not all philosophizing has reflected a genuine pursuit of wisdom, and to this extent it presents itself as a fitting target for caricature and ridicule. Yet, at the same time, a fair-minded person can hardly deny that the pursuit of wisdom is a laudable endeavor. Moreover, whatever the name given to the enterprise throughout recorded history, human thought reveals most convincingly that the human being desires to uncover not only the underlying causes of *things* but the origins of human nature as well. Indeed there seems to be something of a compulsive obsession about this inquiry into the nature of the human person.

For reasons that we will explore, people have learned that as a subject of inquiry they are as elusive and frustratingly complex as they are fascinating. Seemingly, the more they learn about themselves, the more eager they become to learn even more. Every fresh glimpse into the depths of their nature reveals to them that ever greater depths remain to be explored.

The Nature and Scope of This Study

During our investigation of the underlying nature and structure of the human, our principal focus will be on activities that set the human apart from other animals and organisms. Although our investigation includes many levels of the human experience, it should not be confounded with other wholly legitimate and praiseworthy studies of the human that are conducted by biologists, psychologists, sociologists, and other scientists. These studies are limited to investigations of human activities that are observable and testable. They rely, for example, on random samplings, questionnaires, and polls to assemble data from which general, merely statistically probable conclusions can be drawn.

The philosopher, however, employing a different methodology, makes use of the principles of human understanding and *being* itself as the chief tools for carrying out the investigation of human phenomena, thereby seeking their ultimate ground and cause. It is for this reason that the quality of the questions the philosopher will raise differs markedly from the questions raised by the social or life scientists. It is precisely the hidden inner dimension of the human, which cannot be either observed or measured according to the restricted scientific norms, that the philosopher seeks to bring to light.

This, then, explains why it is that the philosophic inquiry focuses on human activities that clearly set the human apart from other animals and organisms, and includes an entire repertoire of questions systematically excluded from the authentic circle of questions raised, for example, by the psychologist or sociologist, since they exceed the limits of detection by the ordinary scientific standard. Among these philosophic questions are those that are concerned with the act of *knowing,* which involves more than the realm of sensory perception; with the act of choosing, which transcends the spontaneity of mere organic stimulus-response; and with the phenomenon of human language, which can convey thought visually or verbally. Such questions and such a focus aim at uncovering a metaphysic of the human.

The principal questions we will be raising during the course of our investigation, therefore, are the most basic questions that we raise about ourselves and our nature; for example, What does it mean to be human? What is the nature of human knowledge and language? What is the nature and what are the corollaries of human freedom? What constitutes a person? How does personality differ from personhood? What are the nature and significance of our emotional life? What is learning and how do we come to learn? What is life, and particularly, what is it that differentiates human life from other forms of living things? What is the origin of human life? What is death and what is its significance to us as individuals?

Historically, these questions are found among the most basic questions that humans have perennially posed for themselves. They emerge from the very nature of our being. While for a time these questions may lie dormant within the human psyche because of immediate concerns, they cannot be permanently suppressed, much less wholly eradicated. They ever lie hidden in the depths of human conciousness waiting for the moment when they might surface.

It should be noted that these and other fundamental questions are raised by the philosopher, not to sow seeds of confusion nor to cause disquiet, but rather to provide people with a fuller understanding of the meaning of human life and thereby to provide them with a better understanding of themselves. It is in this sense, then, that a philosophic inquiry into the nature of the human person is inescapably autobiographical. This should not be surprising, for what ultimately is the value of learning about anything unless it somehow reveals to us more about ourselves? In the last analysis we experience within ourselves the desire to learn more because we wish to come to a fuller understanding of who we truly are and all that the mode of human existence implicitly entails.

This is not to claim that philosophy will provide us with a knowledge of all that we want to know. The claim *is* made, however, that philosophic investigation can provide us with a deeper and broader understanding of who we are, and it can assist us to learn how to learn.

In the course of this study we will not consciously eliminate any of the major facets of human experience. It should be evident, however, that many of these facets can only be touched upon lightly. At the same time it is not our intent to make a mere compilation of the many forms of human experience, but rather to seek from them an underlying unity and meaning. Thus the field of our inquiry is the total complexus of human experience itself; and we will be viewing this complexus from the perspective of its unique situation within the world of existing things.

Consequently, our study will introduce us to a wide variety of seemingly unrelated activities that constitute the human's dynamic world. This must include, of course, the world of sensory activity as well as the worlds of memory and imagination, of understanding, and of willing. Included also is the entire field of human communication: of language and of interpersonal relationships, the phenomenon of emotional experience, and the acquisition and retention of knowledge, all of which include both bodily and mental skills. The variety and complexity of human activity and achievement is truly bewildering. It is this very variety and complexity that we will strive to exploit, for it is intimately related to the profoundest questions surrounding the nature of the human person.

Philosophy and the College Student

Understandably, many college students approach the study of philosophy with a certain reluctance and with mixed feelings. They may have heard disquieting things about philosophy from their peers as well as from their elders. They have probably been forewarned about "how hard" philosophy is, unless one happens to be "really interested in that sort of thing!" Perhaps, too, they have been informed that philosophy is boring. They are almost certain to have heard from several quarters that it is totally impractical. "What can you do with it?" and "How can it help you earn a living?"

Yet, despite the bad press, philosophers continue at their academic posts. Since the time of Plato's academy, philosophic questions have been raised and discussed in an academic setting. Philosophy still retains its power of allurement over young, inquiring minds. Whatever the reason, there clearly seems something endemic to the human person that gives birth to the philosophic question and to the philosophic search. Most people seem instinctively to recognize the truth of the Socratic saying that "the unexamined life is not worth living." So long as we are wakened to examine our lives, philosophy and philosophers will doubtless continue to be a regular fixture in the academic world. At any rate, there is little evidence that the philosopher is on his way to becoming a dying species. But this does not mean that the philosopher's contemporary role is necessarily well understood, much less appreciated. In large part this may be because the philosopher often has failed to communicate successfully to others what his studies are about. But it is simply untrue that philosophers are a strange breed apart. They are simply ordinary persons who are intently interested in knowing what kind of beings humans are.

Viewing the situation from the philosophers' perspective, however, one might say that their task is not an easy one in a world so caught up in the syndrome of the instant-success formula. Philosophy simply is not the kind of undertaking that easily lends itself to fast assimilation. Often philosophers find that they cannot convey what it means to be a philosopher without first introducing their listeners to the intricate, fine web of philosophic inquiry. One suspects, however, that the philosopher is fortified with an unshakable inner confidence in Aristotle's comment that "by nature all humans desire to know."

The often heard charge that philosophy is impractical cannot go unchallenged. In one sense it is the most practical of all forms of study because it assists us in learning how to learn. If it is true that philosophic questions range over the whole gamut of human living and address themselves to that which is at the core of human experience, they can hardly be considered to be impractical or without value. Indeed, what is the value of practical knowledge, if it does not somehow lead people to a better understanding of themselves and of their world?

By nature, philosophy is practical because it is integrating. It takes the long view of human existence. Consequently, its findings are applicable to everyday living, in that they provide the sustaining threads by which the individual, commonplace patterns of life can be drawn together into a meaningful design. Unless we are able to take in the entire human scene, we simply cannot understand any of the details. If one lacks the integrating principle by which the various strands of human experience can be woven into a meaningful whole, one cannot see the proverbial forest for the trees.

These philosophic questions are uniquely human. They are not raised by other kinds of animals. As humans we want desperately to know who we are, and what it truly means to be human. Why this is so, we will examine and strive to answer after we have first considered several other preliminary questions. This, however, constitutes the primary aim and objective of the inquiry we are about to undertake. A prominent humanist has recently stated that just as one studies to understand internal-combustion engines in order to be able to design or build or repair them, similarly, one undertakes the study of philosophy to be able to understand, design, build, or repair a human life (Delattre 1977). If we have no idea of what is worth making or doing, we are reduced to the absurdity of doing what we do simply because we are able to do it.

The point, then, of this study is to provide us with reasons for doing what we do, and to exploit the inherent capability all of us have for asking and reflecting on the enduring questions. This does not mean that philosophizing is not a personal undertaking. It is a task that each of us must undertake and perform for ourselves. It is a task, too, that entails discipline and the willingness to devote long hours to quiet, reflective study. The pages that follow are intended to provide a modicum of assistance to the student of philosophy who is beginning or continuing his or her solitary search.

Summary

In this introductory chapter we first defined the nature of philosophic inquiry. Reasons for the difficulties inherent to the nature of philosophic inquiry were briefly investigated. The nature and scope of the present study were examined, as well as the manner in which philosophic study differs from non-philosophic studies of the human. The relation of the study of philosophy to the college student was discussed. Finally, the main aim and value of philosophy were treated.

Definitions and Conclusions

1. Philosophy is a love of wisdom.
2. Our present study, as a form of philosophic inquiry, is a quest for the unity and inner meaning of the whole range of human experience.
3. This metaphysical study entails a search for the underlying nature and structure of the human being and for their ultimate causes.
4. Philosophers are not a strange breed apart, but ordinary persons intently interested in knowing what kind of beings they are.
5. Philosophy is by nature practical since it helps provide one with the basic skill of learning how to learn. It investigates the learning process itself. And it is a means by which we may find a way to integrate our experiences.

2 The Human Phenomenon of Questioning

To pursue and admire a thing implies the
acknowledgment of one's inferiority to the thing pursued.

Plotinus

What Is Experience?

Since it is not possible for us to inquire into what has not in some fashion been experienced, our inquiry concerning the human person begins where every inquiry must; namely, with experience.

Primary experience cannot of itself be defined. It is simply that which is given; that of which we become aware. Properly speaking, primary experience is of things. It is awareness of things that exist independent of ourselves. In this sense it is whatever we experience directly as "concrete" things that are subject to the action of our senses. A table, a rose bush in a garden, a bird flitting from one tree to another, are examples of primary experiences. We do not need a prior experience to experience them.

There are, however, experiences we have which are not directly of things, but rather are subsequent awarenesses of primary experiences. This kind of experience is derivative; it is not itself primary. I can only experience this second level of awareness if I have already experienced something at the primary level. For example, I can be aware *of my awareness* of the table at which I am writing; I can be aware *of my awareness* of the rose bush in my garden; I can be aware *of my awareness* of the bird flitting from one tree to another. In these instances it is clear that what I am experiencing is the internal experience itself of sensing and of understanding. Such reflective experience is only made possible by a prior act of primary awareness Yet it is important to note that in referring to the first level of experience as a *prior* act it is not implied that the first act of experiencing must cease before the second begins. One can continue gazing at a rose, while simultaneously being aware of one's fascination with its beauty.

When it is philosophically stated that all inquiry begins with experience, the meaning of experience is understood to encompass both types of awareness described above. Furthermore, no inquiry can begin prior to experience; nor does it call into question the fact of a primary experience. Rather it questions the nature and the hidden assumptions underlying that experience. In this sense, every inquiry can be said to go beyond experience or to transcend it. The point of the inquiry is to probe more deeply into the experience. This is precisely what we mean when we state that all inquiry is a conscious effort to explain and clarify the nature of an experience; to seek out its source, or origin, and to uncover its hidden implications.

As stated in the previous chapter, our present study is an inquiry into the nature and meaning of the totality of human experience. The expression "totality of human experience" includes experiences at both the direct and the indirect, or the primary and derivative, levels.

Fundamental Characteristics of Experience

Human experience is identifiable by three distinct, fundamental characteristics. First, it is highly diversified; second, it is fundamentally social by nature; and third, it is capable of growth and development. Let us briefly consider each of these:

First, our experience is highly diversified. Perhaps no facet of our experience is less arguable than the fact that it is highly diversified.

We see things, we hear and touch them, we taste and smell them. We can "imagine" things; we can experience various emotions; we can understand things; we can laugh, reason, judge, choose, walk about, plan, form friendships; we can interrelate with others at many levels; we can eat, play, talk, listen, write; we can remember what we have experienced; we can sing, paint, draw, build, and construct things, etc. The list is endless, and of course each of our activities has its numerous subdivisions. Finally, when our list is completed, we can add to it the many ways we are able to *experience our experience.*

Second, human experience is fundamentally social by nature. What this characteristic of experience emphasizes is simply the fact that our experience always entails an "other," that is, something beyond ourselves. For example, we never just see or hear or understand, but we see or hear or understand *something*, and so it is with all other acts of experiencing.

The experiencing self is never found to be in a state of total isolation. Rather, a non-self, an "other," is always found to be present somehow in and during the experience. So vital is the role of the other in human experience that we recognize that without it no experience were possible. This is pointed up by the fact that our experience varies constantly, as well as by the fact that we recognize our inability to control totally the content of our experience. We find that our experience is highly restricted by circumstances and by our environment. We cannot *see* unless there is *something* to see, or *hear* unless there is *something* to hear. In short, what we experience is not our own creation; we are not the total source of our own experience. Whenever we experience something we are beholden to the "other." A new experience is for us a new *coming to be.* As explained above, "the other" serves as the formal cause of the act of experiencing. That is, it provides the content of the experience. The other is *that which* is experienced.

Third, we note that human experience is also characterized by an incremental or growth dimension. As diverse as human experience may be, it nonetheless tends toward unity and to a measured development. The various forms of experience fall into discernible patterns, which in turn coalesce into an identifiable manifold. No single experience is found to be totally isolable from all other experiences. This phenomenon, which we can recognize as constituting a key element of human experience, indicates the mutual interrelatedness of all individual experiential acts. They may thus be viewed as promoting and reinforcing one another, and even as emerging from, and depending one upon, another.

Through the growth dimension of experience, it becomes understandable how past actions can be carried over into the present, how the present is extended into the future, and how *explicit* knowledge can be derived from a less perfect or merely *implicit* awareness. It is through focusing on the incremental aspect of our experience that we can best come to recognize its significance and meaning. Experience itself has as its goal the development of the individual person to whom that experience belongs.

The above three characteristics of experience provide us with a meaningful introduction to the study of the phenomenon of questioning.

The Phenomenon of Questioning

Asking questions is undeniably a part of the human condition. All of us have been asking questions since the dawn of our own personal histories. Not only do we ask questions, but we do so continuously and about everything. Indeed, perhaps no facet of our total human experience is more easily recognizable than the fact that we humans are incessant questioners. However, *what* a question is, and *why* precisely we ask questions are not quite so obvious. Because of the question's overriding importance and its obvious centrality to all human experience, we formally begin our investigation of the meaning of being human with an investigation of the true meaning of the question.

We are not here concerned with raising questions that address themselves to a limited sphere of our total experience of questioning. Rather what we now wish to question is the question itself; its nature and its meaning. What is a question? What are we doing when we ask a question? What are the conditions necessary for asking a question? What does the act of questioning in general have to tell us about the nature of being human?

These are questions, all of which question the question, for they investigate the meaning and definition of the question itself. Our questioning of the question will serve as a worthy beginning for our search into the authentic meaning of being human, because to question is a uniquely human phenomenon and, as such, can reveal much to us regarding the meaning of being human.

As remarked earlier, the phenomenon of questioning itself is truly common to the human family. The small child's compulsive instinct to ask *Why?* when experiencing something it does not yet fully comprehend is a clear indication of this. It is of course true that the quality and depth of the questions asked will vary with time and with changes in the level and sophistication of one's experiencing. Yet the fact remains that at any level the phenomenon of questioning itself continues unabated. Indeed, it would appear that with the passing of years, and with the increase in experiencing, we seem to question more. Though the questions may become more internalized with the advancing of years, still the questions tend to increase in both frequency and intensity as the scope of their concern broadens.

The Anatomy of the Question

What is a question? What in fact are we doing when we question? First, we may reiterate what has already been observed, namely, that asking a question is closely, even inseparably, related to the act of experiencing itself. Questions can be seen to be a natural and an inevitable outflow from experience. We observe that we never question unless we have first of all experienced something. The question is always a search into the depths of an experience. In a sense the question is a questioning of the experience. It is not a question directed against the fact of the experience, but directed to the nature, the meaning, and the importance of the experience. It may thus be seen that the question is a search for the causes underlying the experience. What is it that I am experiencing? What is the source of this experience? What is the meaning or value of this experience? This is the nature of the philosophical question.

Philosophical questioning originates in a kind of wonder. Confronted with an experience we do not yet fully understand, we inquire further about it. Our wonder has aroused our curiosity, and we set about striving to ascertain the cause of our wonder. What is it that we do not yet understand?

This can be illustrated simply enough by utilizing the example of water that has been frozen. We might suppose that a youngster has for the very first time in its life experienced the phenomenon of a small pond freezing over. What was formerly a liquid is now a solid; water has become ice. If the freeze was heavy enough, the youngster might even now be able to walk across the pond. Naturally, the youngster may be puzzled by the experience and wonder what has happened.

Similarly, when we ask a question, we simply acknowledge that there is something about our experience that we do not fully understand. Truly, something has occurred, but we are unable to explain what it is that has happened. Our perplexity and our underlying desire, however faint, to penetrate into the meaning of our experience find their own articulated expression in the question. We want to know the "why" of our experience, just as the child wants to know why the water on the surface of the pond has turned into ice.

At this point it is important to note that, when we ask questions concerning our experience, it is not the fact of the experience itself which we are questioning but rather *the meaning* of that experience. We are simply looking for the explanation as to why such and such an experience occurred. How is it to be accounted for? Thus the question can be seen to emerge out of the experience and to extend beyond it. In raising a question, therefore, the questioner clearly acknowledges the incompleteness of his own experience. He is, on the one hand, aware that he is experiencing something, while, on the other, it is also clear to him that there is still something about his experience that eludes him.

The question always reveals to us not only that something is *known* but that something is *unknown* as well. It always points to the possibility of further knowledge, thus indicating that there is more to be known than is already known. It can be noted, therefore, that it is a basic and essential characteristic of the question that it rests upon the possibility of there being more to be known than is known.

Consequently, ignorance plays a key role in the phenomenon of the question. A question always will involve an admission of ignorance on the part of the questioner. It only occurs because of an inner drive within the questioner to dispel ignorance through the acquisition of further knowledge. One questions simply in order to come to know what one does not know.

Since the question is a search for the unknown leading out from the known, it plainly involves a recognition of the fact that there is yet more to be known; therefore, there is a true sense in which the questioner somehow knows what it is that he or she does not know. This is the most profound philosophical aspect of the question. In order to ask a question, we must know that we do not know, but such knowledge plainly entails some knowledge of *what* it is that we do not know. At the same time we cannot have a precise knowledge of what it is that we do not know, for this would clearly involve a contradiction of our knowing and not knowing the same thing at the same time and in the same respect. On the other hand, if we have no idea whatever of what it is that we do not know, we have no way of formulating our question, nor would there be any way in which we could later determine whether or not the question had been answered.

To restate this more concretely, let us return to the example of the frozen pond. In one sense the youngster knows what has happened and in another, does not. The child knows, for example, that where previously the pond contained only water, now there is a very hard substance on the pond's surface. Water has been turned into ice; a liquid has become a solid. This much the youngster knows. But to the extent that he or she does not yet know the reason why this phenomenon occurred, the youngster does not *really know* what has happened. To find out what has happened the child must investigate further by asking questions.

"Answer" is the term used in referring to the knowledge that is sought by the question. Therefore, an answer is the knowledge that, in our act of questioning, we recognize we lack. In this sense, questions and answers are correlative. Every correct or authentic question has an answer, and every answer is a response to a previously asked question. This rules out the possibility of there being a question to which there is no answer. It is important to note, however, that this does not imply that someone actually knows the answer to the question.

Regarding the nature of a question, we are able to conclude that every authentic question involves three conditions, all of which are essential. First, I must know or experience something in a partial way. Second, I must be aware that my knowledge is partial—that there is still more to be known. Third, in at least a general or obscure way I must be aware of what it is that I do not know.

The False Question

At this point it will be helpful to introduce into our discussion the distinction between an authentic, or real, question and a false, or pseudo, one. This distinction follows as a corollary from what has been concluded above, and it is important to be aware of the ambiguity that can result from a failure to recognize the validity of this distinction. Frequently it is assumed that there are questions to which there are no answers or, which really amounts to the same thing, that there are some questions that can have several answers.

We have seen, however, how a question always involves ignorance and a recognition of that ignorance. This condition, therefore, eliminates the possibility of our having an authentic question concerning that aspect of our experience we know to be self-evidently true. Thus we can ask authentic questions that relate to conditions of our existence, but it is not an authentic question to ask whether or not we exist; that is, an authentic question arises out of what we know, but it cannot be an inquiry into what we know precisely to the extent that it is known.

To question what is already known is merely to feign a question, since no ignorance is involved in asking such a question. This kind of question is known as a false, or pseudo, question. Though it is grammatically indistinguishable from an authentic question and in its spoken form always ends with a rising tone, it is a question in appearance only. Often such pseudo questions are referred to as *rhetorical* questions and are employed almost exclusively by speakers and writers to emphasize or call attention to a point they wish to make. In this sense the rhetorical question does fulfill a useful function. The point is, however, that it is not a genuine question and philosophically has no real significance.

Closely related to the false, or rhetorical, question is the inauthentic answer to a question. Perhaps this latter phenomenon finds wider application in everyday discourse and is surely the source of considerable confusion in the minds of many. What is at issue here is the distinction between an authentic and an inauthentic answer to a question.

On the prereflective level it is often thought that any response to a question can be considered as an answer. Based on this misunderstanding of the nature of an answer, it is often concluded that some questions at least have more than one answer, since it is obvious that different people do give different responses to the same question.

Yet, if an answer refers to the knowledge which is consciously sought by a question, then only a response providing that knowledge constitutes the answer to the question. Any other type of response is necessarily a false, or a pseudo, answer. Though superficially it may appear no different from the authentic answer, the pseudo answer is significantly different because it does not provide the knowledge essential to the question. It does not dispel the ignorance out of which the question arises; it does not answer the question.

Note, then, that we must distinguish carefully between an answer to a question and a mere response to a question. Though there may be many *responses* given to a question, only one *answer* can be given. The fact that several people may provide different responses to a question does not indicate that the question can be answered in a variety of ways, nor does the fact that we have many responses mean necessarily that any of the responses is the authentic answer.

For example, should someone ask how much seven times seven is, it is clear that the response must have something to do with numbers. Indeed, the questioner is aware in asking the question that the answer must be a number. Consequently, should we respond to the question by saying, "Mount Rainier," we would not have provided an answer, even though, from a purely grammatical standpoint, it would be considered an answer to the question. In other words, if someone should ask how we answered the question put to us, we would reply that *Seven times seven is Mount Rainier* was the *answer* we gave.

While an answer of sorts was given to the question, it was not *the* answer; it did not provide the knowledge that was being sought. Hence, we may refer to it as a false, or pseudo, answer or, yet again, as a mere response.

When it is claimed, however, that every authentic question has an answer, it is crucial that one understand exactly what this means. It does *not* mean, for example, that someone presently knows what that answer is; nor does an authentic question necessarily entail an answer that is even humanly attainable.

First, to state that every question has an answer is not equivalent to stating that the answer is already known by someone. For example, the question How many fish are there in Lake Washington? is a perfectly good question. It does make sense, for it is a question to which there is an answer. The lake is known to exist. Likewise, fish are known *to be* in the lake. Yet the number of fish in the lake is *not* known. Although there is *an answer* to the question, that answer is not known by anyone. Only because the question can be said to have an answer is it an authentic question.

Second, an authentic question does not necessarily entail an answer that is humanly attainable. We can demonstrate this by returning to our example of the fish. No one actually knows the number of fish in the lake. Furthermore, no way has yet been conceived whereby the number of fish in the lake can be ascertained. Hence, though there is a definite number of fish in the lake, and even though that number is either odd or even, no one either knows or can know what that number is. But, at the same time, the question is an authentic question for which there is an authentic, unknowable answer. Similarly, there is no humanly known way by which we might count the number of grains of sand on any beach or the number of stars in the universe. Yet, at any given time, their number is finite and hence measureable, if only we had the means to measure them. The question, "How many grains of sand are there on the beach?" is an authentic question, and so is the question concerning the number of stars in the universe. Nonetheless, these questions remain humanly unanswerable.

The claim that some questions have several answers or that the answer to a question depends on the viewpoint of each individual is without foundation. We can only be led to commit the fallacy of many answers if we have so failed to grasp the conditions of a question as discussed above that we confound verbal responses with authentic answers. A question seeks knowledge that is limited and restricted. As already stated, one cannot ask a particular question without knowing what it is that is being sought. Consequently, to assume that there are many answers to a single question is either to deny outright that there are questions at all, or to mistakenly conclude that what is, despite the linguistic camouflage, two questions, is really only one.

It may, however, prove helpful to distinguish here between an answer that is complete and one that is partial, or incomplete. There is a legitimate sense in which there truly can be many answers to a question, if each answer is understood to be correct but incomplete; providing some of the knowledge sought by the question but not all. An answer can be thought of as "authentic" to the extent that it satisfies some of the requirements of the question. Such a response, however, would not constitute an authentic answer if it were presented as a total response to the question.

For example, if someone asks, "What am I holding in my hand?" and we reply, "Something red" or "A piece of fruit," we have not really answered the question fully, if what the other person is holding is a red apple. Since the apple happens to be red and is, of course, a piece of fruit, we may construe each reply as a partial answer; but, since neither answer fully satisfies the conditions of the question, neither constitutes an authentic answer in the unqualified sense.

Yet it should be recognized that the position argued above regarding the relationship between questions and answers applies only to those questions which might be described as *factual*. A factual question refers either to a present state of affairs or to a past event. Excluded from the above claims, therefore, are all questions referring to the future, since the truth of such questions depends upon as-yet-unfulfilled conditions. Included, then, within this category of non-factual questions are those that might inquire into the nature of tomorrow's weather or the outcome of an event—for example, a political campaign or an athletic contest. Questions such as these do not have answers in the sense in which we have been speaking, since they refer to a merely imagined or projected state of affairs. One can of course give a response of sorts to such a question, but it can never constitute an authentic answer. In such cases, the response can never transcend opinion or simple conjecture. In responding to them one either is stating what one thinks in all probability will happen or is expressing one's hope or wish as to what will happen. Yet all the while one is clearly aware of the possibility that one's response might prove to be inaccurate, even totally untrue.

It is, then, with regard to questions such as these that there can be many different "responses," since at the time the question is asked there can be no actual answer. Indeed, if we analyze carefully what is actually being asked when a question inquires into the future, it is simply what someone "thinks" or "conjectures" *might* come to pass, not what *will* come to pass. For example, the question "Who will win the game tomorrow?" is not really asking which team will actually win, but more modestly, which team you *think* is going to win. To this extent the question can be answered, for the opinion I now entertain as to who is going to win the game exists in *the present* and so is communicable. But it is only to that extent that the question is authentic, for the future does not yet exist and hence is not subject to exact knowledge. The winner can only be known when the outcome of the game has been determined. Consequently, any true response given to such a question can only provide the interrogator with an opinion. In short, in saying that such and such a team will win, we are not, in Howard Cosell fashion, telling it like it is but as we hope or think it will be. The response must remain as tentative and hypothetical as the future event itself.

It is important, then, to note the difference between questions for which there is no authentic answer and questions for which there is an answer that is not known and is, perhaps, humanly unknowable. Who will win the baseball game tomorrow is an unanswerable question today, since the game has not yet been played and, indeed, may never actually be played. On the other hand, the question, How many fish are in Lake Washington? is a question having an answer at the very moment it is asked, even though the answer is not known and is humanly unknowable. Similarly, the question, Does God exist? is an authentic question with an authentic answer. God either exists or He does not, whether we profess to know the answer (one way or the other) or not. Since God cannot both exist and not exist, only one answer can be true.

Finally, it should be noted that some questions appear to have more than one authentic answer for the simple reason that, though in appearance they are one question, they are, in point of fact, multiple. Often, in order to simplify our mode of expression, we combine two or more questions into a single interrogative sentence. In such instances there are of course *as many answers* as there are questions contained within the *single* question. Thus, for example, a question such as Have you given up smoking? might be in fact a double question. It contains the hidden question, Do you smoke? as well as the question, Have you stopped smoking? If the person who has been asked this question is not in fact a smoker, the question is immediately recognized as being out of place. It is clear that the double or multiple question does not deny our earlier claim that every question has but one answer.

Knowing That I Know

Before concluding this section on the nature of the question, one final consideration remains. It has to do with the manner in which we can know that we have successfully answered a question. Briefly, the problem can be stated by asking, How do I know that I know? This is a difficult question, for it strikes directly at the core of the problem of human knowing. Not surprisingly, therefore, this question has long attracted the attention of serious philosophers. It is equivalent to asking, What does it mean to know?

It is not necessary to attempt here an in-depth response to this question since this would require a more detailed analysis than suits our present purpose, carrying us beyond the present stage of our inquiry. It is enough to indicate the direction that the solution to the problem might take. A fuller treatment of the question has been reserved for the chapter on intellection.

It seems clear enough that we have an answer to a question when we are aware that the knowledge we possess satisfies the conditions of the question. The problem, of course, consists in knowing when it is that we have such knowledge. The mind knows that it knows or that it has the answer to its question when it is able to return to the first principle of its knowing; namely, being. It achieves this in confronting its experience with the principle of noncontradiction by which it knows that something cannot *be* and *not be* at the same time and in the same respect. The mind recognizes, in other words, that something is in a certain way and for that moment at least, it cannot be in any other way. It *is* and cannot *not be*.

The notion of necessity thus plays a key role in our recognition that a particular response is indeed an answer to the question asked. The mind is not able to close the circle of its reflection and return to the first principle of being, unless it is able to affirm that a response is true, that it contains the knowledge sought by the question. For example, I know that eight plus seven is fifteen because I understand that it must be such; it cannot be fourteen or sixteen or any other number. Unless one *understands* that it *must be* this way—that fifteen alone is *the answer* to the question How much is eight plus seven?—one cannot be said to have the answer to the question. Only when the mind is able to return to being, understanding that something is in a certain way and cannot be otherwise, can it be said to have completed the search it initiated with its questioning.

In answering a question authentically, one recognizes that the conditions laid down by the question have been fulfilled and there is no longer *more to be known* regarding that question. It is at this moment that the tension of inquiry ceases and the mind experiences a sense of relief, which allows it to pass into a state of repose. The search is over, the question has been answered, the truth is known, and inwardly there is an awareness of a new unity and harmony, where formerly there had been disunity and division. The mind now grasps an intimate and inseparable relationship between elements of its experience which previously it experienced as separate and disjointed. The mind is able to affirm that something is in such and such a way because, were it not, it would be constrained to deny the experience itself.

Thus it is through *being* that all answers to questions are known to be answers. I am able to affirm that *this* is the answer to this question because I have come to realize that the two coalesce, or unite, in being. The *why* of the question gives way to the *because* of the response. Where once there was ignorance, now there is knowledge.

As subsequent investigations will further emphasize, only we humans ask questions, since only we know what more there is to be known. Only we humans at our deepest level are questioners; therefore, only we are capable of answers.

Summary

First, the meaning of experience was discussed. It was presented as being either direct (primary) or indirect (derivative). Experience was also described as possessing three fundamental characteristics: it is highly diversified, social by nature, and susceptible of growth and development. Next, the meaning and significance of the question was taken up. Questioning was defined as a conscious search for further knowledge. Three conditions were said to underlie every authentic question. First, one must have some knowledge; second, there must be a recognition of ignorance, and third, one must recognize that there is more to be known, that is, there is an answer to the question. Next, the distinction between an authentic and a pseudo question was considered, as well as the difference between an authentic answer and a merely verbal response. The chapter concluded with a discussion of why each authentic question has one and one answer only and how, when one has an answer, one comes to recognize that one does have an answer.

Definitions and Conclusions

1. Primary experience is our direct awareness of a thing.

2. Primary experience in the more proper sense is always directly of things; derivative experience extends to an awareness of primary experiences.

3. Experience possesses three basic characteristics: (a) it is highly diversified; (b) it is social; (c) it is susceptible of growth and development.

4. A question is a conscious search for knowledge.

5. An authentic question involves three fundamental conditions: (a) knowledge of something; (b) an awareness of ignorance; (c) an awareness that there is more to be known.

6. Every authentic question has an authentic answer.

7. A pseudo, or false question, either feigns ignorance or does not proceed from authentic understanding.

8. A factual question inquires into an actual state of affairs, whether past or present.

9. A factual question has but one answer.

10. One knows one has an answer when the conditions of the question are consciously fulfilled.

11. All authentic answers entail the mind's return to *being*.

3 The Problem of Human Knowing: A Historical Overview

... it is not impossible to become a competent scientist without knowing much about the history of science, but no man can carry very far his own philosophical reflections unless he first studies the history of philosophy.

Etienne Gilson

Introduction

The problem of human knowing is central to the problem of what it means to be human. It is not surprising, therefore, that the problem of knowing has played an important role in the historical development of Western philosophy. How this problem is resolved does, to a high degree, shape and determine one's view regarding a philosophy of the human person.

A historical overview, however brief and inadequate, will greatly facilitate our understanding of the positions taken by modern and contemporary philosophers. It will, as well, enable us to contrast somewhat the views assumed by more recent thinkers with those of the early Greek philosophers, pointing up the similarities and differences between the two as well as highlighting areas of historical dependence.

Plato (427-347 B.C.)

Plato was the first philosopher to undertake an in-depth analysis of the phenomenon of human knowing. He is without question one of the great intellectual geniuses of the Western world. Indeed, many scholars would rank him at the top.

Unfortunately, since all of the major extant works of Plato are in dialogue form, it is difficult to determine whether or not the views expressed in the dialogues are meant to represent Plato's own views. Therefore, I will make no pretense of presenting an authentic historical account of Plato's views, but instead will provide a brief summary of the *theory of forms*, which seems to have its historical origin with Plato himself. We must leave to the Platonic scholar the ultimate determination of what Plato's own position was with regard to his theory and, particularly, whether he might have changed his views toward the end of his life.

Scholars remain divided regarding the definitive interpretation of Plato's theory of *recollection*, and it may well be that the outstanding historical questions surrounding his views may never be resolved to everyone's satisfaction. For purposes of our present study we assume nothing more than that Plato intended his theory of forms to be taken seriously.

Plato, who was deeply convinced of the intellectual dimension of man, made a sharp distinction between sensory and intellective knowledge. He did not accept the teaching of some of the earlier pre-Socratics, such as Democritus (460-362? B.C.), who viewed all knowledge as essentially one and explained human understanding as merely a refined form of sensation. Democritus conceived of knowledge as an effect of impinging atoms, from which all material things were made, on the senses. To explain the phenomenon of knowledge, Democritus employs what today we would call a mechanistic model, which is based on the assumption that ideas are merely images formed by the patterned onslaught of small particles of matter on the sensory faculties. In short, Democritus assumes a materialist position and sees no fundamental difference in sensing, knowing, and other activities found in nature, such as growth. Further, Democritus is a subjectivist, or phenomenalist, since he also maintains that what we know are the images, or perceptions, within the senses, not the things themselves, independent of the knower.

Plato reacts forcibly against such a view of human knowing, and the general thrust of all his dialogues is to insist on the transcendent dimension of the human spirit vis-á-vis the material world. In his concern to refute the materialism of the earlier philosophers, Plato tends to sharply divide the world of human experience into two domains: that of understanding and that of sensory perception.

Plato is convinced that the human act of understanding involves an activity that totally transcends the world of material objects and sensation. Ideas are universal and abstract and are unlimited by time and space. Consequently, Plato does not see how they could derive from the shadowy world of sense objects where things are in continual flux and are singular, material, and limited; therefore, subject to the limitations of time and space. Because of the dichotomy between the intellective and the sensory worlds, Plato saw no possibility for any real interaction between them, at least not to the extent that the mind is dependent upon the world of material things for the ideas it has. Since ideas are universal and immaterial, they could not derive from the material world where everything is singular. This leads Plato to deny that the material world is truly a cause of our knowledge. He will not deny, however, that the world of sensible things plays a role in our knowing, for it does *occasion* our awareness of our ideas. Yet Plato does not admit that the material world causes that knowledge, and thus he denies that there is any real dependency of the mind on sensible, or material, things. Hence, he must look elsewhere for his explanation of the origin of the ideas found in the human mind.

In order to account for the ideas we have, Plato appeals to a prior existence of the mind or soul. He suggests that prior to birth the soul enjoyed a fullness of knowledge but that, when it was conjoined with the body, the soul lost its conscious awareness of the ideas it once had. Since union with the body induces in the soul a general state of forgetfulness, it is the role of sensible things to stimulate and thus occasion our recollection of the ideas we possess in our subconscious. It is for this reason that Plato is able to say that all learning is merely a matter of remembering and that, consequently, knowledge leads one back to the world of prior existence, where the mind or soul enjoyed an uninhibited vision of truth and goodness, of the ideas it now must struggle to recall through its contact with, and immersion in, the material world, which is really a world of shadows.

From this, one can readily see that Plato's theory of the origin of knowledge is heavily intellectualist and that it attributes minimal importance to the body and to the world of sensible forms. Indeed, Plato views the body as an obstacle to the life of the soul, a kind of prison from which the soul is constantly trying to escape through the acquisition of knowledge. This view is strongly reinforced by Plato's symbolic account of human existence as it is presented in his famous allegory of the cave, in book seven of his *Republic.*

Aristotle (384-322 B.C.)

A pupil of Plato's for nearly twenty years, Aristotle understood Plato's teaching thoroughly, but while he greatly admired his mentor, he was unable to entirely accept Plato's teaching. It should be borne in mind that even though Aristotle's theory of knowledge differs rather substantially from that of Plato's, Aristotle borrows heavily from him and is, in many respects, very much a Platonist.

Aristotle shares Plato's profound conviction regarding the difference between sensory and intellective activity. He agrees that ideas do in fact transcend the material world of sensible things. Yet, at the same time, he does not accept Plato's contention that these ideas are obtained through a prior existence. Rather, he maintains that all ideas in the mind are derived through experience. Thus he views the material world as the cause of our ideas and not merely the occasion of them.

In order to make good on this assertion, Aristotle must show how it is possible for immaterial and abstract ideas to derive from material and concrete things. It is not an easy task, and most of Aristotle's philosophic efforts, as well as those of many of the great philosophers throughout the Western tradition, were directed either toward making such an assertion plausible or toward attempting to show what an impossible task it was.

Briefly, Aristotle's rejoinder to Plato is as follows: All human knowledge is obtained through experience. In the beginning of an individual's life, the mind is like a slate upon which nothing is written. The body must thus share with the soul the task of accumulating knowledge. The body is not the prison of the soul but the instrument whereby it obtains access to the material world. All knowledge must, for Aristotle, come to the mind by having in some way previously passed through the senses. To render such an explanation consistent, Aristotle must view the sensible world, which for Plato is merely a world of shadows, as a world of genuine intelligible objects. The material world was not actually knowing but it was capable of being known; it was intelligible. Aristotle refers to it simply as potentially knowable. The world is intelligible because, in a restricted but real sense, it contains ideas embedded in sensible objects. These ideas or forms, as he calls them, are not actually intelligible because they exist under material conditions, rather the freeing of the material forms from their material conditions renders them actually intelligible.

Thus Aristotle sees understanding as an act by which the mind becomes one with the *other*, the material object. Not in the sense, of course, that there is a *physical unity* of the two, for the stone does not truly enter either into the eye or into the mind, but in the sense that the form or intelligible dimension of the material thing has been assimilated by the mind, and now functions as the form or determining principle by which the mind has been moved from a state of *capacity* to one of *act*. The mind is *in act*—that is to say, actually knowing at this moment—to the extent that it is informed by the other. From Aristotle's point of view, understanding is not remembering but discovering, for it is through understanding that the other reveals itself to the mind. Clearly, then, according to this view, the mind very much depends on the material world, not merely to *occasion* what it knows but to cause it to actually be that which is known. Aristotle also speaks of an agent, or active, intellect which performs the singularly important function of raising the material thing to the level of pure intelligibility. That is, the role of the active intellect is not to change the thing but to dematerialize it, liberating its form from the material conditions which make it concrete, singular, and individual.

Aristotle's explanation places much more importance on the role of body in the human knowing process than does Plato's. In Aristotle there is a marked shift away from an appeal to an other-worldliness to explain knowing, and a pervading dependency of the human mind or spirit upon the body and the world of material things. Yet, at the same time, Aristotle also maintains that the act of understanding is an immaterial operation which transcends the world of sense, even though it does take its rise from that world as regards the content of its thinking. For Aristotle, human understanding is a dialogue with the world of sensible things.

The Beginning of the Modern Era

Alfred North Whitehead (1861-1947) once observed that after Plato all philosophy became little more than a footnote to Plato. It is meant, of course, to be an exaggeration but, if we add Aristotle's name to the list, it does convey a fairly accurate notion of the evolution of Western thought from the third century B.C. to our own time.

Our quest to understand the human being confronts us with the non-self, the world beyond one's immediate reach, and one cannot come to terms with oneself without simultaneously satisfying the questions that arise with regard to one's experience of the totally *other*. Is the other merely an extension of oneself, a product of one's own creative thinking, or is it a wholly separate, distinct entity? If the latter, how then is it related to one? How does one come to recognize the world, and what is its origin? These are the crucial and basic questions all philosophers have asked themselves, and they are questions which every individual somehow answers for himself or herself, either theoretically or practically, because it is impossible to live without assuming an attitude toward them.

It is well to remember that philosophers do not inquire into experiences that pertain to an elitist segment of humanity; instead they inquire into experiences that are common to all humans. Those who are distraught by the spectacle of divergent views of philosophers underestimate the difficulty of the problems philosophers set for themselves and the complications which the historical situation adds to this difficulty. An appreciation of why various theories arose at certain epochs of world history entails some awareness of the continuing dialogue that goes on between one generation and another. Each period involves new experiences to be analyzed and assimilated into the fabric of human consciousness. This process of assimilation can often prove difficult, even painful, and often, until we obtain a particular perspective on the problem, it may cause confusion and be disruptive. In such instances there may be a tendency for people to lose confidence in the past and for them to cast about in desperation for an entirely new account of the human equation, even though what is needed is merely a modification of the old vision in order to update in a satisfactory manner the ongoing human experience.

The French philosopher René Descartes is considered to be the father of modern philosophy. He sought a new method of philosophizing that would permit the philosopher to reach the same kind of certainty that he believed the mathematician and the scientist had achieved. He sought a method that would eliminate all disturbing doubt and hesitancy. Descartes's mistrust of his sensory powers led him to attempt a great modern experiment: to establish the physical world through a clarification of the nature of the knowing subject. This experiment was to become a challenge to the great minds of the seventeenth and eighteenth centuries. Among those who were to seek either to carry out his experiment to completion, to modify it, or to reject it utterly, were the philosophers Locke, Berkeley, Hume, and Kant, whom we will briefly study after our introduction to Descartes.

René Descartes (1596-1650)

Anxious to develop a philosophy that would enjoy the same degree of certainty and acceptance as mathematics and the physical sciences had come to enjoy among the intellectuals of Europe, Descartes elected to strike out in a new direction and to devise a method of philosophizing that would be universally accepted. Descartes set himself no less a task than resolving once and for all, in terms all could understand, the perennial philosophic problems of the nature and origin of knowledge, truth, and certainty.

To initiate his investigation of truth, Descartes was determined to eliminate from the start the historically perennial source of all philosophic problems, error. By eliminating the possibility of error from the outset, Descartes was confident that he would then be able to proceed in systematic fashion to confront all problems of the human mind, and to do so with a professional poise and security similar to that of the great mathematicians and natural scientists.

What, Descartes argued, had frustrated his efforts in the past and had repeatedly led him into error was a naive and childlike trust in what he had experienced with his senses. He considered it most important, therefore, to eliminate this fertile source of error. He resolved to accomplish this simply by bypassing all sensory experience and beginning his analysis through reflecting within himself. It was his own life of inner consciousness that became the field of his inquiry. Descartes's novel philosophic approach thus rests on what he calls *the methodic doubt.* In the state of methodic doubt, Descartes purports to suspend all sensory activity and to reflect on his own inner consciousness, a consciousness uncontaminated by any image derived from sensory experience. It should be noted that the Cartesian methodic doubt differs from a *real* doubt in that it is feigned for scientific purposes. Descartes will pretend or assume that he has no knowledge of the external world, and he will do this to establish his entire knowledge structure on a firm basis.

He extends his methodic doubt to all knowledge, even including knowledge of himself. He will first pretend that he knows nothing for certain. He will assume that everything is doubtful. Yet, as he reflects on his state of universal doubt, Descartes begins to realize that it is impossible for him to doubt everything for, even while he is doubting, he is clearly aware that he is doing so. That is, there can be no doubt that he does doubt. Consequently, something is obviously certain: he is presently doubting and, if he doubts, he must also exist. Following this reasoning, Descartes satisfies himself that something can be known without any dependence whatever on sensory experience. Thus, he concludes that he has broken the great circle of doubt and has established his knowledge on an unshakable foundation.

By extending his reflective analysis, all the while employing his methodic doubt, Descartes discovers that there are other 'truths' which he is aware of in the same clear and distinct manner in which he is aware of his own existence. He discovers that he can think about mathematical theorems without the slightest employment of his senses, and he clearly is aware of their truthfulness. Since, therefore, he has a clear and distinct idea that the sum of the three interior angles of a triangle must always equal 180 degrees, he is certain that it is true. The same he finds to be the case with regard to both geometrical and algebraical formulas. Thus, Descartes concludes that the true nature of mathematics is that it is a priori, or independent of sensory experience. It is precisely for this reason that he can place his trust in this knowledge, since he has been able to eliminate the perennial source of error; namely, sensory experience.

Descartes's reflections upon his own world of inner consciousness unfolds for him what he considers to be the unwavering criterion of truth; namely, ideas which are at once clear and distinct. He notes further that no sensory object, nothing experienced through the employment of the senses, is such that he beholds it as altogether clear and distinct. For example, he would claim that he has no clear and distinct idea that an object, such as a red pen, is what it might appear to be, since he is aware that it does not have to be such. It is noteworthy that for Descartes the notion of universality is latently present in his criterion of clear and distinct idea, and it is precisely because he is aware that mathematical statements, for example, must always be the way they are, that he is secure in their truth and is able to affirm without hesitation that $10 + 5 = 15$, for it cannot be otherwise.

Descartes and the Existence of God

Since, in initiating his philosophical analysis, Descartes has by-passed the sensory world entirely, it is obvious that he could not accept any of the cosmological arguments that philosophers had previously put forward to establish God's existence from reason. This does not mean, however, that Descartes assumed an atheistic or agnostic position, for he did indeed believe that a viable argument could be made for God's existence, beginning from the premises he had already assumed. The argument Descartes construed is well known in the history of philosophy and does not originate with Descartes. It is, in effect, a variation of the argument proposed by Anselm in the twelfth century and is generally referred to as the *ontological* argument, presumably because it begins with an idea rather than an existential experience of the material world.

Striving to adhere exclusively to his newly adopted method of reflection on his own inner experience, Descartes became convinced of the existence of an all-perfect Being, which exists independent of oneself and which is ultimately the source of all of our ideas. The argument he employed to reach this conclusion may be briefly reconstructed as follows: First, Descartes is aware of his possessing an idea of perfection. His own reflections on his inner doubts, which initially led him to explore the possibilities of discovering a new philosophic method, reveal to him his own limitations. Thus, through his own experience of doubt, Descartes is aware of his own imperfection, for doubt is nothing more than an admission of ignorance. To doubt something is to be aware that one does not know. But surely, Descartes argues, it is more perfect to know than not to know. Thus he becomes aware that he could not have conceived of himself as imperfect without his having the idea of perfection, for the two notions are clearly correlative.

As Descartes continues to ponder the implications of this awareness of perfection, he soon becomes convinced that he is not the author of this idea, for how could an idea of perfection proceed from something that is imperfect? In this manner Descartes concludes that there must exist a perfect being who is the author of his idea of perfection and indeed of all other ideas he possesses.

Descartes's argument for the existence of an all-perfect being is essential to his philosophic system, for without such a perfect being he has no way of reestablishing his trust and belief in a material world. The existence of God for Descartes is the foundation stone for his belief in the authentic existence of a world which differs in kind from the world of his own ideas. Because, Descartes argues, God is perfect, He is necessarily just. His justice would not permit Him, therefore, to deceive. Hence, there can be no doubt that my ordinary perceptions of the physical world, even though I have no clear and distinct idea of them, rest on and derive from a reality beyond the reach of my own personal experience. In short, Descartes substitutes a form of belief for actual knowledge of the existence of the physical world and substantiates this belief on the prior knowledge of an all-perfect Being whose existence he has arrived at by reflecting purely within himself. Thus Descartes is ultimately secure in admitting to what he learns from his senses because of his confidence in the faithfulness of God, of whose existence he had become aware without the slightest reliance on his perceptions of the physical world.

Descartes's views bear a recognizable resemblance to the earlier intellectualism of Plato for whom certain, universal knowledge did not arise from the world of the senses, but had been obtained by the soul in a prior life.

Descartes's views are considered to be revolutionary in the sense that they were an important development and adaptation of earlier positions restated within the context of the seventeenth century. For his contemporaries Descartes's methodic doubt signaled a definitive break with the moderate realist position of Aristotle and the medieval scholastics.

Descartes inaugurated this new approach to philosophy in order to bring philosophy into harmony with the latest findings in mathematics and the natural sciences. He wished to place philosophy on a firm footing by applying to it the method which, in effect, he felt the mathematician and the scientist followed in their respective fields. It was the application of the mathematical method to philosophy that constituted the revolution of which Descartes was the author and which earned for him the honorary title, Father of Modern Philosophy. What this revolution was to mean for the succeeding generations makes up a good part of the story of modern philosophy, and it is undeniable that the unfolding of the modern and contemporary periods makes little sense to anyone who is wholly unaware of the nature of the Cartesian experiment. The inventor of a new system often brings about changes he could not anticipate, and what Descartes's attempt to set philosophy on a firm footing resulted in was to have all forms of human knowledge, including the apparently impregnable bastions of mathematics and the physical sciences, brought into question.

Thus his contemporaries and those who came after him were to find cause to direct a large portion of their effort toward the problems that his new philosophic method had raised. There is a sense in which, after Descartes, philosophy was never quite the same again.

John Locke (1632-1704)

There was much reaction on the Continent to the views of Descartes, even though many scholars gave them a favorable hearing. Yet it was in England, where there had long been a tradition of empiricism, that perhaps the firmest reaction to the Cartesian experiment set in. John Locke was the philosopher in England who took the lead in formulating an empiricist response to the Cartesian challenge. Yet, Locke readily admits that Descartes had made an advance in knowledge theory, and he will incorporate a certain amount of Descartes's view into his own empirical theory.

Locke is clearly to be numbered among the empiricists, for he insists that sensation plays an important and central role in the acquisition of knowledge. He repudiates the theory of innate ideas and denies that the human mind can know anything without first beginning its inquiry with the material world. For Locke, all knowledge does indeed begin with the material world; all knowledge does indeed begin with the senses; and in this regard, Locke definitely sides with Aristotle, rather than with Plato.

However, Locke introduces a very basic and, in its implications, far-reaching distinction regarding the nature of sensation. He distinguishes between what he terms the primary and secondary qualities of things. Those qualities are primary that are independent of the sensory act. Examples of the primary qualities that he lists are shape, size, motion, and position.

Secondary qualities are not really *in* the object perceived, according to Locke, but are rather *imposed on* the object by the sensory powers of the one perceiving. Examples of what he means by secondary qualities are color, sound, odor, flavor, temperature, hardness, and softness. Although Locke insists that the secondary qualities of the object are contributions of the sensing subject, he does grant there are certain powers within the material object that give rise to, or occasion, the actual experience of those secondary qualities by the one perceiving.

According to Locke's view, it is perfectly true to say that a thing is in motion, has this or that size or shape, and is in this or that position; however, it is not correct to say that a thing is blue or red, gives off sound, tastes sweet or bitter, is hard or soft, warm or cold. These latter are secondary qualities and only result from the union or confrontation of the material object with the sensing subject.

Locke admits, in addition to the primary and secondary qualities, to an underlying substratum, which he calls substance. This substance, or substratum, is found in the material thing and is the basis for its primary qualities. The substratum, however, is not sensible, since it is not a quality but is a reality to which the mind reasons. It is necessary in order to explain the stability of the primary qualities, which clearly cannot exist in themselves.

Since Locke maintains that there is no innate knowledge, he must explain the reality of general and abstract ideas. He does this by a theory of abstraction, whereby the mind thinks about certain aspects of perceived objects while neglecting to think about others. In this manner he claims to be able to reach a notion of 'cause' and eventually to demonstrate from reason the existence of God. Thus, although Locke insists that all knowledge takes its origin from the senses, he does not end up a materialist.

It is helpful to contrast the positions of Descartes and Locke, for the differences of the two positions serve to bring into clearer relief what each philosopher is affirming and what each is denying.

Locke's distinction between primary and secondary qualities is, in effect, a recognition that he appreciated the dilemma in which Descartes found himself. Descartes separated himself from the sensory world because he could find no firm footing there upon which to build a reputable knowledge theory. Locke feels that the source of the errors which Descartes was attempting to eliminate was not sensation as such but only certain forms of sensation. By his distinction between primary and secondary qualities, Locke could separate the reliable from the unreliable elements and thereby reestablish the possibility of deriving certain and clear knowledge from the sensible world of experience. Secondary qualities were indeed unstable. Different people experienced the color and temperature, etc., of things differently, and this shows that these qualities are not objective. Yet the primary qualities are experienced in a uniform manner by all people, and so they are clearly stable and objective. In this manner Locke feels that he has responded to the fundamental problem which Descartes had struggled with. He has rendered Descartes's revolutionary approach to knowledge, that of beginning exclusively with the knowing subject, both unsound and unnecessary.

However, Locke has gone part way in his attempt to meet Descartes, for his empiricism is not total. By making the secondary qualities dependent on the knowing subject, Locke feels confident that he has eliminated the real source of error in human knowing and has removed the need of doubting absolutely everything in order to put human knowledge on a firm footing. Yet, other philosophers coming after him will see Locke's solution in a quite different perspective and will find serious fault with his views.

George Berkeley (1685-1753)

Recent discoveries had indicated that the world was not as simple as it had hitherto been thought to be, and hence a new theory of knowledge had to be developed that could successfully incorporate the new developments in mathematics and the natural sciences. The views of Descartes and of Locke were, therefore, much discussed in European universities.

One who entered into this debate and developed a theory of his own was George Berkeley. Philosophy students confronting his views for the first time often find them both intriguing and bewildering. Intriguing, because they do catch one up short, coaxing one to think more deeply about views one had come to accept as beyond question; bewildering, because to them it seems very odd that anyone would seriously even consider denying the existence of the physical world. Yet, bizarre as these views may seem, they have exerted considerable influence in philosophical circles and continue to be discussed to this day.

Although Berkeley takes issue with both Descartes and Locke, his principal philosophical antagonist is the latter. Berkeley finds the Lockean distinction between primary and secondary qualities to be inconsistent; for, he states, the same arguments that Locke proposes—in support of his contention that secondary qualities depend on the knowing subject—can be applied with equal force and logic to the primary qualities. Motion, size, shape, position, etc., can all appear different to different perceivers and even to the same perceiver at different times. To one person a flat disk might appear circular and to another, viewing it from a different position, it might well appear elliptical. Consequently, Berkeley argues, Locke did not go far enough in granting that secondary qualities depend upon the knower; he should have included primary qualities because size, shape, position, etc., are subjectively dependent on the knower. To Berkeley, it makes little sense to say that an object of perception moves or is of this or that shape independent of its being perceived.

According to Berkeley, that which is perceived becomes one with the perception itself. There are no objects beyond the act of perception. The sensible world of Locke, even of Descartes, becomes a pure fiction, for it rests on the premise that there are things beyond the act of perceiving. Yet, for Berkeley, there can be no way that one could move from a world where things are real because they are *perceived* to another world where things are real independent of their being perceived. Since for Berkeley "an idea can be like nothing but an idea," the required bridge between two such worlds would be wholly lacking, no more than a chimera, with the consequence that no communication between a world of ideas and a supposed world where *things are not ideas* would be possible. Berkeley sums up his position with the aphorism, *esse est percipi*, "to be is to be perceived." This view, of course, represents a kind of idealism, for it implies that to be real means simply to be perceived.

As a consequence of his view that everything is idea, Berkeley is led to deny the existence of matter. To him, matter itself—what Locke called the *substratum* that underlay the primary qualities of things—can be nothing more than an abstraction, an idea. Obviously, there is no longer any need for such a substratum or substance if there are no qualities for it to support. Matter or substance without qualities becomes imperceptible, which means there can be no basis in experience upon which to ground the affirmation of its existence. In this manner Berkeley totally demolishes the philosophic structure that Locke had erected in an attempt to bridge the chasm between Cartesian skepticism and radical materialism.

Although Berkeley reduces all reality (dependent on perception) to idea, he is not a *pantheist* who believes that all things exist in God, nor a *solipsist* who denies that anything exists other than himself. He maintains that the ideas he has, he has *experienced*, and that, therefore, ideas exist outside of his own mind or spirit. Since, however, *all reality is idea,* Berkeley cannot hold that ideas exist in things, for this he has already denied. Ideas can exist only in mind. Further, since the number of ideas is infinite and he is continually experiencing new ideas, Berkeley concludes that the mind in which all ideas reside is infinite and hence the ideas he himself experiences, while they may be mediated by another finite mind, ultimately originate from a divine mind. In some sense, then, for Berkeley, the human mind is in direct contact with the divine mind and is continuously supplied with ideas emanating from it. Berkeley does not seem to have elaborated further on this theory of "divine illumination."

One can thus observe in Berkeley's view a partial return to the fundamental position of Descartes. Like the latter, Berkeley sees no possibility of obtaining knowledge from the sensible world, if by sensible world one understands a world of material objects where ideas do not already exist in the 'ideal' state. In this sense, his position is a radical rejection of Locke's theory of knowledge. On the other hand, Berkeley opposes Descartes's final acceptance of the existence of a material world, since he insists that whatever is, is idea. Consequently, Berkeley rejects the dualism of mind and body entirely and admits to the existence of mind as the only substance.

David Hume (1711-76)

In terms of influence, David Hume is perhaps the most important philosopher born in the British Isles. This Scottish philosopher developed a philosophy which was to serve as the basic pattern of British and American empiricism. It involves a radical rejection of mind as distinct from body, and of idea as distinct from sensory image. It is at once a reply to Descartes and to Locke.

Hume's theory of knowledge is very uncomplicated, for the simple reason that it reduces all knowledge to the collecting and association of various sense images. He has no theory of abstraction, therefore, and no theory of insight.

Briefly, Hume conceives of everything we call an idea as a sensory impression. Some impressions are, of course, more vivid than others. Those that have begun to fade and lose some of their particular qualities are ideas we may refer to as abstract. Accordingly, for Hume an abstract idea does not really differ from a sensory image; it is a sensory image that the mind now only partially retains. From this, Hume concludes that there can be no universal ideas, no general principles like those accepted by many earlier philosophers. Hume's theory of knowledge is above all a rejection of Descartes's acceptance of clear and distinct ideas which are universally true. For Hume all certainty becomes a matter of mere probability.

Because of his rejection of the reality of universal ideas in the mind, Hume also rejects the idea of necessity. As a consequence, he denies that the causal principle—"everything that comes to be has a cause"—is necessarily true, simply because it entails the notion of necessity. Because, therefore, the cause-and-effect principle is merely the result of custom, it follows that for Hume all reasoning consists merely in an association of one idea with another in a rather arbitrary way. When we experience certain sets of ideas often clustered together or in proximity to one another, we view them as though certain relationships existed between them and refer to one as the cause or the effect of the other.

Hume's rejection of the principle of causality as an authentic, meaningful principle is the point for which he is best known. Certainly it is a most fundamental philosophic point. Consequently, the effects of this rejection are very pervasive and totally radical. Since Hume recognizes the causal principle merely as a sociological phenomenon; that is, as the product of custom and not as a truth-bearing principle of reality implicit in all human experience, he necessarily assumes an attitude of universal skepticism toward the whole of human experience. He is unable to distinguish his own experience, his own impressions and ideas, from their objects, because such a position entails the very principle of causality which he claims to reject; therefore, Hume is reduced to saying that all he knows are his own impressions, for he cannot say with certainty that there is anything which causes those impressions. Furthermore, Hume cannot ascribe any true meaning to I, the subject of impressions, for the totality of his experience must be reduced to what he actually experiences. To argue that there is a subject underlying the experiences or impressions would, once again, entail Hume's admitting to the validity of the principle of causality.

We may now briefly relate the position of Hume to the views of the other philosophers recently discussed. Turning first to Descartes, we notice that while the French philosopher admits to the universal truth and certainty of some ideas at least, Hume refuses to grant that universal ideas are more than the products of human ingenuity produced for purposes of social intercourse. Nonetheless, it should be noted that these two philosophers are wholly in agreement on one rather fundamental point. Both agree that, if our knowledge must be construed as being totally dependent on sensory experience, there is no such thing as universal knowledge, at least not, according to Descartes, in the sense that we can ever be fully certain that such is the case. In effect, that is precisely what Hume is saying.

Contrasting Hume's position with that of Locke, we can note that both agree in emphasizing the fact that there is no innate knowledge; that all knowledge somehow is experienced. On the other hand, Hume finds it impossible to agree with Locke in the latter's explanation of the origin of universal ideas and principles from the experience of sensible things. For Hume, universal ideas have no objective basis, and it is impossible to know anything for certain, since such knowledge implies necessity and the validity of the principle of causality.

The relationship between Berkeley and Hume is one which is perhaps the most difficult to characterize, because even though their views at first appear worlds apart, there is, nonetheless, a common ground underlying both. Berkeley and Hume agree that ideas are merely sense images and that it is impossible to obtain general or universal ideas from a sensory, material world. They thus join forces in opposing the positions articulated by Locke. Yet they disagree in their views on the origin of what Hume terms sense impressions and Berkeley terms ideas. For Hume there is no way we can be certain of their origin. For Berkeley, however, the ideas arise from other minds, either finite or infinite (divine). Yet, even here, one cannot help seeing a common thread of sorts, for Berkeley does not assign a specific source to the origin of each individual idea, and in this way his view does not differ enormously from that of Hume, who likewise does not assign an exact source to the impressions which the mind receives.

Immanuel Kant (1724-1804)

The name of Immanuel Kant is unquestionably the best known of all modern philosophers, and it would be impossible to assess the extent of his influence. A profound thinker gifted with a keen mind and an enormous capacity for continuous hard work, Kant developed a very detailed theory of knowledge by means of which he strove to bring together the views of Descartes and Hume.

Firmly convinced of the validity of mathematical and scientific knowledge, Kant was profoundly shaken by his reading of Hume's critique of human knowledge. From that point on, Kant devoted his efforts to developing a theory of knowledge which would both take into account the criticisms and objections of Hume on the nature and origin of knowledge and provide a firm and unshakable foundation for the universal validity of mathematical and scientific truths.

The key to the system that Kant laboriously devised lies in what he termed *synthetic a priori judgments.* These judgments for Kant are universally necessary and true, and yet dependent in some fashion on sensory experience. That they are universally necessary and true reflects the Cartesian element of his position; that they depend on experience reflects the influence of Hume. In order to clarify what Kant understands by the synthetic a priori judgment and how he arrived at his position, it is necessary to turn our attention to several preliminary considerations.

Aware of the different levels of judgment expressed by the human mind, Kant realized that the reason for their differentiation lay in the diverse manner in which the predicate of the judgment was related to the subject. On this basis he quickly distinguished what he termed *synthetic* judgments from *analytic* judgments. The former were those that added some new cognitive element to the subject. The statement, "this apple is green," is an example of a synthetic judgment, for the predicate *green* adds a cognitive element to the subject *apple*. Knowing that what is in this sack is an apple does not suffice to indicate to me what color it is, for it could be any of several different colors and still be an apple. Because, therefore, the synthetic judgment always adds some new element to the intelligibility of the subject, it always requires what Kant calls *experience* to enable one to give it expression. I simply must experience this apple by looking at it to determine whether or not it is green.

On the other hand, analytic judgments are those in which the predicate is already included in the subject; that is to say, the predicate does not really add a new cognitive element to the subject. As a consequence, it will not be necessary to have added experience to formulate such a judgment; provided I already know the meaning of the subject. An example Kant provides of analytic judgment is the following: "This circle is round." It is clear that the predicate *round* does not add a new element to the subject *circle*. If I know what a circle is, and I know that this figure is a circle, I implicitly know, without further experience, that it is round. Thus, through a mere analysis of the subject, I am able to state "This circle is round." Because no new experience is needed to formulate such judgments, Kant terms them analytic, as opposed to synthetic; and because they do not extend the scope of my knowledge, Kant insists that they are relatively unimportant in comparison with synthetic judgments.

This brief summary by no means exhausts Kant's views regarding synthetic judgments, however, for he goes on to point out that there are basically two different kinds of synthetic judgments and this distinction is of crucial importance to his total explanation of human knowledge.

Some synthetic judgments depend entirely on experience for their truth. The example of the apple is of this type. That "this apple is green" can be known only through direct experience. Knowing that *this* apple is green tells me nothing of the color of *another* apple

I may have in this sack, since not all apples are green. This judgment, dependent upon experience for its truth, Kant terms a *synthetic a posteriori judgment*.

There are other synthetic judgements, however, that, though they rely on experience in some sense for their truth, are of such a nature that they are nonetheless always true and necessarily so; that is, this second class of synthetic judgments is universally true and necessary on the one hand, and on the other hand, is somehow dependent on experience. They occupy a point somewhere between the pure analytic judgment, which is always true but is merely tautological, and the synthetic judgments of the first class mentioned earlier. This second class of synthetic judgments are Kant's *synthetic a priori judgments*. He terms them synthetic because the predicate adds a new element to the understanding of the subject; they are a priori, however, because they do not wholly depend on experience, since they are universally and necessarily true. As examples of such synthetic a priori judgments, Kant presents all mathematical and arithmetical type judgments. He uses $7 + 5 = 12$ as an example of a synthetic a priori judgment. He claims that the meaning of the number 12 is not contained in the meanings of 7 and 5, and for that reason the judgment is not merely analytic.

Because such judgments are synthetic for Kant, they must somehow depend on experience for their truth. Otherwise one could come to an awareness of their truth through simple analysis of the meanings of subject and predicate, and in that sense one would be merely engaged in analytic judgments.

Kant's explanation as to how such judgments are dependent on experience is subtle and difficult to explain briefly, since it involves an understanding of several points we are unable to touch on, save in the most cursory fashion, in this introductory sketch. In essence Kant's reasoning is as follows: One cannot think about any arithmetical or mathematical reality without employing some form of sensual image, which necessarily involves either a spacial or temporal dimension. Since, according to Kant, space and time are foreign to the realm of pure intellect, all conceptions involving either or both of these characteristics must derive from a special sensory power of the mind, which in turn depends on experience for the actual content of what it is that is judged. This internal sensory power, imagination, has two closely related intuitive functions by which it places the data of experience within the twofold framework of space and time. Any judgment that reveals a spacial or temporal dimension indicates straightaway that it is a judgment that relies on sensation, and for this reason it is experiential. Because it is experiential and adds to the reservoir of our knowledge, it is likewise synthetic.

At the same time, the synthetic a priori judgments are for Kant universally and necessarily true, as already indicated; that is, they are unexceptionable. Since, however, universality and necessity transcend the singular world of sensory perceptions and hence cannot be actually experienced, all universally true judgments must also be a priori, prior to experience. As Kant views it, the *form* of universality and necessity that we find in mathematical judgments derives exclusively from the mind, while the material data of the judgment derive from experience. Hence, the synthetic a priori judgment becomes for Kant an amalgam of mind and experience and contains elements both of the analytic judgment and of the simple synthetic judgment, which depends for its truth exclusively on experience.

By this type of maneuvering Kant is confident he has responded to the objections Hume has raised against the idealist system of Descartes in a manner that preserves intact the universality of at least certain orders of knowledge. Kant's achievement is not, however, without its consequences, for in saving mathematics and the natural sciences from the critique of Hume, Kant has sacrificed metaphysics. Kant claims that all knowledge that does not include the delimiting characteristic of the sensuous intuition is tautological and redundant; that is, analytic. Metaphysics is thus reduced to the level of a meaningless, unreal science which is, he says, a transcendental illusion. Following as a corollary of this position is Kant's insistence that all discussion of freedom, immortality, and God is incapable of providing any real answers. Only knowledge that is at once a priori and synthetic provides us with meaningful information, universally and necessarily true. As merely analytic knowledge, all metaphysical questions are useless forms of inquiry, better abandoned. It is this attitude of Kant's toward metaphysics and any search for transcendental meaning that has profoundly influenced the direction of modern philosophy. It is this attitude that largely accounts for the contemporary reluctance to view metaphysics as a legitimate form of human inquiry.

Kant's solution to the Humean dilemma entails a further corollary that constitutes an integral part of the Kantian system. Kant denies that it is possible for the human mind to know things as they are in themselves. What we do know, he affirms, are things as they are presented to us; that is, their appearances, for what is present in our consciousness is the data of experience, ordered and arranged according to the structure of the mind. This structured experience he refers to as the phenomena. Our consciousness extends merely to phenomena. What things (noumena) are like in themselves we can never know. The world of noumena is the source and origin of the data of our experiences; otherwise it remains for us an unknown world.

It can, upon quick reflection, be seen that Kant has attempted a compromise position between the theories of the human person proposed by Descartes and Hume. Kant shared Descartes's enthusiasm for the unquestioned validity of mathematical reasoning and its scientific application to the world of experience. He also shared Descartes's acknowledged goal of putting philosophy on a scientific basis that it might regain its former respectability.

On the other hand, Kant recognized the basic philosophical weakness of Descartes's position; namely, that his confidence in the existence of a material world rested on his first having arrived at a certain knowledge of the existence of a supreme being. In this regard Kant, to a great degree, shared the inclinations of Hume, who insisted that all meaningful knowledge was inextricably bound up with sensory images and impressions. Thus the Kantian position can, with justification, be viewed as a compromise between the Cartesian emphasis on the knowing subject and universal knowledge on the one hand, and on the other, the Humean emphasis on sensory perception and the concrete world of singular things.

The Kantian compromise, however, does not succeed in healing the profound cleft between the Cartesian and the Humean views, with the result that Kant's position remains inherently unstable and in a state of continuous tension. The duality Descartes had introduced between the world of the mind and the world of material things remains essentially a duality in Kant's phenomenal and noumenal world, the world of appearances and the world of things as they are in themselves. Ultimately, Kant has no explanation as to how or why the union between the concrete and the mental realities takes place. In effect, the Kantian position requires an act of faith

similar to that of the Cartesian position, which affirmed the reality
of such a world on the strength of trust in divine justice, which, it
was believed, would not allow man to be deceived on so basic an
issue.

The dichotomy between the phenomenal and noumenal worlds,
which Kant's philosophy introduced into the thinking of the modern world, was quickly recognized even by his own contemporaries.
In a very true sense one could claim that the period extending from
the year 1800 to the present can be characterized as a commentary
on the Kantian theory of man and his knowledge. The aim among
philosophers remains ever the same—an attempt to find unity in
the totality of human experience. Since the time of Kant, philosophers have sought to achieve this either by denying the split between
the world of the mind and the world of concrete reality, or they have
sought to show how these two worlds somehow complement and relate to one another. How this question is resolved, of course, profoundly affects one's view as to what it means to be human, for
humans mirror their world.

Post-Kantian Era (1805-1985)

Kant's single-minded aim was to rescue the science of Newton and
the mathematics of Pascal, Descartes, and Leibniz from the blister-
ing critique Hume had leveled against all universal knowledge. He
wished to explain how mathematics and scientific knowledge could
bear a significant relation to the phenomenal world and still retain
its universal characteristics. At the same time, Kant's solution to the
problem of the origin of universal knowledge required the acceptance of a radical compromise. By his own admission, the sciences
and mathematics could be rescued only by consigning metaphysics
to the flames and the world of real things to the shadowy realm of
unknowability. Metaphysics became a transcendental illusion; the
thing-in-itself, an unknown and unknowable 'entity'.

Not surprisingly, Kant's critique of pure reason met with considerable opposition even within his own lifetime. Initially this opposition came from his compatriot Johann Gottlieb Fichte (1762-1814)
and later it was strengthened by two other powerful German minds,
Friedrich Wilhelm Schelling (1775-1854) and Georg Wilhelm
Hegel (1770-1831). These men were strongly critical of the split
Kant had introduced between the noumenal and phenomenal

worlds. While the views of these three thinkers are certainly not identical in detail, they do substantively agree in their common rejection of Kant's division between mind and thing, the knower and the known. This radical separation rendered it impossible on Kant's own account, to know the thing-in-itself in its own reality; it could only be known as it *appeared* to the knower.

Fichte was the first of the German idealists openly to express his dissatisfaction with this dogmatic tenet, and to point out that if, as Kant claimed, one is incapable of knowing the thing-in-itself, one is equally incapable of affirming that a world of things exists independent of the knowing subject. To avoid the inconsistency of affirming that a world exists that cannot be known, Fichte, Schelling, and Hegel all repudiate the dichotomy (introduced by Kant) between mind and thing, proclaiming them to be but different aspects of one and the same reality. Though variously accounted for by each of these thinkers, the world for all three is a projection of mind. That is, what we ordinarily designate by the term world is, in effect, an idea. In Hegel's view, specifically, the phenomenal world of Kant does not originate from a noumenal world independent of the knower, but is rather to be regarded as a phase in the ongoing developmental process of mind as it comes to an ever fuller knowledge of itself. What at one moment of consciousness is taken to be a world separate from the knower, is, in a subsequent moment, seen to be wholly one with the knower and to have been one with it all along. Hegel explains the whole of experience as a continuing drive of mind toward fuller self-consciousness. Mind and thing are really one to begin with; the seeming opposition between them is merely apparent and illusory. This view is commonly described by philosophers as one of absolute idealism, for nothing exists that is not mind.

But this was not the only response to the Kantian challenge in the nineteenth century. Other thinkers, following the lead of the French philosopher Auguste Comte (1790-1857), reflected the influence of the natural sciences by opting for a radical or empiricist view, which bore a strong resemblance to the phenomenalism of Hume. The positivist approach placed its emphasis wholly on what was sensible, abandoning all talk of universal, necessary knowledge. In this way these thinkers sought to eliminate the gaping Kantian split between mind and thing. Only the aspects of experience that could be verified in sense experience were to be considered authentic. Universal ideas and principles were viewed as being mere human constructs, conventional approximations and probabilities, but not universal and necessary truths. From the positivist view there is no single valid viewpoint for all humans, nor does anyone really know what might count as a good answer to a question. For the positivist there are only facts, not reasons, and the only real meaning to truth is that it is a simple recognition of what works. This singularly pragmatic, utilitarian viewpoint has found more than a few adherents during the post-Kantian era, and many among these have been, perhaps quite understandably, thinkers closely allied with the physical and natural sciences.

Although there are important differences between those who generally or generically describe their position as positivist, there is nonetheless a rather significant common ground they share. Some describe themselves as naturalists, others physicalists, or logical positivists, or analytical philosophers, or philosophers of ordinary language. All of these agree that sensory perception is the highest form of knowledge. Some of the more prominent names of those adhering to this school are Bertrand Russell, Ludwig Wittgenstein, Gilbert Ryle, and A. J. Ayer, all of England, and John Dewey, W. V. O. Quine, Donald Davidson, Hilary Putnam, and Richard Rorty of the United States. In his most recent work *Philosophy and the Mirror of Nature,* Richard Rorty of Princeton University starkly sums up the reluctance of the positivist philosopher to view human intelligence as qualitatively distinct from sensory and even mere physical activities by remarking that we humans are not "irreducibly different from inkwells or atoms" (Rorty 1981, p. 373).

Because of the impersonal and depersonalized view of the human championed by the positivist, and because a not altogether dissimilar impression was left by the German idealists for whom the individual all but drowned in the tide of universal consciousness, other thinkers of the nineteenth century opted for a highly personalized, highly individualistic philosophy. Thus the perceived trivialization of the human by both positivists and idealists gave rise to a new current of philosophy whose almost single aim was the promotion of the individual. Later this view came to be described as existentialism because of its frequent emphasis on how the human actually lived his life in the everyday world. In the nineteenth century the Danish philosopher Søren Kierkegaard (1813-55) and the German

Friedrich Nietzsche (1844-1900) were the two leading proponents of this at once anti-scientific and anti-rationalist view of the human person.

Existentialism was a reaction to the perceived excesses of German idealism more than anything else, and while displaying generally a disdain for universal and necessary knowledge, it did not repudiate the Kantian view entirely. Although it rejected the synthetic a priori of Kant, it did embrace Kant's position concerning the practical intellect, whereby Kant had exalted the freedom of the individual and made him the ultimate ground of all law. For the existentialist, there are no essences in the traditional sense. Though the human is acknowledged to have an essence of sorts, that essence is "no-thing"; it is freedom itself. It is wholly up to the individual to create his or her own life and assume full responsibility for it. For the existentialist there are no laws that ultimately are not of one's own making. One's obligations are to oneself alone. Though rejecting universal knowledge the existentialist absolutizes human freedom.

Existentialism found numerous adherents among continental European philosophers of the post World War II period, and somewhat later it also received a sympathetic hearing in various parts of the Americas. It has exerted considerable influence in the areas of psychology, religious studies, and ethical theory. Among the better-known philosophers of this century who are commonly identified with the existentialist movement are Martin Heidegger, Karl Jaspers, Jean Paul Sartre, and with notable qualifications, Gabriel Marcel.

Phenomenology is another philosophical movement of this century that is a spin-off from Kantian critical idealism. As a reaction to the nominalism of Locke and Hume and the positivism of subsequent thinkers, phenomenology focuses exclusively on the given in consciousness. Claiming a purely descriptive methodology, the phenomenologist seeks to uncover the pure essences of things as they appear in consciousness. Using a more traditional terminology, we might say that phenomenology concentrates on ideas as they are found in the mind, prescinding entirely from the reality of which they are ideas. Since ideas are the appearances of things, phenomenology is a philosophy of appearances, which is what the Greek word *phaenomena* means.

Speaking generally, then, we may say that phenomenology is a derivative of the philosophy of Descartes and of Kant, combining a modified version of the methodic doubt of the former with the transcendental or critical idealism of the latter. Phenomenology's acknowledged founder, the Austrian philosopher Edmund Husserl (1859-1938) actually sought to purify the Kantian system of its inconsistencies by employing a mitigated form of the Cartesian methodic doubt. Husserl will not block out all consciousness as Descartes had sought to do, but only those aspects of consciousness related to space and time. For purely methodological reasons he will proceed as though there were no such thing as a thing-in-itself. These ideas or essences within the mind are considered pure essences because they are removed from all individuating characteristics and are thus universal in character. Husserl will claim that his method is presuppositionless since his analysis begins with what is immediately given in consciousness. He further claims that the phenomenological method is merely descriptive; its sole intent is not to explain but merely to relate or describe the immediately given.

Although Husserl's understanding of his own phenomenological method underwent considerable development during his lifetime, and even though toward the end of his career he moved closer and closer to a transcendental idealist view, his voluminous writings have been enormously influential, especially among many important continental philosophers of this century. A list of these would include Martin Heidegger, Max Scheler, Alfred Schütz, Jean-Paul Sartre, Maurice Merleau-Ponty, and Paul Ricoeur.

As already indicated, in his later writings Husserl tended increasingly to adopt an idealist position, bending the phenomenological reflection farther and farther back into the hidden reaches of human consciousness, so that the world of transcendental human consciousness and the pure essences of things within the mind became ever more blurred. As Kant had before him, Husserl found it increasingly difficult to account for the differentiations of consciousness and to uncover a link by which the givens of inner consciousness might be traced to a world whose existence was independent of the human knower.

It was to alter the direction of this development of Husserl's phenomenology that some of his disciples have modified the latter's emphasis on pure consciousness by including the temporal and spacial within the horizon of the phenomenological reflection. These philosophers attempt to exploit the advantages both of existentialism's emphasis on the individual and phenomenology's emphasis on inner consciousness. Accordingly, this modified form of phenomenology is commonly termed existential phenomenology. It strives to preserve the phenomenological method and the reality of universal ideas while at the same time incorporating into its reflections the concrete, sensible world of everyday experience. Martin Heidegger, Maurice Merleau-Ponty, and Paul Ricoeur are perhaps the three best known of the philosophers who can be considered existential phenomenologists.

A closely related development, and one many see as growing out of the phenomenological movement itself, is that development commonly referred to as hermeneutics. The term owes its origin to the Greek word *hermeneia* whose first meaning is "interpretation." Accordingly, hermeneutics considers the primal task of the philosopher to be that of interpreting the human experience; that is, of clearing a path through the forest of experience so that its true meaning might appear. The hermeneuticist characteristically underscores the complexity of human knowing, emphasizing especially the temporal, historical context of all human experience and insisting that the meaning of experience must be constantly mediated by interpretation. For the hermeneuticist the meaning of experience can only be unfolded through a primordial clarification of language, since language is the indispensible mediator of experience itself. What differentiates this new hermeneutical development from the more classical and existential phenomenology is its focus on, even preoccupation with, the role language plays in the conscious world of the human. From the hermeneutical viewpoint the first and principal task of the philosopher is to clarify the manner in which language is used in the experience of the human. Indeed, in its more radical stage it reaches a point where the meaning revealed by language becomes one with language itself; language and its interpretation become one with understanding and insight. By seeking to establish beforehand the meaning of language and to uncover the structure of interpretation as a precondition for understanding, one can discern an affinity of the hermeneutical view to the Kantian position of laying bare a theory of knowing before taking up the inquiry into the metaphysics of being. Both in turn share the Cartesian view that a method of procedure in philosophy is a necessary preamble to the study of philosophy itself.

Although hermeneutics was, in its original form, a development of nineteenth-century German thinkers, spearheaded notably by Friedrich Schleiermacher (1768-1834) and Wilhelm Dilthey (1833-1911), it seems to owe its origin as a distinct philosophical method to the twentieth-century German philosopher Martin Heidegger (1889-1976). The latter's hermeneutical theory is an attempt to reformulate the transcendental phenomenology of Husserl, which Heidegger viewed as wholly removed from the temporal and historical dimension of human existence. Yet Heidegger sought to lay emphasis not only on the historical dimension of the things experienced but on the subjects of knowledge as well; that is, on the temporality of the individual knowing subject. Husserl's transcendental subject had not been affected by the historical conditions and contingencies of human existence.

For Heidegger there is no way for the subject to transcend the limitations of time and history and to assume a perspective that is transhistorical. So profoundly does temporality pervade the human condition that there is no escaping it. No knowledge is possible that does not involve the unique historical condition of the knowing subject. Hence there can be for Heidegger no serious talk of the human's attaining a universal viewpoint whereby lasting knowledge can be obtained. Heidegger refers to this inability of humans to transcend their own individual conditions as the hermeneutic circle.

In its later development Heidegger's philosophy takes more and more a linguistic turn. It is language that becomes the principal focus of his concern. The language of which Heidegger now writes, however, is not a language in the ordinary sense. It is not one of the languages we humans now employ. It is, instead, a language that strives to express the inexpressible—*Sein*, or "Being". As a consequence, Heidegger's later writings abound in poetical and mystical expressions which he seems to find more congenial to the task of uncovering the uncoverable (Being) in all its totally indeterminate and undifferentiated generality. Since Being is "no-thing," it cannot really be expressed in words. As it turns out, the authentic mode of the language of Being is nothing other than silence.

It is, however, a former student of Heidegger's, Hans-Georg

Gadamer, who is generally credited with the development of the former's ideas regarding a philosophical hermeneutic. Today Gadamer is looked upon as the founder and principal spokesman for the hermeneutical school.

The prominent French philosopher Paul Ricoeur has in his more recent writings shown great interest in the hermeneutical dimension of phenomenology and has made a considerable contribution toward clarifying its aims and method.

Structuralism, a derivative of the Heideggerian hermeneutic, lays claim to having drawn inferences from the latter's implications. In taking up the late Heideggerian theme of language, the French structuralist Jacques Derrida opts for a language not of Being but of Nothing, of total negativity. For Derrida, words always have more than one meaning. Consequently, no single interpretation of any sentence or text is possible. Everything has a plurality of meanings. For the structuralist, objective interpretation is an unrealizable goal. A text means what I want it to mean; whatever I read into it. The sheer contingency and uniqueness of the individual experience prevents one from ever obtaining a reliable set of criteria according to which an accurate and authentic interpretation can be made. It is, in short, impossible to know the whole without first knowing the parts; and the parts cannot be understood as parts without knowing the whole. The hermeneutic circle can never be breached, and there is no such thing as an authentic interpretation. No two readings of a text can in effect ever be the same, for each reading involves a creative act fashioning a wholly new meaning. In this way the hermeneutical problem dead-ends the search for universal and necessary knowledge. This, in brief, is the position assumed by the leading spokesperson for the structuralist school.

In this view, philosophy becomes essentially a "conversation" wholly wedded to the present moment. It involves relativizing both knowledge and values. Only through dialogue does the truth emerge, and its lifespan is precariously brief, safeguarded only by consensuses. Truth has been *sociologized*, becoming in effect a societal by-product. For the structuralist there is no genuine content to knowledge; there are no opposites nor are there contradictory principles; indeed, there is not even a principle of non-contradiction. That is why one contemporary scholar T. K. Seung concludes that Derrida's language of total negativity is "the language of nirvana" (Seung, 1982, p. 278).

Thus the contemporary resolutions of the problem that Kant bequeathed to the modern world ends, at least temporarily, on a destructive note. The only meaning of experience is assumed to be the experience itself as immediately given in the present. Such experience cannot be transcended. On the basis of these developments one may surmise that there are significant facets of the human experience that have been systematically omitted from Kantian and post-Kantian experiments.

This concludes our brief account of the development of modern philosophy from the time of Descartes to the present. The philosophy of this period is fundamentally transitional in that its chief concern is the adjusting of philosophic theory to the advances and discoveries recently made in the area of the natural sciences, mathematics, and technology. There can be little argument that the experiment inaugurated by Descartes and modified by others leads us to view the human being as a deeply divided person within, uncertain of an identity.

One cannot help but be profoundly struck by the similarity of the contemporary philosophic questions and those first raised centuries ago by the Greek philosophers Plato and Aristotle. Obviously, we humans have yet to solve the mystery which is ourselves. The quest of the question and the questioner continues unrelentingly.

Summary

In this chapter we have made a historical overview of the problem of human knowing. Beginning with Plato, we examined briefly this great philosopher's teaching regarding the nature of human intellective knowing and its origin. We saw that Plato often explained the general, universal idea as having its origin in a prior existence, since the sensory world could not adequately account for the immaterial and unchanging nature of those ideas. This view was seen to be a reaction to the position of Democritus and other pre-Socratic philosophers for whom human knowledge was essentially identified with sensory awareness.

In his adaptation of the Platonic theory, Aristotle sought to explain the origin of intellective knowledge by placing the ideas in things, rather than by assigning them to a separate intellective world. To explain, then, the possibility of the sensible world's being a genuine cause of our knowledge, Aristotle distinguished between an active and a receptive intellect. The former illuminated the sensible experience, making what was potentially intelligible actually intelligible, while the latter was the receptacle of the newly illuminated ideas. For Aristotle, therefore, knowledge was viewed as deriving from the sensible world even though human knowledge itself in its highest form transcended the world of singular existents.

Passing over for the moment the contribution the thirteenth-century philosopher St. Thomas Aquinas made to the development of the Aristotelian position, we next examined the views of the sixteenth-century French philosopher René Descartes. Striving to accommodate the method of philosophy to that of mathematics, Descartes chose as his philosophical starting point the internal awareness of his own existence as spirit. Descartes was convinced of his own existence and of the reality of mathematical truths because he had a clear and distinct idea of them as being independent of all sensory perception.

Next, John Locke's views on the nature of human knowledge were examined. This English philosopher was seen to have fundamentally disagreed with the experiment initiated by Descartes and to have insisted that all knowledge begins with the senses. However, by distinguishing between the primary and the secondary qualities of things, he did acknowledge a certain indebtedness to the French philosopher but felt that the doubts the latter had had with regard to sensory awareness could be allayed. Locke proposed that primary qualities were found to exist in the singular thing while secondary qualities were the responsibility of the knower.

Berkeley's reaction to Locke's distinction between primary and secondary qualities was then considered. Berkeley was seen to deny all forms of empiricism by denying the existence of matter. For Berkeley, "to be is to be perceived," so that things for him were identical with ideas or perceptions. Nothing existed outside the mind. What does not exist in any human's (finite) mind, must, if it exists at all, exist in the infinite divine mind.

The skeptical position of the Scottish philosopher David Hume was next examined. Hume attacked all previous theories of knowledge by calling into question the very principle by which any viable explanation could be effected. Hume denied any validity to the causal principle, arguing that one could not with certainty conclude that, just because something came to be in some way, it was therefore caused. His argument rested on his contention that each of the ideas of cause and of effect can be thought of separately without one necessarily including the other. As a result of his skepticism regarding the causal principle, Hume further concluded that we could not say with any certainty whether our knowledge proceeded from us, from things outside ourselves, or from the author of our being.

The next philosopher considered in this overview was the German critical idealist Immanuel Kant. Because he felt that Hume's critique of Locke's and Berkeley's views was telling, Kant strove to answer Hume in a manner that would preserve intact the necessity and universal validity of mathematical and scientific knowledge. Kant's response to Hume consisted in his developing his now-famous distinction between synthetic *a posteriori* and synthetic *a priori* judgments. In his view the synthetic *a priori* judgment is both universally true and dependent upon experience, not in the sense that it arises out of experience but in the sense that it involves experience. Kant views the mathematical judgment to be a perfect exemplification of the synthetic *a priori* judgment since it is universally and necessarily true and since it always involves an imaginative or sensuous component. As a corollary of this view, all metaphysical knowledge is illusory, maintains Kant, since it totally transcends experience and is hence always analytical. A final result of the Kantian critique was that the mind could never know reality as it actually was but merely *as it appeared* to the knowing subject. Our knowledge was, Kant claimed, not noumenal but phenomenal.

Lastly, the impact of the Kantian position on nineteenth- and twentieth-century philosophy was briefly reviewed. It was noted that most of the major branches of contemporary philosophy have their source in attempts by philosophers either to modify the Kantian critique of knowledge or to overcome it.

As early as the late eighteenth century and continuing into the nineteenth, German idealist philosophers strove to unite the phenomenal and noumenal worlds of Kant by identifying world with idea. The positivist view, which can be seen as a development of the philosophy of David Hume, was next considered. The positivist philosopher restricts the area of human experience to the sensible, or observable, world and responds to Kant's critique by denying all validity to his views concerning a priori knowledge. Finally, the phenomenon of existentialist philosophy as a reaction to the exaggerated claims of absolute German idealism; and phenomenology, as both a modified return to Cartesian and Kantian methodology and a reaction against the mechanizing tendencies of positivism, were considered along with the recent development of hermeneutics and structuralism.

Definitions and Conclusions

1. Plato's theory of forms explained the origin of universal and immaterial knowledge by positing an experience of the soul before its union with body. In this view sensory perception would be an occasion of our knowing, but not an actual cause. *Knowing* for Plato is equivalent to recollecting.

2. Aristotle placed the intellective forms within the material things themselves. Existing within the material world in a potentially intelligible state, these forms can only become actually intelligible through the mediating influence of an illuminating and active intellect. Knowing is not recollecting but rather the uncovering of the real through an illuminative and abstractive process.

3. Descartes began his philosophy with the axiom: "I think, therefore I am." Whatever he experienced in a clear and distinct manner he held to be true. According to this norm, the validity of mathematical truths could be established as well as the existence of an all-perfect Being from whom he received his existence as well as his ideas.

4. John Locke held that all knowledge must begin with sensory perception. Primary qualities exist independent of the knower, while secondary qualities exist dependent upon the receiver. Substance is the ground of primary qualities and is defined as "I know not what" by Locke.

5. George Berkeley identified reality with perception. *To be* was, for him, *to be perceived*. The distinction between primary and secondary qualities advanced by Locke he rejected as involving a contradiction. To maintain that a material world existed which was unknown was, for Berkeley, the surest road to skepticism.

6. David Hume viewed the causal principle as a mere psychological rule having its origin in custom. Consequently, there exists no general or universal knowledge for Hume, and there can be no certain knowledge of things since such knowledge would depend upon the

validity of the causal principle. What is known is only our impressions.

7. Immanuel Kant held that the only universal knowledge which was also *real* was found in the *synthetic a priori judgment.* Kant responded to Hume's critique of knowledge by granting that universal and necessary knowledge could not find its origin in mere experience. He held that the form of universality was imposed upon the matter of the experience by the knowing subject. The resulting knowledge was what he meant by the term *synthetic a priori.* Since in the very act of knowing, the knower modified whatever it was he knew, Kant denied the possibility of our ever knowing the thing as it is in itself. He also rejected metaphysics as a science of the real, or noumenal world.

8. *Absolute idealism* seeks to close the breach between the Kantian phenomenal and noumenal worlds by viewing the world as a projection of mind.

9. *Positivism* restricts human experience to the sensory, or empirical world, by accepting as real only what is observable or in some way measureable.

10. *Existentialism* reacts to absolute idealism by fixing its attention on the unique temporal dimension of human experience; and reacts to all forms of positivism by exalting and absolutizing the freedom of the individual.

11. *Phenomenology* seeks to uncover the pure essences of things as they appear within human consciousness, employing a modified form of the Cartesian *cogito.*

12. *Existential phenomenology* is an adaptation of phenomenological inquiry that includes temporal consciousness of perception as part of its reflective world.

13. *Hermeneutics* as philosophy is a development of phenomenology; its chief difference exists in its insistence that a methodological interpretation of meaning precede the investigation of essences. As a consequence hermeneutics focuses its attention on language, even identifying it with meaning itself.

14. *Structuralism* is a radicalization of hermeneutic theory in that it denies a distinction between idea and language and at the same time denies the possibility of objective interpretation of any single linguistic event.

4 Sensory Consciousness

*By a 'sense' is meant what has the power of
receiving into itself the sensible forms of things
without the matter.*

Aristotle

Preliminary Notions Regarding Sensory Consciousness

The material in the second chapter on the phenomenon of the question, and the brief outline in the preceding chapter on the human act of knowing from a historical perspective were intended to suggest the complexity of human knowledge. Knowing is, above all, an activity, although it is neither the only kind of human activity, nor is it an activity that is restricted to sensation, or sensory consciousness. In the present chapter our consideration will focus, however, on the nature of the sensory act.

Since it is apparent that the range of human activity is extremely broad, it is most important that one understand *why* our investigation begins with the sensory act, or sensory consciousness, and that we do not take this to mean that human activities can actually be compartmentalized as though one kind of activity were unrelated to others. By concentrating on sensory consciousness we do not assume that such awareness is found in isolation. The division, or separation, we make in studying the various levels of human activity is mainly a pedagogical device we employ in order to more easily understand the totality of our human experience. From the standpoint of lived experience, there is no such thing as a purely sensory consciousness.

There is no way in which it can be proved that we sense. The fact of sensory experience, which we humans share in more than a metaphorical manner with the animal world, is clearly a given. That we see, hear, touch, taste, and smell are facts that are obvious to each of us. These are activities that we clearly discern in others. However, what sensation is in itself, the nature of sensory consciousness, and the manner in which it is differentiated within itself are questions that require examination.

Sensory Acts Contrasted with Vegetative Acts

It will help if we begin our investigation of sensory consciousness by contrasting it to activities with which we are equally familiar and which bear some similarity to sensation. For example, in some form the vegetative acts of digestion, intussusception, growth, and repair are noted in all living organisms and are familiar to us on the level of everyday experience. By the ingestive act, food is taken in, digested, and converted into the tissue of the hosting organism. Through the metabolic process there is effected a union between two distinct, individual substances—between food and the consuming organism.

It is not difficult to detect a similarity between such an act and that of sensation. In the latter there is, first of all, always another that is sensed. We never, for example, just see or hear. Rather, it is always *something* that we see or hear, and this something is clearly distinct from both the sensory organ and the sensation itself. This is made evident to us by the fact that we do not always see or hear; neither do we continually see or hear the same thing. Sensation, therefore, depends upon an "other."

The manner of dependency of the digestive and sensory act, however, is seen to be quite different. What is taken in by the organism as food is consumed in the digestive process. It loses its identity, becoming one, in a physical sense, with the organism that has consumed it. On the other hand, the object which is seen or otherwise sensed, though it becomes one with the sensory act, remains totally unchanged. It is not diminished in its own being; it is not consumed; it does not lose its identity. The sensory act, therefore, respects the integrity of that which is sensed.

In order to distinguish between the union that is effected through the acts of ingestion and intussusception on the one hand and that of sensation on the other, philosophers employ the term *intentional union* to characterize the latter. Intentional union is not a *physical* union but a union of *forms* only. The sense has become the other, not in a physical way but, rather, it has been determined or *informed* by the other. The nature of the sensory act has been accurately and succinctly expressed by Aristotle when he stated that *the sense* in act is *the sensed* in act; that is, there is one activity but two components of the act, the sense and the other. We will return to a fuller consideration of the nature of this intentional union when we discuss the individual acts of sensation and how they are differentiated one from the other.

The Diversification of Sensory Consciousness

It is idle to question whether or not human beings enjoy sensory consciousness; that is, whether or not there is an intentional union of the human with their environment that transcends the merely physical type of union illustrated in the act of ingestion. To deny the act of sensation would render impossible the very discussion from which such a denial would originate, for we could not make such a denial without indicating it either through speech or writing, both of which depend upon sensory acts for their transmission. Indeed, the history of philosophy teaches that whenever our human sensory consciousness is minimized or neglected, a distorted view of the human inevitably results.

The acts typifying our sensory consciousness are those with which we are familiar on an everyday basis; that is, those of seeing, hearing, tasting, smelling, and touching. Our present intent is to probe into the nature of such sensory acts and to explain in a fundamental way what the conditions are for their possibility. We shall also inquire into the fact of the differentiation of sensory consciousness, seeking to explain the multiplicity of such acts.

In the preceding section we already touched upon the dependency of all sensory consciousness on something other than itself. It is always something that is seen or heard, etc., and that which is seen or heard is that which explains the actuality of sensory consciousness within us. When no other (object) is present, we are incapable of seeing; we see nothing. The *other* in sensation is that which presents itself before the sensory organ and somehow activates it. This other has come to be termed *object*. The root meaning of the Latin word *objectum* is "that which is hurled against something." An object, therefore, is that other which presents itself to the sensory organ. In the case of the sense of sight, the state of *can see* moves to the state of *actually seeing*. Thus, the act of seeing consists in the sensory organ becoming the other. It is a kind of union between sense and object.

But, of course, we also readily experience different kinds of acts of sensation. Within the realm of sensory consciousness we are aware that seeing is quite a different kind of activity from hearing or any other sense activity. That is, we are conscious of seeing as an act distinct from hearing and vice versa. Upon closer scrutiny we also observe that the act of seeing reveals something to us about the object sensed that is provided by no other sensory power. Only through the sense of sight do we become conscious of the color of the object sensed. I may hear the automobile driving past me, but if I do not see it, I cannot answer the question, "What color is it?"

Yet it is important to note that what I am aware of is not, for example, color alone or sound alone but the total thing that possesses color and gives off sound. What is sensed as a whole by all of the sensory powers can thus be designated as the *total object*, while that aspect of the total object which uniquely activates a particular sensory power we can conveniently designate as the *formal object*. Employing this terminology then, we can, by taking an object of sensation such as an orange, easily designate what the formal object of each of the five special senses is.

As already noted, the *formal object* of the sense of sight is *color.* We know the color of the orange only from the fact that we are able to *see* it. Similarly, the formal object of the sense of hearing is *sound.* If I allow the orange to drop onto the table, it is only the sense of hearing that registers the sound of the orange hitting the table. In the same manner, the sense of taste is activated by the *flavor* of the orange; the sense of smell, by its orange *fragrance*, or *odor*; and the sense of touch, by its *hardness* or *softness* and by its *temperature*—whether or not it is warm or cold.

In all of these instances of sensing, *that which* is known is the same. The total object is *the orange* for it is the orange that I see, hear, taste, touch, and smell. Yet each of these sensory activities receives its stimulus from a different aspect of the orange. One power is activated by its color; another, by the sound it gives off; another, by its flavor; another, by its scent; and another, by either its hardness or its temperature. Each of these sensory activities contributes to our knowledge of the orange in its own unique way; seeing is not the same as hearing or any of the other sensory acts.

Lastly, and of considerable significance, is our awareness that sensory activity is highly varied. We sense different things at different times, and the time span of individual acts of sensation is often no more than a fleeting one. Our attention is directed from one sensed object to another, frequently in a spontaneous manner. For example, a sound or pattern of sounds intrudes upon our consciousness without warning, only to fade away as quickly as it came without our being the cause either of its coming or going.

It is this transitory nature of our sensory perceptions that clearly indicates that they are not of our own making. Each of our sensory acts is dependent upon the existence of an *other* for its very occurrence. In order to see, we are dependent upon the existence of an other, something that is separate from ourselves. The phenomenon of sensation unmistakably indicates that a world of things exists independent of our knowing it. This world is not there *because we sense it*; rather, we sense it *because it is there*.

Common Sensibles

As already explained, each sensory power is activated by a unique characteristic, or quality, of the individual sensible object, and it is through this special characteristic or formal object that we are able to distinguish one sense from another. Seeing is defined as that sensory activity by which I know physical objects inasmuch as they have color; hearing is defined as that sensory activity by which I know physical objects inasmuch as they give off sound; and so forth.

Yet, having said this much, we by no means wish to limit the above sensory acts to providing a knowledge of things merely inasmuch as they possess the one specific characteristic capable of actuating each of these separate powers. Obviously we see more than the color of an object. We see that it is a particular size, has a particular shape, and is either in motion or at rest. In the instance of the orange mentioned earlier, besides the color, clearly one sees the size and shape of the orange and one can also see how it falls to the table.

Further, the sense of touch clearly indicates to me the size and shape of the orange. And even if my eyes are closed, by touching the orange I can ascertain whether or not it is in motion. Characteristics of things—such as, size, shape, motion—that can be sensed by more than one sensory power are ordinarily referred to as *common sensibles*, for they are shared in common by two or more powers.

Precisely, however, because they are shared properties, they do not serve to differentiate one power from the other. Hence, we are unable to define sight as the power by which we know the size or shape of a physical object, since the same certainly can be said of the sense of touch and even to some extent of the sense of hearing. What we call common sensibles are identical to what Locke labeled primary qualities. Further, what we have called the formal objects of the sensory powers, Locke designated as secondary qualities. It is important to note the difference, however, between Locke's explanation of the origin and significance of this distinction and the one given above.

The foregoing considerations allow us now to formulate, along with Aristotle, the following general principle: Powers are *known* in their acts, and acts are *specified* according to their *proper formal objects*. This principle sums up briefly what we have observed above from our reflections on the phenomena of sensation. It indicates that we can detect these powers or capabilities only through their activities and that these activities can be distinguished or differentiated to the extent that one can detect that they are related to uniquely distinct properties of sensible things.

The Role of the Sensory Image in Sensation

The final aspect of the sensory act which deserves our attention is that of the role of the sensory image. From the preceding analysis it is clear that the senses require a stimulus from the object to activate them. Were the senses independent of the external object for their activity, there would be no accounting for the variation in the sensory act nor for the fact that we are not always seeing or hearing, etc.

It is further obvious that the object sensed does not enter bodily into the sensory power. At the same time, the object is present in some way. The reason, for example, that I am unable to see with my eyes closed is simply that nothing external to the sense is then capable of rendering itself present to the sensory power and of thus activating it. It is why the blind cannot see and the deaf cannot hear. The fact that we may experience a brief continuation of seeing after the eyes have been closed or of hearing after the sound has ceased does not gainsay the above claim. Such phenomena can be readily explained by a continued internal stimulation of the sensory organ caused by the original stimulus. However, the ability we have to retain what we have sensed long after the act has ceased is a different matter, involving as it does the imaginative and memorative powers, which will be considered in the following chapter. The eye (a similar case can be made for the other senses) cannot move from a state of *can see* to actually seeing unless it is activated by something other than itself; that is, by the sensed object through the medium of that object's likeness. This provides the only explanation, it appears, as to why we are not *always* seeing, nor always beholding the same thing. Neither the eye nor any other sense is sufficient unto itself; it simply cannot function without having been brought into union with an other's likeness. This activation takes place through a likeness, or representation, of the object which is found within the sensory power.

The likeness, or representation, of the other does more than facilitate the act of vision; it renders such an act possible. Without the vicarious presence of the other in the organ of sight, there can be no initial act of vision. This brings us to the crucial point regarding the function of the likeness of the object. To assume that it is the likeness that is *first seen* and from that assumption to attempt to reason to the existence of the object of that likeness, is to fall victim to the criticism of Berkeley and other philosophers who argued against such a copy theory of knowledge. The copy theory can never establish that the image in the eye is a copy or similitude of an object existing outside the eye. It is just such an approach that ultimately leads to the skeptical position assumed by David Hume.

Because such an approach leads to a dead end, rendering it impossible to affirm with any assurance that what we sense or know is truly something distinct from the perceiver, it is crucial to view the form, or object, which activates the sensory power, not as *that which* is sensed but rather as that *by which* the sensory act can occur. By means of the image within our eye we see that *of which* it is a likeness. As a sign, the image leads us to a knowledge of the other. But the image is a formal and not a material sign.

A sign is that which, when known, leads one to the knowledge of something else. In the case of a material sign, first the thing itself is experienced and then we are led to what it signifies. Such is the case of a stop sign at a street intersection. First it is observed as a post of a certain size and color and then it is recognized for what it *signifies*; namely, that one coming to this intersection should make a complete stop before proceeding through. However, the sign of which we are now speaking, the sensory impression within the sense organ, is not what we first *sense*, but as indicated, it is that by means of which the object is sensed. Hence the sensory impression is not a *material* but a *formal* sign. We have no conscious knowledge of it as a sign *before* knowing *that which* it represents. This occurs simultaneously in one act.

As already stated, were I to affirm that the image in the sensory organ of my sight is that which the eye beholds, I would then be *affirming* that what I really know are my own impressions. I would then have no way of avoiding a thoroughly subjective theory not only of sensation but, ultimately, of all knowledge. I could never really establish that the impression which I claimed to know was really an *image* at all; I could never show that it pointed to something beyond itself.

Thus we can appreciate why it is that sensation involves a form of union of the knower with the other, or the known. That which I sense has somehow become one with me, not in its total physical structure but vicariously through the sensible form, or object, by which the sight has been activated. This sensible form is that by which I see, and it controls and measures totally the act of seeing. I see only to the extent that my sight has been activated by something other than itself. Thus, I cannot receive the likeness of a *tree* within the organ of sight and see, for example, a *mountain*. The object sensed cannot activate the sense in any manner save that according to which it itself is. It is a tree; this is the way it is, and thus it cannot present itself as being other than *it is*. In short, the object cannot falsify itself. To imply that it does, or could, is to assume a position that is patently contradictory. Such a position would lead us to believe that the object presenting itself to the sensory power is really not one thing, but rather a plurality of things at one and the same time; and in anthropomorphic fashion would have us attribute to sensed objects qualities that are exclusively human, implicitly having us view them as being capable of masquerading their true identity.

Of course it is true that some plants and many animals are capable of ingenious camouflage by which they seek to escape detection. Yet this most interesting phenomenon found in nature in no way contradicts what was said above even though it might well appear to. It is important not to confound the act of the special sense, such as that of sight, with acts of the interior senses and the intellect, which judge and evaluate the meaning of *what it is* that is sensed. The interpretation made of the experience of what is seen or heard, for example, can be erroneous, but the original sensed experience can only be authentic. What the eye sees is simply what is present to it under the formality of color; it does not *judge* what it sees, so that, regardless of whether the object seen is engaged in an act of expert camouflage or not, the eye merely sees it as *it is*. Its task is not to discern what it is that is seen, but merely to pass on to other cognitive powers the visual characteristics of the things it sees.

It is helpful to recall here what was remarked at the beginning of this chapter; namely, that the process of human knowing is a complex one and that the activity of the special senses is merely one phase of the total cognitive act.

Let us then reemphasize what we have already stated, that each of the special senses, senses the total object, the singular individual thing existing independent of the sensory power, but yet attains to it in an incomplete and restricted manner, since each sense is only formally activated by one aspect of what it senses. Thus, for example, the eye in beholding a portrait of former President Lincoln sees what is to be seen, but cannot penetrate beyond the color, the shading, the size, etc. of the portrait. It remains oblivious to what lies outside the field of its formal object and common sensibles. The eye beholds the portrait materially but not formally; that is, what it sees is a portrait, but it does not see *that it is* a portrait. This latter recognition is an interpretive act which can only follow upon the initial act of seeing. The sensory act of the exterior sense generates the question What is this? but the sense remains blithely unaware of all properties and intelligibilities of the sensed thing except those made accessible to it through its own formal object. What the eye beholds is simply a colored thing. It does not see the *what* of what it sees, since that *what* is not visible. Such fuller awareness of the sensed thing must involve the activities of powers that follow the visual act; namely, the interior senses and the intellect.

Similarly, in the case of animal camouflage, the eye reports with unerring accuracy what it beholds, a colored patch. The discerning of what this signifies and of the nature of the creature sensed, even whether or not it is camouflaging itself, is a judgment to be made by another, higher power. The special sense itself is not licensed, as it were, to wade into these deeper waters, but must limit its activity to the more modest though indispensible task of providing the sensing organism with the first raw data of sense experience. It is clear that the phenomenon of the optical illusion can be explained in much the same fashion that the phenomenon of animal camouflage has been explained. Here again the senses report what is *there* with unfailing accuracy, but because of a certain complexity of what has been sensed, what they report can be ambiguously interpreted. The conclusions just reached seem to be strikingly borne out by recent studies pertaining to vision in the new born, which indicate the need to clearly demarcate the actual vision from its interpretation, for they show that the infant requires a good deal of time and practice before it learns to distinguish objects one from another so as to be able to identify the use or function of these objects. What, of course, the infant is doing is learning how to interpret what it sees, so that color patches gradually become known to it as familiar color patterns with associated meaning.

The foregoing explanation of the sensory act also offers us a consistent account of how it can sometimes happen that one can have one's eyes wide open, yet remain oblivious to what one is looking at or even that one is looking at anything. Unless there is a minimum of concentration while one is sensing, which entails an involvement of the interior senses and the intellect as well, there is really no authentic act of seeing at all. The exterior organ is receiving its sense stimulus from the object and indeed is in act, but because the act is not in turn acted upon by the other sensory powers, there is no awareness of what is being seen. If one's attention is distracted from what one is sensing with one sense organ, it is just as though that sense were not activated at all. The sensing does take place, but it is not accompanied by a subsequent interpretive activity, with the result that it becomes a meaningless act.

For the purpose of this discussion, the assumption is that the sensory organs in question are healthy. Historically, particularly since the time of Descartes, part of the skeptical attitude concerning the untrustworthiness of the sensory act, can be traced to philosophers who have unduly stressed and incorrectly interpreted those instances where the sensory power is in some way defective and, therefore, incapable of functioning normally. The phenomenon of color blindness is often adduced to support the contention that seeing is an activity subjectively conditioned by the one sensing.

In the case of color blindness, however, one still observes a constancy and regularity in how the sense of sight receives its object. The color blind person sees objects in a consistent manner; a red object will regularly appear, for example, as amber. But it is precisely because the anomaly is constant that it can be detected and diagnosed as such. Such detection rests squarely on the premise that it is the object that controls the content of the sensory act. Only because the sensory act is cbjective can the pathological condition of the sensing power be uncovered. In short, such anomalies as color blindness merely serve to reinforce the claim that the sensing powers truly sense things as they are.

In concluding this chapter on the intriguing but elusive phenomenon of human sensation, it is important that one recognize its unique character and appreciate that sensation is truly a form of authentic knowledge. It is not the *totality* of knowledge, to be sure, but it is an authentic form of it, and one whose role must be seen as complementary to other forms of knowing. Otherwise we cannot hope to avoid the pitfalls of a rationalist or reconstructionist theory of human knowing.

The reader is cautioned once again, however, to recall that the total phenomenon of human knowing is a harmonious, unified process which constitutes a cognitional whole. Hence, the mere fact that we begin our investigation at the sensory level of awareness does not prejudice this truth and above all does not suggest that sensation either precedes intellection in a temporal sense, or that it is a mode of knowing which merely parallels the intellective process. Human sensation finds its true goal and purpose in understanding; it is not an end in itself but contains an inherent order beyond itself.

We conclude with one final but general observation regarding sensation. This marvelous capability of sensing puts us in contact with the entire world of sensible things. Everything that is sensible can be sensed. Even on this level of knowing there is an openness approaching almost to infinity. The sensory power of sight makes it possible for everything that possesses color to present itself to me; for me to enter into a kind of union with it, somehow to become one with it. Knowledge is thus seen to be an activity that is intrinsically relational. It is essentially a social activity relating me to another, and even allowing me, in a qualified sense, to become the other. Aristotle expressed this with customary succinctness by stating "the sensory power in act is identical with the sensible." Since, then, the sensory power is naturally ordered to all sensible things, it is potentially all sensible things.

Summary

In this chapter we have discussed the nature of the sensory act and the manner in which it is differentiated. The sensory act was first contrasted with the organic act of ingestion and was seen to be of a higher order since it implies a union that respects the integrity of its object.

Next, in order that we might intelligently distinguish between one kind of sensation and another, the distinction between the *total* and *formal* object was introduced. Subsequently, the difference between the formal and common objects was examined. It was seen that the formal object was unique to one individual sensory power, while the common object was capable of activating two or more powers. These reflections on the nature of sensory powers and their various acts led us to formulate the following principle relating to the knowledge of these powers and the distinction of their acts: Powers are known in their acts and distinguished by their formal objects.

Finally, the role of the sensory image in the various acts of sensation was examined. The sensory image was seen to be *not that which* is sensed, the material object, but rather that *by which* what is sensed is sensed. The sensory image was thus seen to be a *formal* rather than a *material* sign of the sensory act, for the sensory power itself has no conscious awareness of the image within it by which it is reduced from a potential to an actual state.

Definitions and Conclusions

1. Sensory consciousness is but an aspect of the totality of awareness that we identify as human consciousness.

2. Our study begins with human consciousness because the sensible thing is the ultimate source of our human, intellective awareness, and not because sensory activity occurs first in the order of time or in isolation from other aspects of human awareness.

3. The sensory differs from the digestive act in that the former does not alter the nature of its object but allows it to remain intact. It is a union which is thus less material than that by which food is digested and assimilated.

4. The total object of a sensory act is *that which* is sensed: tree, dog, house. The formal object is that aspect or quality of the material object *by which* a given sensory power is *uniquely* activated: color, sound, flavor, odor, temperature.

5. A common object is the quality of a total object that is capable of activating more than one sensory power: size, shape, motion.

6. As purely potential in the order of activity, powers can be known only in their acts, while their acts are distinguished according to their formal objects.

7. The sensory image, or likeness, is not *that which* is sensed by the power but is rather that *by which* the material object itself is sensed. It is thus a formal and not a material sign.

5 The Internal Senses

And I discern the scent of lilies from that of
violets while smelling nothing; and I prefer
honey to grape-syrup, a smooth thing to a
rough, though then I neither taste nor handle,
but only remember.

Augustine

The Coordinating Sense

We have examined the orientation and nature of the sensory powers,
which link the knowing subject to the real world of physical objects.
Because each of these senses is restricted in what it is able to know,
they are often called "special" senses. The range of activity of each
of these senses is especially ordered to respond to a single activator,
or quality, inherent in the sensed object. Thus, for example, the
sense of sight is incapable of detecting sound because the latter is
not inclusive of color, the formal object (activator) of sight; that is,
the formal object of seeing (color) is lacking in the formal object of
hearing (sound), and vice versa. The special senses are also referred
to as the "external" senses, because they traffic directly with the
world of things that is extrinsic or external to the sensing subject,
the knower.

How many of these external or special senses there are and precisely how they are to be subdivided are matters of dispute. But the
question regarding the number of these senses is of no great concern

to the philosopher and can readily be left to the other disciplines for further study. For example, it does not serve our purpose to make any judgment here concerning the nature of the vestibular, the kinesthetic, and the organic senses. The *vestibular* refers to our sense of gravity and our ability to maintain our physical balance. The *kinesthetic* refers to the internal sensations we have of our physical motion. The *organic* refers to our sense of such things as hunger and thirst. The vestibular, kinesthetic, and organic senses can be considered independent senses, or they can be regarded as subdivisions of the sense of touch (somesthetic sense). From the philosophical standpoint these are not questions of great concern. What is, however, of concern to the philosopher is the reason *why* man and the animals possess sensory powers, and the way in which these various sensory powers are *interrelated.*

The first of these questions we have previously touched upon. Sensation provides a flexibility and a manifold of activity that implies for the sensing subject a much greater freedom and independence from its environment than it otherwise would have. Through sensation any animal, including the human, is able to seek nutriment in a way that safeguards its health and well-being. Thus, sensation is much more than a mere adjunct of the organism; it is an essential dimension of it. So important is the sensory activity, that any animal is incapable of surviving without it. All sensing organisms depend upon their ability to sense in order to maintain and nourish themselves and to reproduce their kind. In short, their development and survival are directly dependent upon their ability to make sensitive contact with the world that surrounds them. Sensory knowledge is for the animal truly a necessary way of life.

From this it is clear that the coordination of the various sensory acts of the animal organism is of paramount importance to its well-being. It is imperative that the act of seeing be coordinated with the act of hearing, and that these sensory acts be likewise related to acts of touching, tasting, and smelling. At the same time, however, it is equally clear from our foregoing analysis of the special senses that such coordination and differentiation of these sensory activities cannot be effected by any of them alone, because each special sense is restricted to its own formal object. It is for this reason that a further capacity is necessary to the sensing organism, if it is to organize the various sensory activities. An apt name for this capability is the *co-*

ordinating sense, for its fundamental activity is to differentiate and to coordinate the activities of the special senses.

It is clear that this coordinating sense must have as its material object the impressions of all of the special senses. Otherwise, it would be unable either to differentiate or to correlate them. Its formal object, that unique perspective according to which the total, or material, object is viewed, would then be these same impressions to the extent that they are related one to another or that they are distinguished one from another.

The special function, then, of the coordinating sense can be viewed as a monitoring of the activities of all of the special senses in such a way that the raw data of these sensory acts may be organized and patterned according to the nature of the sensible objects that present themselves to the external senses. The activity of the coordinating sense permits the sensing organism to become aware of the manner in which these sensory activities are related, so that it is able to know that what it sees is also what it scents, and that what it scents is also what it hears, and so on with the activities of the other senses in any possible combination.

For example, let us suppose that we see a bird perched on the limb of a tree. Our sense of sight does not inform us of its chirping, for that information comes to us solely through our sense of hearing. Yet when we see this individual bird on the limb, we are aware that it is the same one that we hear chirping. The union of these two acts of sensation is the accomplishment of the coordinating sense.

The activity of the coordinating sense performs a function of irreplaceable value to the sensing subject, who is continually faced with the herculean task of coordinating and differentiating a great variety of sensory impressions. We shall study later how this clustering and organizing of our sensory experiences into patterned data assists, in a very important manner, the intellective activity of the human.

The Imagination

The retention of sensory images is an obvious dimension of the human experience. Once acquired, the patterned images of the coordinating sense are not lost but are stored within the psyche, where they can be combined with other sensory experiences and utilized in various ways. Indeed this storage of images is what we refer to as sensory experience, even though such experience is always enlivened and transformed by an accompanying intellectual awareness, which we shall consider later. Because of the continual flood of fresh impressions, or images, coming through the special and coordinating senses, retention of these images is essential if we are to profit from our experiences of the past.

The act of retention is clearly distinguishable from the act of the coordinating sense, and Aristotle has even assigned a separate inner power to account for this function, which we commonly call the imagination. The word imagination derives from the Latin *imago*, which in turn comes from the verb *imitari*, meaning to imitate, or be like another. An image, then, is a likeness, or a representation, of another; that which imitates another. The imagination stores impressions (likenesses) that have been received through the special senses and unified by the coordinating sense, and it can make use of these impressions in any number of complex, even fanciful, ways.

As a distinct power, imagination must have its own proper act, which in turn is distinguished by its own *proper object*. The *total*, or *material object* of the imaginative sense is understood to be all of the images that originate directly from the activity of the special senses and are formed and collated by the coordinating sense. The *formal object*, or the unique perspective, of the imagination is simply the images in themselves which, though derived from, have also been freed from, all attachment to the sensible world of concrete things; they are freed from the experiences that originated them. This means, therefore, that the imaginative power receives and stores images in a manner totally *independent* of time and change. This unique function of the imagination by which it timelessly stores the images and impressions of previous experience has brought in its train consequences that have played an important role in the development of Western philosophy. The methodic doubt of Descartes and the phenomenalism of Hume can be traced to problems that "unattached" images of the imagination raise in connection with the question of certainty and truth.

It is the memorative act that traces impressions back to their point of origin, where they are sequenced according to a before and an after. It is memory, not imagination, that renders possible the experience of time. Understanding the timelessness of the imaginative act is essential if we are to recognize this distinction between imagining and remembering. Such understanding helps to render intelligible the phenomenon of dreams.

At this juncture it is important to emphasize that the *creative* imaginative act is quite distinct from the *fundamental* imaginative act. Whereas the fundamental imaginative act is concerned chiefly with storing and retaining images, the creative imaginative act is more closely associated with bringing these images together in a way not previously experienced. The creative imagination explores the outer limits of possibility and human ingenuity.

Although there is abundant evidence that animals possess an imaginative power that enables them to retain impressions of objects sensed, the creative imaginative act, which requires conscious reflection, is only realized through the influence of the intellective power of the human. It has no counterpart in the animal world.

The creative imaginative act enables us to freely associate imaginative images one with another in wholly novel and previously unexperienced ways. The result of such haphazard associations is the constitution of new patterns and images ranging from the very plausible to the singularly bizarre. Through the employment of this creative dimension of the imaginative power, people have constructed fictional images of great complexity and grandeur. Witness the great epics of literature, Homer's *Iliad* and *Odyssey,* Virgil's *Aeneid,* Dante's *Divine Comedy,* the plays and sonnets of Shakespeare, the plays of Racine. On a less elevated plane there are the ingenious animated cartoons of Disney, the intergalactic battles of *Star Wars,* the delightful nonsense scenes of the Muppets, and the special world of Charlie Brown.

It is the human's power of imaginative association that accounts for the literary phenomenon of the metaphor. Derived from the Greek and meaning etymologically "to transfer" or "carry across," metaphor results when one uses an image from one channel of experience in place of an image or impression from a distinctly different channel of experience, implying a likeness or comparison of things experienced independently of each other. Involving a novel use of sensory images, the metaphor always bears with it a sense of unreality, and we recognize this quite readily. Nonetheless, we find this form of "image play" both entertaining and meaningfully suggestive, never tiring of striving to piece together fresh combinations of metaphorical images, mainly because they allow us to share almost mystically in a creative act and to personalize our experience.

Thus, for example, through the free merging of images and interplay of diverse modes of experience, we create expressions such as *fleeting days*, *whispering wind*, and *blind hands*.

It is through an extended use of the creative imagination that humans are able to create new worlds and environments. It is this dimension of the imaginative power that permits us the development of the fictive act. Music, drama, literature, sculpture, painting, architecture, motion picture production, tapestry weaving, the graphic arts, are all subsets of this world of fiction—products that humans have imagined and woven together from items of experience previously obtained. It is the rootless character native to images that makes possible this marvelous fictionalizing activity.

With the aid of fiction we humans seek and find a certain temporary release from the concerns of everyday life, an escape, as it were, from the constraints of our own finitude. Through our literary and artistic creations, we experience in a very limited way the power of the creative act, whereby we are able to bring into being something that did not previously exist. The human creative act, however, is of a constructionist nature, for it is basically a form of "reconstitution." However fascinating and brilliant this reconstitution may prove to be, it has emerged from something else that already is. What we humans are able to achieve is the organization of our experience in a manner in which it has never before been organized. For creative organization to take place, however, it is essential that the "material" to be organized already possess the capability of being "shaped" by the creative power of the human act. This means, in short, that all human creation is an act of discovery, an uncovering of the previously unknown, which elicits from the discoverer the response of wonder and surprise.

Before concluding this brief section on the imaginative power, it will be well to reemphasize what has already been mentioned at the beginning; that is, the *primal* function of the imaginative power is not that of fictionalizing, or "reconstitution," but rather that of storing and retaining the patterned images received from the coordinating sense, as well as those creatively formed by the imagination itself. It is precisely because these images are ontologically cut off from the initial sensory experience that generated them that they can be considered as *things* in their own right and related with one another in all of the various creative ways that we have just considered.

From the foregoing, then, it is easy to appreciate why it was that Aristotle referred to imagination as the source of error. The very fact that the stored sensory images can be viewed apart from the original experience, which gave them rise, and the fact that the imagination itself has creatively clustered them in an unexperienced way readily suggests how it might prove difficult on occasion to separate the imaginary, or fictional, world from the world of authentic experience. Indeed, beginning with Descartes, many modern philosophers have been vexed by this problem.

One can readily appreciate how, from such a potpourri of real and unreal experiences, the problem of the *real* and the *unreal* may arise. Not only occasionally but each day, we humans must struggle to repossess our world of authentic experience and carefully differentiate it from the twisted and gnarled world of unreality—the free scenario we commonly call dreams. In the creation of dreams, the imagination, without conscious direction from the knowing subject, pieces together bits of experience in a totally haphazard fashion, thereby creating a *new world* that inevitably mixes with the dreamer's authentic experience that has been obtained from an encounter of the special senses with the sensible world. The question of dreams serves to lead us directly to the next topic for our consideration, the phenomenon of remembering.

The Memory

Besides being a remarkable accomplishment, which we tend to take for granted, the act of remembering is so vital to human development and so central to the acquisition of a human personality that its importance can hardly be exaggerated. The distinction between the acts of imagining and remembering is undeniably quite subtle, but it is crucial to understand the difference between these two acts if one is to have a reasonable basis for a theory of knowledge that would not ultimately fall prey to subjectivism and consequently deprive knowledge of its only true value. It is through memory that we are able to trace the impressions and images stored in the imagination to their actual point of origin and thus to distinguish the authentic image from one that is the product of creative fantasy or the spontaneous result of subconscious mental activities occurring during sleep.

When I say that I "remember" something, I am, first of all, referring to an event in the past, which was once as real and as present as the activity I am at the present moment engaged in. Thus memory has to do with not what is but what once was; in this sense memory deals with the *what-is-not*, or *non-being*.

Yet, although memory is of what-is-not, it is nonetheless an activity present to me in my consciousness at the moment of my remembering. At the same time, this presence is of an absence, for in remembering an event I am fully aware that what is present to me in my remembering no longer enjoys a real existence apart from that conscious awareness. That is why Aristotle refers to the memorative act as one by which I am aware of the *past as past*. It is in this sense that remembering differs from the fantasy world of imagining; in the former, I am aware that what is now present to me in my consciousness was once present to me as a *real event* and once determined and shaped my consciousness.

It is for this reason that, although I can imagine that I am presently in Mexico City or that I once was there, I cannot say I *remember* having been there unless, in point of fact, at some time in the past I actually visited that city. Remembering, then, is an act which oscillates between the past and the present, the real and the unreal, being and non-being. It seeks to rescue from oblivion the valued threads of past experience and to extend into the present what now no longer is. Perhaps it is true that no human act more dramatically underlines the fragile nature of the human condition than this phenomenon of human remembrance.

We may then sum up the results of our reflections on the memorative act as follows: (1) Remembrance is always of an event that actually occurred at some time; (2) that which is remembered is no longer really in existence but has ceased to be; (3) the remembered event which is no more in its own reality is nonetheless present to me in my consciousness; and (4) in remembering I am aware that what is present in my consciousness is now totally past in its own actuality. Since remembering is an act whereby one is consciously aware of the *past as past*, it is clearly distinct from an act of merely retaining sensory images and of collating such images in a wholly fanciful way. The *material object* of the memorative power is all past events, and the formal perspective, or *proper object*, of the memorative power, according to which these past acts are viewed, is precisely that of their *being past.*

The memorative act is intimately related to my awareness of time, for it is through the act of remembering that my consciousness of time arises. Through memory I am able to distinguish the present from the past and both the present and the past from the future. Time, after all, is nothing more than the sequential property we note in the order of events. It is the numbering of events according to their order of precedence, according to a *before* and an *after.* Time is thus a property of change, and the memorative power is that capacity by which the knower is consciously and expressly aware that change has taken place. Memory is the *time* power.

Our unique human ability to remember is, of course, very closely linked with our intellective prowess, for this is what provides us with the power not only to recognize that certain events have transpired but also in what sequence they transpired. It also makes possible the remarkable phenomenon of *recall,* whereby one can bring to consciousness a selected array of past events dependent in good part upon one's own desires and preferences.

Even a slight impairment of our memorative ability so handicaps us in our effort to function as humans that we find it impossible to conduct our affairs in a normal way. Practically every activity we perform depends in some way upon our conscious retention of past acts and events. Speech and all forms of communication, for example, are unthinkable procedures without the presence of the memorative act. Indeed, all forms of learning are somehow dependent upon memory. In fact, who I am as an individual, my own personal identity, depends upon my being able to remember my past actions, experiences, etc., as belonging to me, and as having somehow shaped and formed my personality. In addition, my memory also retains my personal evaluations of what I have experienced, including my emotional reactions to particular occurrences. Thus I can recall the pleasure I once experienced from a particular food or drink as well as the joy or anger felt on a particular past occasion.

Though the imaginative power retains all experiences, it is the memorative power that *conserves* their *meanings*, for it alone enables the individual to relate them to their original source, thereby grounding our contact with the real. The memorative power provides us with the criterion whereby an actually lived experience may be distinguished from a purely imaginary one. We know that we have actually visited a certain place if we are able to associate it with a situation and an experience that at one time engaged our special senses with a concomitant sharing and involvement of the body. For example, if I have never been to Miami, I recognize the statement "I have visited Miami" as having no personal meaning for me. It differs little from the meaninglessness of my supposing that I have visited some far distant galaxy which is light-years away.

We have already considered how human achievement that is expressed through the wonders of music, art, literature, etc., is made possible by the free state in which sensory forms are preserved in the imaginative power. Such unattached retention permits us to reflect on these forms as being independent, isolated units and, prescinding totally from their point of origin, to construct from them new and wholly creative patterns of experience. This condition of independence from the originating reality which authored them permits us the possibility of fashioning within our minds *realities* of the most bizarre nature, of which the animated cartoon may be perhaps the most striking and familiar example. There is little danger of confounding the well-known characters of the Disney cartoons with any experience of the real world. These personages are unmistakably creations of fantasy.

The memorative power, on the other hand, is precisely that which allows us to formulate the distinction between what actually happened and what we merely imagined to have taken place. Thus this remarkable power allows us to keep in contact with the source of our experience and, from this perspective, can accordingly be viewed as a power by which we are enabled to relate successfully the world of inner consciousness with the sensible world of concrete things.

It is, then, important to note that one can remember only what actually happened. Memory itself is not fanciful or merely imaginary. Nonetheless, it should be pointed out that it is possible for us to remember a purely imaginary happening inasmuch as we can actually remember having imagined some event or other, such as having recently vacationed in Spain. Yet, even here, one can only say,

"I *remember* having imagined vacationing in Spain," because I am aware that I *really did imagine it.* The distinction may appear to be somewhat subtle but it does allow us to differentiate clearly between pure imagining and authentic remembering.

Earlier we referred to memory as the inner sensory power of self-identity. It may prove helpful to expand on this point before concluding this section on the memorative power. Without the power of memory, my ability to know *who I am* and *what I have done* would be wholly lacking. Since past actions no longer exist in themselves, it is only in memory that they are present, and it is in this manner alone that one can be aware of past events. Through the recollection, or representation, of past events, one's own personal selfhood is built up and developed, and the life of individual consciousness becomes a span of continuity rather than a mere single point in the present. Through memory the events of a lifetime are gathered into a unity that is constitutive of our life of inner consciousness and self-awareness, enabling each of us to identify our individual self as a unique personality. Memory is truly constitutive of personal history, because it makes possible an awareness of time, which is nothing more than change viewed as having a *before* and an *after.*

Because all human actions occur within a temporal context, that is, successively, one action must necessarily follow upon another. Each new action or human event announces the demise of the one that preceded it. Memory, then, performs the unique function of retaining these diverse experiences as unified and interrelated and as dependent, both upon each other and upon the environment from which they took their rise.

The phenomenon of memory makes it possible for me to speak of myself as 'I', an enduring subject that possesses certain past actions, constituting a manifold of diverse experiences. This 'I' awareness is possessed by the human alone. Other animals lack an inner awareness of their own personal history. Consequently, they do not study themselves nor do they strive to improve upon their past record of achievement. They are creatures of the present. Although they have a history, they are not party to its unfolding. The study of animals must, paradoxically, be left to the authentic memorative animal, the human, who knows infinitely more about animals than animals *know* about themselves.

These reflections serve not only to illumine the import of the human memorative power in developing our sense of personal awareness but they should also further sharpen our understanding of what a truly remarkable animal the human is. They should also serve to emphasize our need continually to exercise and to develop our memories, for it is clear that without conscious and untiring effort it is difficult for us to assimilate and coordinate the vast array of events and experiences that form the rich fabric of our individual lives.

In conclusion, a few words need to be said about the difference between the memorative act in the human and in the animal. Aristotle ascribed both memory and imagination to the animal but he sharply limited their range of activity. In the case of memory, he argued there is clear evidence that animals have the power to recognize things previously experienced. Yet for Aristotle, this power of recognition is of a spontaneous nature, rising from an ongoing sensory stimulation from an object earlier experienced. A dog, for example, does recognize its master. What Aristotle denies to the animal is the ability freely to recall an experience when the object formerly sensed is absent. The ability to do this he terms reminiscence, which is a uniquely human prerogative. Reminiscence is the ability consciously to search for, and to identify, the source of sensory impressiions.

Aristotle's view has not been disproved. There is no data to suggest an animal possesses more than a passive quality of memory. The explanation Aristotle offers for the difference between the memorative ability in the human and the animal is that the human's intellective power overflows, as it were, into the sensory sector, permitting the latter to transcend the limitations of a purely sensory activity. Reminiscence is the aspect of memory that, reinforced by the proximity of the human intellect and employed as its instrument, actively recalls the originating source of past events. Human memorative power is an *active,* rather than a passive, or spontaneous, recall.

Forgetting

To complement his profound analysis of memory found in *Confessions*, Augustine includes some comments on the phenomenon of forgetting. Forgetting is not merely a simple non-knowing, or ignorance, of something. Forgetting is closely related to knowing, and indeed in one sense it is a form of knowing, for we do not say we are forgetful of something without simultaneously implying that at one time we had knowledge of it. It is impossible, therefore, for me to say that I forget what I never knew. Forgetting is much more than merely being ignorant; it is a living testimony of my once having known. In this sense, then, forgetting is actually equivalent to a partial remembering. It is a kind of *twilight knowledge* which seems to waver between knowing and not-knowing. If I once knew something and now have no recollection of it whatever, it would not be accurate for me to say, "I forget." I should say, "I do not know," which would mean "I do not know that I ever knew."

Since forgetting is a form of partial, or imperfect, remembrance, it will necessarily consist in my inability to trace to its originating source in consciousness some particular experience. A simple example may help to illustrate this. Let us suppose that someone shows me a picture of an individual and asks whether or not I have ever met him or her. Let us further suppose that the picture is quite familiar to me so that I am easily able to say, "Yes, I have met that person." If, then, I am further asked to indicate where it was that I met this person and what this person does for a living, etc., I may easily recognize that I once could have answered these questions but at this time I am unable to do so. Hence, I reply, "I forget," or "I do not remember." This *forgetting* consists essentially in my being unable to connect images relating to the activity of this particular person with a concrete sensory experience involving the activity of the special senses.

As we reflect on the phenomenon of forgetfulness, we are clearly aware that it is an experience common to all of us and that the number of things we have experienced which we are unable to recall either in whole or in part is vast indeed and provides a shadowy backdrop for all of the things which we actually do remember. Such a phenomenon ought not really to surprise us when we bear in mind the manner in which our knowledge comes to us. The ability, or capacity, to forget is the price we humans pay both for our having to know things successively and for our being able, as seen, to know such a wide variety of things.

In a truly basic sense, we humans are condemned to forget in order that we may know, for as we pass on from one experience to another, we must leave all prior experiences behind and suspended in a state of forgetfulness. Forgetting, in this most basic sense, is a necessary condition for the acquisition of further knowledge. Such forgetting, which constitutes an inevitable dimension of the human condition, we may refer to as ontological forgetfulness. Recalling what was previously said about questions and answers, we can readily connect the two phenomena and appreciate the fact that forgetting, like questioning, implies a form of incomplete, or partial knowing. All knowledge is of being and all questioning is, in a sense, a search for the being that lies beyond the being of our present awareness. It is a striving to remember what at present we only vaguely and incompletely know.

We can tie together the phenomenon of questioning and forgetting with that of philosophizing, for the philosopher seeks above all to harmonize and to make present within consciousness the totality of human experience, and this the philosopher can do only by remembering the interlocking links and relations of what he or she knows, what he or she knew, and what he or she can know, all of which come under the common name of *being*. The philosopher, in short, is one who strives to overcome the shortcomings of *Seinsvergessenheit*, an ontological forgetfulness, or loss of being. Perhaps it is this notion that Plato was advancing when, referring to all learning as remembering, he conceived of our present state as a cave existence that necessitated a continuing and radical forgetfulness.

The Evaluative Sense

Sensation is clearly a purposeful activity, but sensation is not an end in itself. The goal of any sensory act transcends the act itself, for it aims at the well-being of the entire sensing organism. This is most evidently true of the sensory activity we note among the animals. This activity for them is not for mere entertainment or enjoyment. Rather, it performs for them a vital and indispensable service. They require it for their very survival. If an animal loses its ability to sense in the manner with which it has been endowed by nature, or even suffers a marked diminution of this ability, it is almost certainly doomed to die either through starvation or its inability to ward off its natural predators. A blind squirrel could hardly fend for itself; a fox that had lost its ability to scent could not survive for long. Animals are provided with their sensory powers in order that they can defend themselves and otherwise provide for their needs.

From this it follows that since animals are able to perceive their environment, they need the ability to evaluate the vast array of objects, living and nonliving alike, that they sense. Not everything the animal encounters in its environment is of value to it. And what is savored by one kind of animal, such as thistles by a horse, may well prove to be less than appetizing to most other animals. This means, therefore, that the individual animal exercises a certain discretion or judgment in selecting what it will eat or otherwise select for its needs. The animal actually does evaluate what it senses in terms of whether or not it finds a thing suitable to itself.

It is to account for such behavior that Aristotle and others after him argued that there exists a special *estimative sense*, which today we can simply call the *evaluative sense*. This act of evaluation cannot be identified with any of the other sensory acts previously examined. It is an activity that has a function all its own and possesses its own formal object. Its function is to assess the value of the thing experienced; that is, to point up the relationship between the sensing organism and the object sensed inasmuch as the latter may contribute to the perfection and development of the organism itself. The evaluative sense power does not have as its unique perspective, or formal object, any particular quality of the thing sensed, like the special senses do, nor does it have for its formal object the retention of the sensory images, like the imagination does; rather its formal object is the total sensed object, assessed as being in some way useful or harmful, desirable or undesirable to the organism sensing it. The material object of this power is made up of the sensory impressions of all the other senses (special and inner) previously considered, whereas the *formal object* is made up of these same impressions viewed from the aspect of their *value* to the sensing organism.

For example, when we see a deer flee from a wolf or a cougar, we can assume that the deer's instantaneous evaluative sense has appraised the presence of the wolf or the cougar and concluded it is necessary to flee. This appraisal is the result of an instantaneous interpretation of the presence of one of its predators. Its flight from the scene is proof that just such an interpretative evaluation has preceded, because the deer would not flee in the presence of every animal. It *knows* when to flee, when to stand its ground, or even when to attack.

What in animals we call the evaluative sense is commonly referred to in the human as the *cogitative* sense, or the particular reason. Like other sensory powers it is organic. Yet owing to its proximity to the intellective power in the human, its activity transcends that of the evaluative sense in the animal.

For Aristotle and Thomas Aquinas the cogitative sense shares in a certain overflow of the intellective act into the region of the senses and is guided and directed by it. It is thus the cogitative power which directly funnels the intelligibility perceived organically by the senses to the intellect, making possible a universal understanding of the singular, sensed thing. This point will be discussed further in the chapter on intellection.

Instinctive Knowledge

A brief consideration of the phenomenon of instinctive knowledge in animals can serve as a useful transition from the analysis of the sensory act to that of the intellective operation wholly peculiar to the human.

Not only is the phenomenon of instinctual behavior in the animal a source of wonderment to us but also it can prove highly instructive to us in our efforts to appreciate the nature of human activity. It is helpful to contrast the presence of instinct in the animal with the need for learning in the human.

Earlier in this century, psychologists commonly shunned the use of the word *instinct*, but this fortunately is no longer the case. At the least, instinct is now a term that one finds in psychological literature, so that its employment need no longer be defended. Detailed observation of many species of animals within recent decades has made it increasingly obvious to the unbiased observer that not all animal behavior can be satisfactorily explained by the overly simplistic stimulus-response formula.

The enormously complex and intricate activities that many animals perform, without their having had any observable learning experience to account for such behavior, indicates that these animals, to a greater or lesser degree, possess a kind of knowledge that can very accurately be termed *innate*, or *a priori*. Generally, however, when speaking of such awareness in animals, we employ the term "instinct." For example, bees do not learn how to construct a hive; birds do not learn how to fly; nor do spiders take lessons on how to spin webs. Without any kind of apprenticeship, these animals rely upon their instinct to perform these and similar activities in an almost flawless manner. Recent discoveries in molecular and genetic biology now permit us to understand somewhat how such instinctual behavior, unique to each species of animal, is encoded into the genes and chromosomes found within every cell of the animal organism. These skills are provided by nature.

Some animals are much more dependent upon instinctual knowledge for their behavior than are others. In general, animals possessed of a lower life-form depend more on a nature-given code to direct their activities than do animals of higher life-forms. Further, it is also a matter of simple observation that the more an animal depends upon instinct for its activity, the less flexible and more restricted that activity is. For example, insects demonstrate the more spectacular instances of instinctual behavior in the animal kingdom, but they also demonstrate that they are severely limited in their repertoire of tasks. It is also important to note that there is no variance in the activity patterns of those animals most heavily dependent upon instinctual knowledge for their behavior. What they do, they do with consummate skill, but they perform identically the same tasks day after day, year after year, generation after generation. Instinctual, or a priori, knowledge is thus seen to have its price. It is fundamentally inhibitive of behavioral change.

Many birds, insects, and other animals extant today are known to have acted in exactly the same manner for thousands of years. Their activity can clearly be seen to be rigidly coded genetically as one generation after another tirelessly continues to carry on the forms of behavior unique to that particular species. Indeed, we may further note that the wondrously harmonious interplay of nature and the stability of the present environment itself would be seriously upset were the established, unvarying patterns of behavior found in the animal world suddenly and irreversibly to undergo change. The inherited programming we find in the various species of animals renders virtually unnecessary their need to acquire through a slow learning process the means of doing what they must do to survive. On the other hand, because they are provided with "knowledge" at birth, they lack the freedom to learn. Because they are programmed, they are not free, and freedom, from the ontological standpoint, is not something one can acquire but is, rather, a characteristic one must possess from birth. This observation, extremely important in terms of its meaning for humans, tells us that the human is actually *born free.*

Summary

In this chapter the internal senses have been considered. By applying the principle that powers are known in their acts and that these acts are distinguishable by their formal objects, we learned that, in addition to the five special senses, four other organic, cognoscitive powers can be identified.

First, it was seen that, owing to the limited field of activity of each of the special senses, there was need for an additional power to account for the manner in which these activities are correlated. This power, referred to as the *coordinating* sense, has as its material object the activities of all the special senses, and as its formal object those same activities once they have been correlated, or differentiated, one from another. Through the activity of this coordinating power the diverse operations of the special senses can be brought into focus and their fundamental underlying unity within the sensed object made available to the sensing subject.

We then turned our attention to the *imaginative sense.* It was noted that coordinated images are retained by the knowing subject and are not permitted to dissipate into oblivion, although the original sensory stimulus has ceased. Since this act of *retention* is an operation quite distinct from the *formation* of these complex images, it requires a distinct sensory capability. Serving as a permanent reservoir of the impressions formed by the activities of the special and coordinating senses, the imagination has as its material object the images received from the coordinating sense; and by its retention of these images after their originating stimulus is no longer present, the imagination can view them as being independent of the material things they represent. The formal object of the imagination consists precisely in these free images, independent of their sources. It was then observed how this fact makes it possible for humans to experience those kinds of activities that we specifically identify as creative, imaginative acts. In these instances the imagination coordinates various sensory images in highly original and unique ways. The reason such formation is viewed as creative and different from the coordinating activity of the coordinating sense is that the imagination can unify images without reference to any originating experience.

We also noted it is the imaginative sense that makes possible the employment of metaphor and provides a basis for the phenomenon of all possible art forms.

Next, the power of the *memory* was scrutinized. This power differs from the imaginative power in that its unique function consists in tracing the stored images, received through the special and coordinating senses, to their originating source. Thus, remembering is a unique activity, by means of which the past is known as past. Its material object is composed of those sensory activities that are past, and in this sense the memory has to do with what no longer is. The formal object of the memory was then seen to be these same sensory perceptions, but in this state they are traced back to their originating cause. Remembrance is always of an actual past event that no longer exists in its own reality, but does exist in consciousness.

This memorative act, since it can render a conscious awareness of the succession of events, is the origin of one's experience of time. We reflected on the significance of the memorative act in the development of the human psyche and personality, and on the intriguing phenomenon of forgetting.

Our study of the internal senses concluded with a consideration of the *evaluative* sense. It was noted once again that all sensory activity is purposeful and aims at the well-being and development of the sensing organism. The sensory experience is not had, therefore, merely for its own sake but is ordered toward further action to bring the sensing being to completion. It was seen that the *discernment of the value* of the various sensory experiences was not an operation that could be identified with any of the other activities previously uncovered. Hence the need for positing a special, or separate, evaluative power whereby the sensed object itself could be assessed as pleasant or unpleasant, useful or harmful. Thus the material object of the evaluative sense was seen to include the entire range of the sensory activities, while the formal object consisted in these same activities being viewed from the standpoint of their use or value to the sensing organism itself.

Lastly, the phenomenon of instinctive knowledge in the animal was considered. The invariant behavioral pattern noted in the animal presents a striking contrast to that of the human, who must painstakingly mold patterns of behavior from the reservoir of personal experience. This consideration helpfully serves as a transition to the following chapter, in which the human intellective operations are for the first time directly investigated.

Definitions and Conclusions

1. The *coordinating* sense is an inner sensory power which differentiates and coordinates the activities of the five special senses.

2. The *imagination* is an inner sensory power that conserves the images and impressions of the coordinating sense.

3. The *memory* is an inner sensory power whose function it is to link all inner images and impressions with their originating source. The memory thus knows the past as past.

4. *Reminiscence,* a memorative activity possessed only by the human, consists in the ability consciously to search for, and to identify, the source of sensory impressions. It is made possible by the human intellective power, which employs the sensory memory as its instrument.

5. *Forgetting* is partial remembering. In the act of forgetting one is consciously aware that he once knew something that he does not at this moment fully remember. It is made possible by the inability of the memory to uncover completely the origin of an impression present to its consciousness.

6. The *evaluative* sense is an inner sensory power whose function it is to discern the value of what is experienced in terms of the well-being of the organism experiencing.

7. The *cogitative* sense is an inner sensory power in the human, paralleling the evaluative sense in the animal, which judges impressions of the other sensory powers relating to the sensed objects. It

also provides the vital link between the world of sensible things and the immaterial activity of the intellect.

8. *Instinctual knowledge* is behavioral programming not acquired through experience. It is essential for the development and activity of animals, since they lack the intellective capability of the human to develop and fashion their own patterns of behavior.

9. Because of the behavioral coding which instincts provide, the animal has little need of learning. At the same time it is incapable of significantly altering and expanding its range of activities, which are determined for it by nature.

6 From Sensation to Intellection

The pivot between images and concepts is the insight.

B. J. F. Lonergan, S.J.
*Insight: A Study of Human
Understanding*

The Unspecialized Nature of the Human Body

The time has come to turn our attention away from the purely sensory world of the animal and to focus it once again on the more complex world of the human. Whereas the animal is initially supplied with most of the knowledge and skills necessary for it to move successfully through its normal life span, the human possesses at birth no specialized talents or skills whatever. Instead we are gifted with an uncanny ability to learn, and our very survival depends directly on our acquisition of numerous abilities and skills.

In contrast to any other animal body—which is highly specialized and ingeniously ordered and fitted to assist it to accomplish tasks essential to its own survival—the human body is totally unspecialized. There are no specific tasks that the human anatomy is naturally ordered to perform, other than those of digestion and reproduction. In all other respects the human body is generalized and extremely flexible.

As a consequence the human child requires many years of nurturing and attentive care before it arrives at physical maturity and can, in any realistic way, be considered capable of providing for its basic needs, of becoming even moderately self-sufficient. Because the human is not equipped at birth to perform specific or detailed tasks, it must acquire at least the skills necessary for survival.

Clearly there is an intimate tie-in between our human anatomy and our complete lack of inborn or instinctual knowledge. Further, there is an undeniable relationship between both of these and our ability to think, plan, and develop multiple modes of behavior, which enable us to perform tasks of an almost infinite variety. Our freedom of action, however, exacts its own price, for although we can learn to perform innumerable tasks, we are left to find meaning within our own inner experience and to provide for ourselves what nature provides for the other animals.

However, what may seem at first to be a significant imposition and disadvantage soon appears to be a great boon, for if we consider the fact that we humans can draw meaning out of our experience and can fit these experiences together to broaden our own horizons of knowledge and activity, then we can appreciate the value of our being left uncoded in our behavior. We are, that is, free of the behavior controls we observe to be so pronounced in lower animals; and as a consequence, we are free to program ourselves. This has proved to be an advantage. For whatever nature has provided other animals we humans have been able to outstrip in truly spectacular fashion by the subtle workings of our minds. We are capable of transforming our world by reshaping it to the image of our own thoughts, which we fashion from a painstaking and prolonged dialogue with our environment. This reshaping of the world, which simply consists in reordering the elements of the world we experience in new and previously *unthought of* ways, is accomplished through what we currently call art and technology. In short, we are the world's greatest doers and makers precisely because we are unexcelled in the world of thought. Our true strength lies not in our bodies but in our minds. It is primarily the human mind that differentiates humans from all other animals.

The investigation of questioning in chapter two illustrated that we humans are not limited in the scope of our questioning. This means that the human mind is not limited in what it can know. Unlike the special senses, the human intellect has for its point of departure not some particular aspect of things but rather whatever is. That is to say, the formal object of the human act of knowing is not a particular quality of a thing, but simply the *being* of the thing itself. The human can know everything because it possesses a power, an intellect, which is ordered to things not because they are in *this* or *that* way but simply because they *are* in *some* way. In whatever way they *are*, they can be humanly known. This means that the *material object* of the human intellect is whatever is, while the *formal object* is the *being* of whatever is.

Although the human is born with a mental power for obtaining limitless knowledge, still human behavior is limited. This limitation derives, however, not from the mind so much as from the conditions of the human body and the material conditions of that which is known. Put another way, the constraints of time and space and the physical laws of nature profoundly affect the manner in which the human acquires the knowledge he needs to lead a human life.

To this end the human body can be seen, as remarked earlier, to mirror in a spectacular way the limitlessness of the human intellect; for lacking a specialized structure itself, it stands ready to respond to the myriad demands placed upon it by the human mind. Thus the human body, after its own fashion, shares in the universality of the human mind and is able in a truly remarkable way to complement and even to share in the intellective activity of the human knower.

The hand of the human offers us a striking example of an inborn flexibility and adaptability, which perfectly matches the unstructured activity of the human intellect. Not fashioned to perform any specific task well, the human hand can be *trained* to do such disparate tasks as to take food to the mouth by using fingers or a variety of utensils; to play a variety of musical instruments that require different handling and fingering; to play ball with balls as varied in shape and size as a baseball, basketball, football, golfball; to handle small tools and large tools with which to repair watches, to create paintings and sculpture, to build buildings, to lay roadways, to plant and harvest crops; to manipulate all kinds of machinery; to communicate by means of writing with every kind of implement from a quill pen to a word processor and to perform such a simple human act as to shake hands with someone. Lacking an inherent structure designed for the performance of highly specialized tasks, the human hand is radically different from the claw or paw of any animal, including the hand of the primate. Its structure is open and adaptable to the needs of the human mind.

Archimedes and the Gold Crown

As an example that demonstrates the unique reality of human knowing and how it differs from sensory acts, perhaps there is none more fitting than a discovery that took place more than 2,000 years ago. In the third century B.C. in Syracuse, Sicily, there lived the most renowned mathematician and scientist of the ancient world, Archimedes, who was in the employ of Hiero II, the ruler of Syracuse. Archimedes was called to the palace one day and asked to provide a solution to a puzzle that was troubling the king. Hiero had ordered a certain goldsmith to fashion a crown. The commission specified that the crown was to be of pure gold. As the story goes, after receiving the crown, Hiero began to wonder whether or not it was truly of pure gold. The reputation of the goldsmith was not entirely above reproach and the king had grown suspicious. But how could he tell whether or not the goldsmith had cheated him? Without tampering with the crown or melting it down, he could think of no way of resolving this question. Thus puzzled, he called in Archimedes and asked him to determine whether the crown was genuine. Archimedes left the royal palace in a quandary for he had no idea how this puzzle might be resolved.

According to the story, it was at one of the public baths that Archimedes discovered a way to answer the king's question. There he observed the change of water levels in the pools as people stepped in and out of the baths, and it was this observation that led him to the solution to the king's problem. He realized that all he needed to do was to weigh the crown in water. That was not really all, but weighing the crown in water was the key. What he did was to place the crown on one of the two trays of a balance (scale), counterbalancing it with gold coins on the other. Then he submerged each tray of the balance into its own basin of water. If the crown and the coins remained in perfect counterbalance while immersed, the crown must be pure gold.

The reasoning behind this is fairly simple. If the crown and the coins, known to be of equal weight before immersion, still register identical weights when immersed, this can only be accounted for by the fact that they are displacing an equal amount of water—their volumes are equal. And if the volume and the weight of both are the same, then the density of both are also the same; therefore, the crown is the same material as the coins, which are known to be gold. If some other metal had been alloyed with the gold in the crown, the crown would have weighed less in the water than the coins and the two trays would no longer have been in balance.

Thus, Archimedes had a solution to his problem insofar as he had discovered a method that would infallibly indicate to him whether or not the crown was of pure gold. He arrived at his discovery by fusing several ideas that had not previously been connected in his own thinking. Prior to his "miraculous" experience in the baths, he had known that gold was the heaviest of metals. He had also known that identical amounts—equal volumes—of the same substance had identical weights. What he had not known was how he could determine the volume of the crown without destroying or otherwise damaging it. Though he had been aware that something would weigh less suspended in water than it weighed normally, Archimedes had never before made the connection between weighing something in water and ascertaining its density. What he realized was that the amount of water an object displaced was the volume of the object. Archimedes' discovery was clearly an act of the mind. It was not merely a matter of simple observation. Though he now saw how he could solve his problem, it was an inner vision that he had had and not merely an act of external observation.

Historically we do not know whether or not Archimedes found that the gold crown was actually of pure gold. For our purposes, this is of no importance. Let us assume, however, that he did find the crown to be genuine. We can easily imagine Archimedes at the palace breathlessly telling Hiero of his important discovery. But is the king convinced? Might not the king wonder whether Archimedes himself is telling the truth? Might not the king then inquire as to how Archimedes determined that the crown was of pure gold? Let us suppose that Archimedes explains to the king the discovery he made in the baths and how, in implementing his insight in the laboratory, he found that the crown and the gold coins weighed exactly the same.

Unless the king *understands* Archimedes' explanation of why the crown must be of gold, he is no closer to solving his riddle about the crown than he was before. Unless the king grasps the *why* of it all, he really does not know, and he is reduced to having to place his trust in Archimedes.

The point to be made of this story about Archimedes is that what we are dealing with is a type of activity that is essentially different from an act of mere external measurement or observation. What we are dealing with is an act of an inner awareness whereby we recognize if two things are identical to a common third, they must be identical with each other. If the weights of the crown and the gold coins remain in balance when weighed in water, then the crown and the gold coins must consist of the identical substance; since the coins are known to be pure gold, the crown, too, must be of pure gold. From the scientific standpoint it matters little whether or not the crown turns out to be of pure gold. What does matter, however, is that a method has been found for determining the answer.

We should note, therefore, that Archimedes' confidence that he has found the answer to his problem never does consist in the fact that he observes that the crown is of pure gold. He never does *see* that it is of pure gold. Rather, he *understands* that it is. The experiment itself is set up and carried out within the context of the discovery Archimedes has made. Had he not made his discovery, there would have been no experiment, for the latter is really nothing more than a concrete implementation of the insight itself. The experiment, then, does not *prove* the validity of the insight that Archimedes had in the baths. The experiment is merely the *application of his insight* and has no value whatever unless the insight itself, independent of the experiment, is valid. It is solely the validity of the principles of hydrostatics that Archimedes can feel exultant about. Unless the king, too, understands what Archimedes discovered in the baths, the weighing of the crown in water is to the king merely an eccentric act of an odd scientist who apparently has spent too much time either at the baths or at one of the taverns.

Inferences Drawn from Archimedes' Discovery

From the story concerning Archimedes and the crown, it is possible to draw basic inferences from his dramatic discovery:

(1) Archimedes' insight came as a response to a previous act of questioning. The tension resulting from the search for an answer to his question was there, for Archimedes had been wrestling with the question for some time. As far as we know, it was a question that had never been answered by anyone before, so there was no one to whom he could turn for an answer. He had to work it out on his own within the quiet recesses of his own mind. Had Archimedes not had a problem when he went into the baths at Syracuse, his observation of the fluctuation of the water in the pools might have meant nothing more to him than it meant to the hundreds of other people who visited the baths.

(2) The insight came to Archimedes suddenly and completely without warning. When he entered the main entrance of the baths, he had not the slightest inkling that, a short while later, he would exit from them with the solution to his vexing problem. As he was relaxing in the baths, something about the motion and buoyancy of the waters became enormously meaningful to him. Had he told a friend that he had noticed a change in the water level as bathers stepped in and out of the pools, his friend would most likely have considered his comment to be a trivial observation.

Yet, for Archimedes it was significant, for in his mind he had linked the fluctuation of the waters with the problem he was trying to solve, and of a sudden it dawned on him that he now had a sure way of determining whether or not the crown was of gold. Further, he was aware that he could reach this conclusion without damaging the crown.

That is the way it is with *understanding*. We cannot predict when it is going to come, nor can we set up rules or experiments to lead us to it. Understanding comes suddenly, unexpectedly, and with conviction.

(3) Insight is much more a matter of inner awareness than it is of outer circumstances. Thousands of people had frequented the baths of Syracuse. They had observed the same external phenomena as Archimedes; they had noted the same fluctuation of the water in the pools; but they failed to behold with the mind's eye what he beheld. It was what Archimedes already knew when he visited the baths that made the difference in what he *saw*. He had come with a question and a mind finely honed in mathematics and the science of nature. The insight that Archimedes obtained could actually have come to

him almost anywhere, but in point of fact, it occurred in the baths of Syracuse; consequently, those baths occupy a place of honor in the annals of health spas. They are famous because they are where Archimedes gained insight into one of the basic laws of hydrostatics.

(4) Insight is a pivot between the tangible and the abstract. Archimedes' problem involved an individual gold crown. Yet the solution to the problem was mental and not limited in its application to this particular object. As a result of his discovery Archimedes had at his disposal the means for determining the purity of any irregularly shaped gold vessel or figure immersed in water. Moreover, there was no time limit on the applicability of his discovery. Its value transcends the era of Archimedes and its truth is independent of time and space.

Because insight emerges from a sensory problem and, perhaps even more, because it can be reapplied to the sensory world of our environment with direct application to the physical sciences and technology, it can truly be said to be a pivot between the tangible and the abstract. Though mental in its natural state, insight *derives* from the sensory world and can be *returned* to it. This points up what is perhaps the most extraordinary and unique of all the characteristics of human knowing, for it clearly shows that human understanding finds infinite resources in the confines of the material world by means of which it is enlivened and motivated. In essence, understanding is a true dialogue between matter and spirit.

(5) Insight passes into the permanent texture of the mind. Once gained, it can easily be reactivated to meet future needs. The initial, spontaneous, and unexpected discovery becomes a permanent possession and can be summoned up again to our conscious presence almost at will. With the passage of time, the elements of spontaneity and surprise, which characterized the initial acquisition of the insight, gradually disappear. We even come to take very much for granted an act of understanding which once may have caused us many hours of impatient searching prior to its coming and led us to experience a deep sense of satisfaction and positive exhilaration at the moment of its arrival. This may be replaced later with our viewing what once seemed to be an impossible achievement as something relatively easy, perhaps even ridiculously simple.

(6) Insight is universal and inherently communicable. It tran-

scends the limitations of the individual mind which grasps it and is thus, by nature, a *public* event. Insight may begin with an individual but it is not the private possession of any one person. Others, too, can obtain the same insight. Thus the insight Archimedes gained while relaxing in the baths spread to the four corners of the world and is as much an insight of our contemporary world as it was of Archimedes' world more than 2,000 years ago. The task of the communication of insight is, and will ever remain, one of the principal tasks of humankind, for of such communication is civilization born, nourished, and enhanced.

New insights lead to fresh questioning on yet higher levels, and the search for deeper and more enveloping insights continues. The mind builds upon what it has already learned and there is a sharing of insights with others. Indeed, the dynamism of human intercourse itself exists at this level of mental interchange where idea leads to idea so that the roots of human progress and civilization are ever increasingly developed and extended. The learning process is itself a dizzying assimilation of insights and questions that expand and intertwine in ever greater patterns of complexity.

The example we have been focusing on of Archimedes and the crown is a dramatic instance of an insight. We have analyzed it to obtain an insight into insight; that is, to better understand the phenomenon of understanding itself. By singling out and reflecting upon this instance of insight that Archimedes had more than 2,000 years ago, perhaps we can better appreciate the nature and characteristics of insights which we ourselves have had and can thus more clearly differentiate between the sensory and intellective activity we possess as human knowers.

Extraordinary as insight is in its nature and momentous as some of its effects can be for the individual and for the human race, it is, nonetheless, an altogether ordinary and everyday occurrence in the experience of an intelligent human. But however ordinary it may be in human experience, it is absent in the subhuman world and, ultimately, is that which, from the experiential side, sharply demarcates the human from all other living things. How this is so, precisely, constitutes much of the search for the underlying meaning of what it means *to be* in a *human* way.

Summary

This chapter marks the beginning of our systematic inquiry into the intellective capability of the human. The sharp contrast between the limited scope of animal behavior on the one hand and the enormous flexibility of human behavior on the other was examined. The human was seen to possess a body that displays a minimum of specialization. The inference was made that the unspecialized quality of the human anatomy was the result of the human's possessing an intellective capability.

The dramatic discovery of Archimedes, whereby he learned how to determine whether the gold in the crown of Hiero had been alloyed with other metals helps to illustrate six fundamental axioms regarding the nature of human insight, or understanding.

Definitions and Conclusions

1. While the animal body is highly specialized, the human body is almost totally unspecialized.

2. Lacking instinctual behavioral patterns comparable to those of the animal, the human requires years of care and instruction before reaching full maturity.

3. The generalness of the human hand is a striking example of the inborn flexibility and adaptability of the human body and evenly matches the human's developmental capability through intellective knowing.

4. The human intellect is a cognoscitive power which has the entire range of being as its object.

5. Insight possesses six basic characteristics:
   (a) Insight comes as a response to a previous act of questioning.
   (b) Insight comes suddenly and completely without warning.
   (c) Insight is much more a matter of inner awareness than it is of outer circumstances.
   (d) Insight is a pivot between the tangible and the abstract.
   (e) Insight passes into the permanent texture of the mind.
   (f) Insight is universal and hence its findings are inherently communicable.

7   Intellection

... The nature of truth is first found in the intellect when the intellect begins to possess something proper to itself which the thing outside the soul does not have.

St. Thomas Aquinas
On Truth

The Moderate Realism of St. Thomas Aquinas (1224-1273)

The dramatic discovery of Archimedes was presented in the preceding chapter as an example of human insight. It was pointed out that insight is characterized as a pivot between the tangible and the abstract, and by the act of human understanding, which is more a matter of inner conditions than it is of outer circumstances.

Now it is time to resume the question of the human's intellective behavior and to complete our investigation into its nature and how it develops. In doing so, it is important to remember that the total act of human knowing entails much more than understanding alone, for it presupposes sensory acts that provide the content of that which is understood. Therefore, it should be borne in mind that the human act of knowing is a dynamic continuum that cannot be artificially divided into segments without destroying its authentic reality.

To assist us in our reflections on the nature of human intellection, we shall rely on the genius of St. Thomas Aquinas, whose philosophic synthesis still remains the most complete and the most profound of any that has so far been achieved. Thomas Aquinas was a thirteenth-century philosopher-theologian who devoted much of his singular intellective talent to reflecting on the philosophic legacy of Aristotle. On some points, because of his Christian commitment, Aquinas was unable to accept the teaching of Aristotle without modification, but on the whole his views represent a true development of Aristotle's position. There is little question that his basic philosophy is Aristotelian, even though he was also influenced by Plato, Augustine, and certain of the Arabic philosophers.

Since Aquinas's intellective theory moves within the framework of the Aristotelian vision, it is clear that his position must be described as realistic. Aquinas opts for a knowledge of a world wholly independent of man himself as a knower, and as primordially accessible to him through the senses. Thus for Aquinas, as for Aristotle, there is, prior to sensation, nothing in the mind other than its own basic structure and pure, illuminative power. Consequently, for Thomas all knowledge which individuals possess is acquired, and has somehow been transported across the great barrier reef of the senses. To employ another metaphor, one might regard the senses as the bridge across which the content of all human thought must pass.

Aquinas's position is opposed to all forms of innativism. All knowledge that the intellect possesses has come to it through the senses, even though intellective knowledge pertains to a completely distinct genre of knowing. In the beginning the human intellect is comparable to a blank slate on which nothing has been written. While it is open to knowledge, initially it possesses none, and whatever knowledge it will later acquire must be derived from its contact with the world of sensory objects.

At the same time, while Aquinas's view is clearly opposed to the innativism of Plato and the Platonists, it is, nonetheless, strongly opposed to the sensism of David Hume, who reduces all ideas to mere sense impressions, and hence for whom intellective knowledge is lowered to the level of sensory perception itself.

Following the lead of Aristotle, Aquinas teaches that the intellect does know the material world, although not as a material world, but rather, immaterially. The material thing he finds to be potentially intelligible, since it is composed of an essential principle, a form, which in and of itself is neither material nor singular, even though it happens to exist in this particular thing under these particular conditions. Human knowing, for Aquinas, therefore, becomes explicable only in terms of an abstractive process whereby the intellect is capable of drawing from the material object some of its intellective content; that is, for Aquinas the original content of all human knowledge is drawn from the sensible world, which is known by the intellect in a way that it cannot be known by any sensory power.

To explain the abstractive process, Aquinas introduces Aristotle's dynamic intellective principle which he calls the *active intellect*. It is the function of the active intellect to draw the intelligible content from the material thing as it has been presented to the senses. Aquinas frequently refers to the internal, complex sensible image found within the senses as the *phantasm*. The phantasm represents sensibly that which is experienced, so that for Aquinas there can be no understanding of any kind unless there has been first a sensory experience. Aquinas's theory is aptly described as "moderate realism," since, on the one hand, the content of knowledge derives exclusively from experience and, on the other, it is only through the illuminating activity of the active intellect that such knowledge is made possible. For Aquinas the intellect knows the material thing experienced, but knows it *immaterially.*

The specific role of the active, or agent intellect, is that of illuminating the sensory experience, or phantasm, thus rendering it actually intelligible. Active intellect accomplishes this by freeing the content of the phantasm from its material conditions. This immediately permits the implantation of the new liberated intelligibility within the receptive, or passive intellect. It is this intelligible form, which Aquinas often refers to as the *intelligible species,* or idea, that owes its origin to the active intellect's illumination of the sensible experience (phantasm) and the elevation of that experience to the intellective level. Thus it is important to note that, for Aquinas, the intelligible species *derives from* the phantasm but is found as such *only in the passive intellect.*

The reception of the intelligible form by the passive intellect has moved the latter from a state of *potentially knowing* to *actually knowing.* With the idea fitted into place, as it were, the circuit is closed, the light goes on, the intellect is activated to understand a particular thing. What we have earlier described as insight is precisely this process outlined above whereby the intellect is moved from a state of can know to actually knowing. In short, the intelligible species is the very internal, determining principle whereby the receptive intellect is in act.

Since the intelligible species is abstracted from the material conditions of the thing known, it is no longer singular but universal. It is in this fashion that Aquinas explains the origin of universal ideas. Although intellective knowledge begins with the singular thing, and it is the singular thing that is first known, the modality of existence of the intelligible species differs from the modality of existence of the thing from which it derives. This is why Aquinas is able to say that the human intellect knows the material thing immaterially, through the modality of universality.

Thus the universal ideas that Plato claimed the mind knew in an existence prior to its union with body, Aquinas finds potentially present in the sensible world. That world is truly a *cause* of intellective knowledge, but it is not the total cause, for without the illuminating power of the agent intellect, the hidden, universal dimension of the sensible thing could not be uncovered. In this way Aquinas avoids the exaggerated realism of Plato, as well as the critical idealism of Kant, on the one hand, and the phenomenalism, or sensism, of Hume on the other. It is because Aquinas's view occupies a place roughly midway between these two fundamental options that it is most aptly described as moderate realism.

Somewhat parenthetically, it may prove helpful to point out that the process described above, whereby the intellect is engaged in an interplay between the concrete data of the sense's experience of material things and the abstract conceptualizations of mind (passive intellect), is wholly one with the phenomenon of questioning discussed in chapter two. Above all, the questioning process represents the mind's hovering over the datum of experience and inquiring into its intelligibility, or meaning. The intellect first formulates its questions by expressing its ignorance or failure to comprehend the what, the why, and the wherefore of that which lies before it. What is it? Why is it the way it is? Why does it exist? are typical of the kinds of questions that spontaneously emerge from the simplest, everyday kinds of experience; that is, from the mind's ordinary confrontation with the sensible world.

Aquinas is quick to point out, however, that the idea, or intelligible species, is not, properly speaking, that which the intellect actually knows. What is *first* and *directly* known is not the idea within the intellect but rather *that of which* the idea is the likeness—the material thing initially reached by the exterior senses. This point is crucial to an understanding of Aquinas's position regarding how the human intellect knows. It constitutes, for example, the fundamental difference between Aquinas's position and those of Locke, Berkeley, Hume, and Kant, each of whom in some way inverts Aquinas's order of knowing by assuming that what the mind first knows is the idea within it. Unlike Aquinas's point that the mind knows things that exist, the opposing view is forced to conclude that "to exist" means "to be known." Consequently, as the history of philosophy itself clearly illustrates, it is impossible to establish the existence of objects independent of the ideas themselves. There is no way open by which one could establish that ideas are *copies of things* without assuming what one wishes to prove. One cannot consciously proceed from mind to things. It was to avoid this skeptical impasse that Aquinas insisted that that which the intellect first knows is not its own ideas, but rather the material thing itself of which the idea is a likeness.

According to Aquinas, the idea, or intelligible species, which is a likeness of the sensible thing, is that *by which* the object is known; it is not that which is first known. From this, however, one ought not to conclude that Aquinas denies the possibility of the intellect's knowing its own ideas. Such a conclusion would not accord with his view. What he denies is that the intelligible species is that which is first known, or in other words, that which is truly the object of human knowing. Yet at the same time he strongly affirms that the intellect can, and does, *know* its own ideas, although secondarily.

Aquinas's explanation as to how and why the intellect knows its own ideas is as follows: owing to the immaterial nature of the intellective act, the intellect is capable of knowing its own act, and therefore, it can know secondarily the nature of the intelligible species by which it knows the object. In this way the intellective act, while at once wholly immanent to the knower, is an act that brings the intellect into oneness, or communion, with the physical world. It is for this reason that the formal principle of the intelligible species is derived from, and hence shared by, the material thing. Briefly, in the act of knowing, the intelligible species is the means by which the *material* thing is contained in the intellect in an *immaterial* way. Thus, to the extent that both share a common form or perfection, the intellect and the object are *one.*

This means, then, that the material thing known is a true *cause* of the intellective act. It is not a mere occasion of it. The material thing is not, of course, an efficient cause of knowing, since it does not bring about intellection through its activity, but it is a *formal cause* because it lends its likeness to the intellect, which likeness, or intelligible species, is the form by which the intellect is in act. The actual nature or content of this particular act of knowing is thus totally dependent on, and determined by, the form that has been elicited from the phantasm by the active intellect. The material thing known is but one of the causes of the intellective act. It cannot impress itself on the passive intellect without the simultaneous collaboration of both the sensory powers and the agent intellect. The latter alone possesses the power to disassociate the material form from its individuating conditions and to render it capable of determining the receptive intellect. The nature of the union resulting between the intellect, its intelligible species, and the thing known is commonly designated by the term *intentional.* An intentional union is thus distinguished from a *physical* union, and serves to call attention to the unique kind of *comm-union* that characterizes the knowing act.

The Role of the Active Intellect

Owing to the crucial role played by the active intellect in Aquinas's explanation of the intellective act, it will be helpful to devote several extra paragraphs to it in an effort to clarify its underlying function. Because Aquinas, like Aristotle, firmly maintains that all intellective knowledge originates in the experience of the senses, and because, at the same time, he defends the intellective act as inherently immaterial, he must offer an explanation as to how such knowledge can be derived from the sensible or material world. It is the *agent intellect* that performs this mid-wifery task. Because Hume, Descartes, and Kant do not postulate an agent intellect, they must hold either that all universal and necessary knowledge is immaterial and hence *a priori*, or that it is inherently material, and hence *sensory.*

The metaphor Aquinas himself regularly employed in attempting to clarify the function of the agent intellect is that of light. The agent, or active, intellect serves to illuminate the sensory image by penetrating it, suffusing it with its light, and thus freeing its inner intelligibility from its material restrictions. It is to be noted that, just as light does not change the nature of what it illuminates but merely renders it visible, so in a similar way the light of the agent intellect does not modify or change the composition of the phantasm but merely renders it intelligible. Through the illuminating process of the agent intellect the sensible thing is raised to a higher order, thus permitting the receptive intellect to read within it what was always there, but which was beyond the limited powers of the senses to discover.

Comparable to an X-ray machine that scans the inner recesses of the body and uncovers the skeletal framework, exposing it to the eye's vision, so the active intellect scans the phantasm, unveiling, as it were, the intelligibility contained within the material thing. Indeed the word *intellect* derives from the Latin word *intelligere* which in turn is composed of the two words, *intus* (within) and *legere* (to read). Thus *intellect* taken etymologically simply means *to read within a thing* and clearly suggests the notion of reading that which cannot be read with the naked eye alone. Therefore, the agent intellect can be described as the power that penetrates to the inner nature of things and uncovers the very inwardness of their being, their essence, or nature.

To employ another analogy, the role of the agent, or active, intellect, might be likened to the role performed by the light in a slide-projector machine, which illuminates the image on the slide by shining through it. The light does not fashion or in any way modify the image. What appears on the screen is a likeness of the image contained on the slide. With each new slide, the image on the screen is correspondingly altered. If, however, the light is turned off, no slide can be projected onto the screen. If, on the other hand, the slide is removed and none other replaces it, the screen is still illuminated, to be sure, but now no image appears on it. Only if the beam of light first passes through the slide, does an image appear on the screen.

The slide thus performs an essential role in the projection process, along with the illuminating role of the beam of light.

Similarly, the agent intellect *causes* the image to be projected onto the screen of the passive intellect, not in the sense that it is determinative of what actually appears there, but in the sense that without its illumination no intelligible species could be elevated from the phantasm, any more than the image on the slide could be projected onto the screen unless the light behind the slide were allowed to pass through it. Thus the active intellect functions not as a formal, or determinative, cause of the act of understanding, but as an agent, or efficient cause. It is precisely for this reason that it is called the *agent* intellect.

From the foregoing it can be seen that for Aquinas the intellective act is mediated by the activity of active mind working upon the experiential given of sensory consciousness. The human intellective act thus effects a junction of two worlds, those of sense (or matter) and spirit. The act of intellect thus unites the thing known with the intellect itself precisely because the content of the intellective act is identically the content of the thing known. Understanding is a mediating union between these two worlds, for, in a very significant sense, only the human has the power to bring these two worlds together and to anneal them into one dynamic entity. Human understanding provides the annealing process that results in a dynamic entity of remarkable power and creative resourcefulness.

Aquinas's Theory of Knowledge Contrasted with Those of Other Philosophers

To contrast Aquinas's views on intellection with those of other philosophers serves not only to clarify the position of Aquinas but to clarify the positions of those with whom he is being contrasted.

Turning first to Plato, it will be recalled that he does not view the material world as a genuine *cause* of human knowledge, but views it instead as merely an occasion of what we know intellectively. Consequently, there is not to be found in Plato's explanation of knowledge anything to correspond to Aquinas's *insight* into phantasm. Nor does Plato make any mention of an active intellect, for in his view intellective knowledge is not derived from the sensory world of shadows, since it is gained in an *a priori* existence.

A similar observation can be made with regard to the position of Descartes, who held that necessary and universal ideas are discovered within the thinking consciousness and are found to be wholly independent of sensation. According to Descartes it is precisely because universal ideas are totally independent of sensation that they are universal and necessary, a position that Kant was to assume as his own.

The position of John Locke is somewhat more difficult to characterize, even though he does not deny that universals derive from experience and are not *a priori* givens. Locke does not speak of an active intellect and has no need of one, since his notion of universal is more a matter of a *statistical generality* than it is one of authentic universality and independence from matter. He considers the universal idea to derive expressly from a repetition of experiences; that is, from an induction of individual instances of experience. (It is precisely this view that Hume was later to attack so vigorously.) In sum, Locke does not speak of insight in the sense in which we have understood it.

Berkeley's theory of knowledge leaves no room for an active intellect, since he expressly repudiates any form of abstractive process. In fact, his denial of a material world is made precisely in order to avoid the skepticism he feels such a position necessarily entails. Since to Berkeley everything is idea, it is evident that there is no place in his philosophy for the phenomenon of insight.

David Hume has insisted that all ideas are nothing more than sense impressions, and thus he disallows any objective validity to general, or universal, ideas. Consequently, he sees no need for an active intellect to account for the origin of such ideas.

The position of Immanuel Kant is more complex, but he, too, has no need for an active intellect in order to account for the existence of general, or universal, ideas in the mind. The forms of universality and necessity are, for Kant, purely *a priori*, and hence *do not arise out of experience*. There is no such thing for Kant as insight into phantasm. Kant does, of course, speak of a *sensuous intuition*, but he employs the term *intuition* to mean that mind or imagination *imposes* its own *a priori* structure on experience, rather than that the mind *discovers* the universal in the experience.

This brief comparative overview of insight and active intellect should serve to clarify their role in the history of knowledge theory, and to provide a useful criterion for evaluating the knowledge theory of the better-known philosophers.

Understanding and Judging

In a discussion of the various levels, or phases, of understanding, it is helpful to first clarify the significance of, as well as the need for, the distinction between the acts of simple and complex understanding—between understanding and judging.

Understanding first comes about through insight. It is the first step in the process whereby the intellect becomes one with its object. It is through insight that the likeness of the thing known is introduced into the intellect. The activity of the intellect that follows upon this determination is, properly speaking, the act of understanding.

Insight, then, refers most properly to that aspect of intellection by which the intelligible form is derived from the sensible world or from experience. This is not the totality, however, of the intellective process, but in one sense it is merely the beginning. Insight accounts for the origin of the content of the act of understanding, but it does not adequately account for its totality, nor does it sufficiently point out the unique dynamism present within the intellect as it truly understands.

The acquired form of the object, the intelligible species, is the formal principle of the act of understanding itself; that is, the intelligible species is that which determines and shapes the intellect at the very moment it is understanding. The intellect is one with the object simply because the very form by which it has been activated (through the instrumentality of the active intellect illuminating the phantasm) derives exclusively from the object known. The act of understanding is the intellect actualized. Through the reception of the likeness of the other, the passive intellect has gone from a state of *can know* to *actual knowing*. Nor has the intellect remained wholly passive. In receiving the form of the other it has gone into act by producing a likeness of the very form that it has received, which likeness Aquinas calls the concept. It is in and through the concept, the likeness of the other, that the intellect knows the other. Since the intellect is, in producing its concept, identical with the other, in know-ing itself it knows the other. The *I am* of the intellect thus is the *it is* of the object known, the two having now become formally one. Intellect is now in act, but only in a limited way because the form by which it is actualized is a limited form. Still, intellect is in a state of actuality once it has been moved to act through the presence of the immaterial form within it.

Through the presence of the intelligible form within it, the passive intellect is now no longer fully *itself*; that is, it is not that which it was. Rather it has become whatever has informed it—the object that is known. The act of understanding, therefore, is a relational act. The relation, or ordering, of the act of understanding to the object known is precisely what is meant by the term *true*. Truth is not a thing, but a relation of identity, which one thing has to another, aris-ing out of the fact that the intellect is aware of its own formal identity with the other. In short, truth is in the intellect in the fullest sense inasmuch as the latter knows its own conformity with the other.

If we ask, then, whether the intellect is true in the act of under-standing, the answer must be that it is. Every act of understanding is essentially and necessarily true, simply because, through the act of understanding, the intellect is one with the object known. Yet, the fullness of truth is lacking at this point, because the intellect is not yet fully aware of its own truth, of its conformity to the other, and this brings us to the second act of understanding which traditionally is called judgment.

The word judgment, as it is commonly employed non-philosophically, has a legal connotation and is related to a judge's opinion in a court of law. Yet philosophically speaking, the unquali-fied term judgment, when technically used, refers to the intellective act. It is that phase in the process of human understanding when the intellect judges, or acknowledges, the source of that by which it knows. The intellective act of judgment is the intellect's coming to a full appropriation of its own act of understanding, whereby it pin-points *what* it is precisely that it knows. Briefly, in the act of judging, the intellect completes its act and comes to full knowledge.

All simple acts of understanding—every act in which the intellect becomes one with another through insight into phantasm—are fol-lowed by the second act of judging. The two acts ought not to be artificially separated, therefore, but viewed rather as complementary phases in one continuing process of understanding. To understand why judgment is the inevitable consequence of a first act of simple understanding, it is essential to recall what has already been said about the immaterial nature of the intellective act.

Precisely because through insight the object cognized becomes present to the intellect immaterially—separate from the physical conditions of quantity and extension—not only is the object present to the intellect through its likeness but the act of intellect itself is present to the intellective power. The immateriality of the intellective act of understanding renders possible a complete reflective act whereby the intellect is present to itself, and thus knows the nature of its own act of understanding, which is precisely that it is one with the object experienced.

Such a complete reflection is not available to the sensory powers, and this explains why the sense of sight, for example, does not see its own seeing. Because the sensory act engages its object precisely on the singular level, and thus within the context of its material conditions, it is incapable of fully reflecting on itself and its own activity. For that reason the act of seeing is incapable of seeing its own seeing. Contrarily, however, the intellect, *immaterial* in its nature and its operation, is open to itself and its own act; consequently, it can know *that it knows* and it can also know *what* knowing is. This act of self-knowledge, therefore, is said to be reflective, since it involves a *bending back* upon itself. The second act of understanding, or judgment, is that act in which the intellect, in knowing its own intellective act, knows the nature of that act, which is that it is to be conformed, or identified, with that which is experienced. It is this known conformity that most properly constitutes the true dimension of the knowing act. This is the reason why only an intellective being knows the truth, since it is only in and through the intellective act that the relation of the knowing act to the other, the object, is fully known. This is why Aquinas simply states, "Wherefore the intellect knows the truth accordingly as it reflects upon itself" (*On Truth*, q. 1, art. 9).

The act of judging can be called the *truth-act*. According to Aquinas, "... the perfection of the intellect is truth as known; therefore, properly speaking, truth resides in the intellect composing and dividing . . . ." (*Summ. Theologica I*, q. 16, art. 2). What he understands by the intellect composing and dividing is the intellect in its second act, the act of judging. Judging can also be defined as *the understanding of understanding*, for through judgment the intellect understands its own understanding. It is, therefore, futile to attempt to *prove* that when it understands, the intellect knows the truth—as though the concepts of truth and understanding were alien to each other and needed to be brought together. The point is that if it were possible to understand without knowing that what one understood were true, there would be no way of establishing that any act of understanding were true, since, by the faulty definition, an act of understanding need not be true.

This second act, whereby the intellect knows the nature of its own act and hence its conformity to the object that has determined it, is traditionally referred to as an act of judging because in this act the intellect judges, or discerns, its own present state of understanding—it discerns that it is active because of something other than itself, which has moved it to this determinate act. The intellect *is* in this way because something other than itself has caused it *to be* in *this* way. This simultaneous affirmation of the nature of its own act of understanding and of the nature of the *other* is what is designated by the term *judgment*.

Finally, in Aquinas's view, it is because intellect does know itself that it can know another. There is, therefore, no need to account for a transition from the *I am* of the intellect to the *it is* of the object. Since in the act of knowing, intellect is formally identified with the other, it cannot recognize its own state of being without at the same time recognizing the actuality of the other.

This *I am* of Aquinas's needs to be distinguished from the *I think* of Descartes's. For the latter, *I think* is without content, while for Aquinas *I am* cannot be uttered without the intellect's first having been shaped by the content of the other. Thus it always is "I am in this way or that way" and never a pure or merely empty "I am" as it is for Descartes.

Similarly, the "it is" of Aquinas—whereby the intellect affirms the existence of the other—is far removed from the contentless and impersonal "it is" of Kant for whom the thing-in-itself remains forever unknown in its own reality, since it can only be known as it appears. Rather Aquinas's *it is* involves, and is identified with, the very manner in which the knowing subject is in its act of knowing. To every *it is* there is a corresponding *I am.*

Existential and Essential Judgments

From the foregoing it is clear that judgments are essentially affirmations made on the part of the intellect as to an other's state of being. All judgments fall into one of two classes. They are either what can be termed *existential* judgments or *essential* judgments.

An affirmation, or an assertion, can be seen as a response to a question, for understanding itself is always preceded by a search for knowledge. Questions, moreover, can be of two kinds. They can ask (a) whether something is, or they can ask (b) *what* it is. The first class of questions is of course existential, since they inquire *whether* something exists. The existential judgment responds to the existential question and is simply expressed linguistically by affirming that something *is.*

On the other hand the essential judgment responds to an essential question, which has to do with the *manner in which* something is, and asks *What* is it? *How* is it? *Why* is it? The essential question properly presupposes the existence of that which is inquired about. If one should ask what the weight of a particular apple is, one has already satisfied oneself that the apple exists. To respond to this question, therefore, a more complex affirmation is required, one that involves some determinate characteristic or property of the thing. But, to the question, What is this? the reply might be, depending on the circumstances, This is a rose. In this instance the intellect is discerning what it is that it is conformed with. The judgment is thus an essential and not merely an existential judgment which does nothing more than affirm the existence of an existing thing— affirm that something is. Because the essential judgment is complex, always coordinating a determinate property with an existing subject, it is comprised of the three logical elements of *subject, copula,* and *predicate.* The subject is *that* about which something is said. The predicate is *what* is said about the subject, and the copula is the *link* connecting the two. In the example used above of an essential judgment, This is a rose: *This* is the subject of the proposition, *rose* is the predicate, and *is* is the copula. In the judgment all three elements are understood as dynamically united. Though according to its mode of signification the predicate lies outside the subject to which it refers, yet according to that which it signifies the predicate refers to a reality entirely internal to the subject, indicating simply in *what* way the subject participates in being.

The Significance of Judgment in the Human Intellective Act

Earlier it was stated that the act of judgment irrevocably follows the first act of understanding, resulting from the active intellect's illumination of the phantasm. A brief explanation of this statement is now in order. Since the first act of understanding is incomplete, a second act is necessary in order to progress to an understanding of the act of understanding and to bring to completion the first, or original, act of understanding. Why is this so? Ultimately the answer lies in the abstractive mode of knowing, which the human intellect must follow. Since it comes to know its existential object through the acquisition of a likeness of that object, it can only come to know it piecemeal and by degrees. With its dependence on the active intellect's illumination of phantasm, the intellect focuses now on one aspect of its object, now on another, and in each instance it is activated by a separate immaterial likeness of the object which the active intellect has abstracted from phantasm. Yet in each instance it knows the thing as it actually is, even though incompletely. Through judgment it coordinates these various perfections of the object known, relating them back to the subject in which each was initially experienced.

For example, one might observe that a particular pen was blue. One might further observe that the same object was of a certain weight, that its surface was smooth, and that it was made of a hard material. Each of these observations constitutes a separate judgment, for each indicates one manner in which the pen *actually* is. These judgments can of course be synthesized so that each original predicate becomes a part of the subject. Once it has been observed that an object is a pen, it is then possible to say This pen is blue. Other essential judgments can be combined, This blue pen is heavy. This heavy, blue pen has a smooth surface. In this way the intellect attests to the unity of the singular judgments which have preceded, indicating that each merely reflects but a partial aspect of the total existing object. Clearly, there is always more to learn about any known object.

The examples we have used of existential and essential judgments have all been positive or affirmative. It should, however, be noted that judgments not only signify union or composition but they may also signify separation or division. Such judgments are said to be negative judgments. Thus the statement This pen is not red, is an example of a negative judgment. Through the negative judgment the intellect is discerning that there is a lack of identity between objects or aspects of objects that it has experienced. It could be affirmed that Plato and Socrates are both Greeks, but in a negative judgment it could be denied that they are the same individual.

The division of the human intellective act, therefore, into simple and complex understanding, or understanding and judgment, is the direct result of the abstractive manner in which the human intellect must cognize its object. The very fact that the human intellect must question its experience, must search out and uncover its intelligibilities through intelligent inquiry is the very reason for the multiplicity of human intellective acts in the first place and lays the groundwork for the phenomenon of human language, which we shall soon investigate.

It is this obvious phenomenon of the truly enormous multiplication of intellective acts which provides one of the great anomalies of modern epistemological theory. While all philosophers acknowledge the fact, few seem concerned with the need of explaining the cause behind it. The reason why the human is condemned to acquire knowledge piecemeal and through time is *not self-evident*, and surely is deserving of a genuine philosophic explanation.

Reasoning: The Mind's Struggle for Further Understanding

The concluding remarks in the preceding section naturally lead us to the phenomenon of reasoning. As already remarked in the first chapter on questioning, the human mind is ceaselessly in search of new knowledge. Its horizons of knowing are unlimited because as an intellective power it searches out things from the perspective of *being* itself. Hence it is capable of knowing whatever is. Because understanding is an activity free of all physical constraint, it is capable of reflecting upon itself. This makes it possible for the intellect to know the nature of its acts of knowing as well as its own nature. Furthermore, it is capable of comparing, contrasting, and unifying the varied and multiple forms of knowledge it has acquired through union with the objects in its experience. This process—whereby the intellect seeks to consolidate and classify the knowledge it has acquired through time—is called reasoning.

Through reasoning, the mind ascends in its knowing to a higher ground or to a higher viewpoint. Through a synthesis of its knowledge, it is able to formulate more general and universalized acts of understanding. It is in this way that the sciences and arts are generated; moreover, it is through this reflective synthesis that philosophy itself is born.

Taken in its most general sense, reasoning can be understood as any activity of the intellect that leads to understanding. In a narrower sense, reasoning refers to that intellective process whereby the intellect derives new knowledge from knowledge it *already* possesses. Understood in this second sense, reasoning terminates in a new act of understanding whereby, as already suggested, a new and higher synthesis of its knowledge is formed. What was *implicitly* present to the intellect is made to be *explicitly* present.

A detailed study of reasoning and the manner in which the human intellect achieves its new syntheses must be reserved to logic, which is properly concerned with the laws of human reasoning. Briefly, however, we can note that the term *reasoning* indicates a connecting of reasons or ideas within the mind. The Greeks employ the word *syllogizesthai* to refer to the same reality. This word literally means *to deduce* or *draw out* something from a plurality. Accordingly, the word *syllogism* means a complex act of understanding that involves two judgments being joined together to form a third. Through the syllogism a new judgment is formed that is implicitly contained in the two preceding judgments. The resulting judgment is called the conclusion, and the judgments from which it immediately derives are called the premises.

Let us turn to an example of syllogistic reasoning: Suppose that through previous acts of understanding it is known that (a) every living thing is corruptible; (b) all animals are living things. From these two statements we are able to conclude that (c) all animals are corruptible. Logically presented:

All living things are corruptible
All animals are living
All animals are corruptible

We may observe in analyzing the above that it is impossible for the conclusion not to follow if the premises are granted. There is a necessary relationship between these judgments. The mind, by reflecting upon the first two judgments which it already possesses, understands that the third or concluding judgment is inseparably united to them.

Reasoning is crucial to the human because of the great number and variety of intellective acts. Through reasoning the human's knowledge is condensed and ordered; thus, it is brought to a closer unity. The human mind is ever seeking to unify its knowledge in this manner, and it is this very unification process that necessitates the phenomenon of questioning we have already explored. Through reasoning and questioning, the mind is in search of the causes of things. It wishes to know more fully what it already knows; to explore relationships among the things it knows. As Aristotle pointed out in *The Metaphysics*, it is the mind's search for the *ultimate* causes of things that constitutes the highest branch of human knowledge, which we call first philosophy, or metaphysics. Inasmuch as the human mind is driven to find out the causes of things, the human is indeed a philosophic, or metaphysical, animal.

From the foregoing it is clear that reasoning is itself merely propaedeutic, a necessary preparation, to understanding, and its goal is a new judgment that will provide a higher viewpoint and allow wider vistas of understanding. However, the new judgment, or act of understanding, leads to yet further inquiry and further judgments. The drive toward unity and synthesis is unending and relentless. Each act of understanding brings in its train fresh questions that always proceed from a higher viewpoint, and any new knowledge serves as a source for further inquiry and as a guide for further experience. This relentless thrust toward new understanding is the work of the active intellect, which constantly probes the hidden meaning of what is experienced.

It should be emphasized, however, that like the phenomenon of insight, understanding does not ordinarily come easily or automatically. Often it is the result of lengthy and painstaking probing and searching as in the case of Archimedes and the gold crown. At what point the experience being analyzed will yield its secrets under the illuminating light of being, is unpredictable. When understanding does come, it comes suddenly and unexpectedly, accompanied by the indubitable awareness that what we understand is *this way* because it *has to be* this way. Understanding is the act by which intellect synthesizes within the very light of being. The synthesis itself is accomplished through the intellect's having returned to being. This is precisely what reflection is: intellect's return to itself. The intellect *sees* that something is and cannot *not* be. As Aquinas says, the intellect reaches understanding and concludes its inquiry when it returns to the first principles of understanding: identity, non-contradiction, and cause. It is at this moment the intellect grasps that something is in this or that way and cannot be otherwise. All judgments and all acts of understanding thus rest on necessity, the awareness that something must be. Such awareness is exclusively a human phenomenon.

Thinking as Imperfect Reasoning

Not every act of reasoning results in new knowledge. Often we experience within ourselves an inability, for the moment at least, to complete the circle and to effect a complete reflection. In short, it is abundantly clear that we can raise many questions for which we cannot yet find an answer; we can also raise questions for which we cannot foresee a way in which we might ever be able to obtain a proper answer. Yet this very casting about for further knowledge; this attempt to delve more deeply into our conscious experience and to forge new relationships out of individual acts of understanding; this looking for the intelligible matrix within a segment of our experience so that we can unify it further and draw it together under manageable (intelligible) form, is a genuine reasoning process in itself, even though it does not succeed in producing the intended results. This is reasoning at the first level. It is simply the mind in its natural restless state of seeking new understanding and of probing relentlessly for further light and meaning within its present world of experience.

In so doing, the mind sends out feelers, as it were, and formulates statements, the truth of which it has not yet grasped. It constructs syllogisms of various forms, testing for the truth of being and casting about for new insights and ever deeper understanding. If insight and new understanding is not forthcoming, the effort remains incomplete, and the mind is left with the evidences of its struggle, but it is not freed of the painful reminder of its own ignorance. It is forced to conclude that it *has not* concluded. At this point the intellect cannot yet say with regard to the question raised, I now understand. Its proposals and mental structures remain as empty scaffolding, providing lingering evidence of an unsuccessful struggle.

Reasoning in the sense described is thus one with the very process of thinking. It is the intellect in an imperfect and intermediate state. It is similar to moving toward one's destination as compared to arriving; to questioning as compared to answering; to searching as compared to finding. At this point the intellect has fallen short of understanding and is in a state of conscious awareness of its own ignorance. (This is the state of mind Archimedes was surely in on his way to the Syracuse baths on the day that he made scientific history.) The statements that the intellect employs at this level of its testing for new knowledge are often of its own fabrication. They are proposed by the intellect and utilized by it precisely in order that it might see what truth is in them; and whether or not such propositions might in actuality be full-fledged judgments.

As the Cartesian experiment clearly attests, it is crucial that the distinction between propositions and judgments in the proper sense be maintained. A proposition is that which the intellect puts forward as probably true, but which it does not yet understand to be true. It is a statement that needs to be examined in the light of experience and in the light of being for the evidence of its truth. A judgment, on the other hand, is a statement that is known to be true; it is an authentic act of understanding.

The reason it is important to make the distinction between proposition and judgment is that on the surface they appear identical. In mere external form they do not differ. There is no difference linguistically between the assertion that *All triangles are three-sided* and *All triangles are four-sided.* Both are constituted of subject, predicate, and copula, and both make an assertion without qualification. Yet the first is a judgment because it expresses an authentic union between the subject and predicate, and is itself the product of an act of understanding. The second statement, however, attempts to unite contradictory notions. By definition a triangular form cannot be simultaneously four-sided. The second statement, therefore, does not rest on, or presuppose, an act of understanding. It is merely an affirmation made without understanding and cannot be a judgment.

Of course, not all propositions contain contradictory qualities such as the one just considered. Indeed, most propositions fall under the classification of being probably true, and thus can be viewed as probable judgments. For example, I may know it to be true at this moment that it is raining outside. The statement *It is raining* is a judgment. However, should I say *Tomorrow it will rain* I have merely stated what I think will occur, or what is most likely to occur, because it is clearly impossible to say with complete assurance that it will or will not rain. It may well rain, but one cannot claim to understand that it *must* be so. Hence, such a statement, while it may become true with the passing of time, is not true at the time it is uttered and for that reason is not a judgment.

Similarly, without actually knowing, one might assert that there were two dozen cookies in a particular jar. In that case the statement *There are two dozen cookies in this jar* would not be a judgment, but merely a proposition. Note, however, that this does not mean that the statement *may not* be true. The statement, which we have defined as a proposition, can be considered a probable judgment until such time as it becomes known by counting them how many cookies are actually in the jar. It is important to note, therefore, that a probable statement, or proposition, is one that may or may not be true, and as long as it remains probable, whether or not it is true is *unknown*. A probable statement is not an authentic judgment.

Understanding and Error

We conclude this chapter on intellection with several comments on truth and error. To claim that all authentic judgments are true must seem to be both dogmatic and a display of profound ignorance about the stark reality of human error. Yet the claim is not made uncritically, nor does it entail an outright denial of error within the ambit of human experience.

Viewing the matter first from a negative perspective, let us suppose that authentic intellective judgments *can be* erroneous. Under such a supposition, clearly one could not rely on one's power of understanding to discern whether or not any given judgment were true or false, for it is the very ability of the understanding to know truth that is being challenged. In such a case, how could an erroneous judgment ever be corrected? How could one come to recognize that he or she had, in fact, erred?

In point of fact, to assume that understanding is not of its very nature true is to begin one's intellective analysis with the premise that no question can be answered, since affirmation depends upon understanding. One could not even ask a question, for every question rests on some prior affirmation. If the initial assumption is that understanding is not of itself a reliable witness in its own defense, one is straightaway condemned to a pervadingly skeptical view, or, to paraphrase Hegel, "To an eternal night in which all cows are black," which is tantamount to an unconditional denial of knowing anything at all. This follows unless, of course, one makes an appeal to a higher court, as Descartes did, in seeking to validate his own knowledge by grounding it on his trust in an all-good God not to deceive him.

The claim that knowledge is not of itself true is self-defeating, for it places one in the awkward conflicting position of asserting simultaneously that one *knows* that one does *not know.* For if one cannot know, then one cannot know even that one does not know. The unreality of just such a claim was clearly uncovered earlier in connection with the nature of the authentic question and its underlying presuppositions. That is, all questions arise out of knowledge. Although it is true that they reveal there is yet more to be known, yet without the rock foundation of true and authentic knowledge to begin with, the phenomenon of the question is reduced to being chimerical.

The distinction previously made between judgments and propositions is crucial to the ultimate resolution of the problem of human error. Let us now seek to illustrate positively how this is so by taking as an example a simple statement such as *This is an apple.*

First, in order to make such an assertion in an authentic way, I must know *what an apple is* from prior experience, and I must recognize it when I see it. Yet there is nothing to prevent me from affirming that an object before me (which indeed is an apple) is an orange or a cat or a toy. When I affirm that *This is an orange,* when in fact it *is* an apple, I cannot possibly understand that it is an orange; assuming, of course, that I understand the meaning of those words in English and I appreciate the distinction between an apple and an orange. Thus the affirmation *This is an orange* in this context is not a judgment but a proposition, a mere juxtaposition of terms, because it is not true. And, of course, I *know* that it is not true.

But how, one might ask, do I explain the fact that I made such an erroneous statement? How do you explain the existence of error in human discourse or in human thinking? There can be many reasons, but in terms of the example employed above, none of them has anything to do with the apple. That is, the apple cannot be held responsible. I could merely have been teasing or joking or responding to a challenge: "I dare you to call that apple an orange!" Whatever the reason, it was a reason extraneous to the apple. This is another way of saying that I made the statement because I saw some value in doing so, even though I recognized the statement to be false. Error does, on occasion, pay. In short, error can be explained as the product of the will's moving the intellect to simulate knowledge when in fact it is lacking; to pass off as a judgment a statement which is not supported by the evidence at hand.

That all of us value rather highly our ability to answer questions is obvious. We are often ashamed to confess that we plainly do not know the answer to a question, and we take pride in being able to figure something out all on our own. Even from a psychological standpoint, gaining an insight provides us with great satisfaction. All of which can pressure us into simulating an answer even when we do not have one; to claim to know when in fact we do not. This is not to suggest, however, that outright dishonesty need be involved. It can easily be a case of rationalized self-deception when emotional pressures serve to render plausible a faulty claim and prevent us from fully realizing that our knowledge in support of it is weak and merely probable. Since we want so badly to be able to say that we understand, it is easy for us to wink at the lack of evidence we actually have for our claim and to rationalize its validity. Such yielding to group pressure is especially noticeable in small children, who often pretend to have answers to questions put to them by their peers or their elders, so as to hide their ignorance and impress their interlocutors. Thus a mere affirmation differs from a judgment in that the former is not grounded on knowledge, while the latter is. To put it another way, the judgment rests on insight, while the mere affirmation does not.

Lastly, it can be noted that the claim that all authentic judgments are true does not in the least entail the denial of the possibility of a genuine growth in knowledge. Although in making a judgment one is saying *something* true about the object, one is not thereby saying *everything* that can be said about it. There always remains something more that can be said about it because our grasp of the real is always limited and dependent upon the special perspective of our own experience. Hence, knowledge among individuals may vary greatly, in that some will have a fuller understanding of certain things than others, but this does not prevent all from having a true and authentic understanding of them. Diversity of knowledge in this sense is no support whatever to the sophistical claim that knowledge is relative.

Thus, in affirming *This is an apple,* I am merely attesting to the kind of fruit that it is. I have not made an assertion, to this point at least, about the kind of apple it is; whether or not, for example, it is green or ripe; where it was grown; how much it might cost; how many calories it might contain; let alone how many atoms might comprise it. As already noted in an earlier chapter, every authentic response to a question invites further questions. There is always more to be known; more questions to be asked; more judgments to be formed. Furthermore, an affirmation that is neither understood to be *true* nor is inherently contradictory is immediately transformed into a judgment the moment an insight is gained, whereby an affirmation becomes grounded in the experienced *being of the other.*

Summary

This concludes our consideration of human intellection. We have learned that human intellection derives its content from the sensory world and thereby depends upon insight into phantasm through the illuminating activity of the agent intellect; further, that it is immaterial in nature. The three levels of the intellective act were considered. The act of simple understanding was differentiated from that of judgment and both of these from the act of reasoning. Judgments were defined as being either existential or essential, and all judgments were understood to be the necessary complement and fulfillment of the simple act of understanding by which the intellect understands the nature of its own act and can therefore grasp its essential union with that which is known. The judgment as the second act of understanding is necessary precisely because the content of the intellective act derives from the sensory world through insight. We have also learned how reasoning can, in its turn, be divided into *reasoning as a complex act* terminating in a fuller act of understanding what is already understood, and reasoning as a quest for understanding, which is indistinguishable from the general process of thinking. The judgment was distinguished from the mere proposition, which is a tentative, probable judgment lacking the supreme validating factor of insight. It was also noted that it is through insight that a proposition or proposed judgment is transformed into an authentic act of judgment, whereby the intellect recognizes its identity with the other and hence the formal truth of its own act.

In a discussion on the problem of error, authentic judgments were shown to be always true by their nature, since they are based on reflective insight or a conscious return to phantasm; but erroneous affirmations were shown to be statements made without the accompanying evidence of insight and were ultimately explainable as phenomena by the intellect's being moved to a premature assent to something being true when there was no full, requisite intellective grounding in being. Finally, the manner in which knowledge is developmental and capable of growth was discussed, and the distinction between mere affirmation and authentic judgment revealed the basis upon which all authentic questions rest.

Definitions and Conclusions

1. The intelligible species is an immaterial likeness of the material thing *which has been abstracted* from the phantasm through the illuminating activity of the active intellect and by which the receptive intellect is formally activated.

2. The phantasm is the complex sensory manifold from which the

agent intellect abstracts an immaterial likeness or intelligible species.

3. The agent intellect is an intellective power always in act with regard to the intelligibilities of material things, whose function it is to activate the receptive intellect through the illumination of the phantasm.

4. The receptive intellect is an intellective power potentially oriented to all material things, but depending on the action of the agent intellect for its actualization through its reception of the intelligible species.

5. The intelligible species is not *that which* is first known but rather that *by which* the thing of which it is a likeness is known.

6. Reflectively and secondarily, the intellect knows the nature of its own act and hence the intelligible species within it by which it has come to understand.

7. Understanding is, properly speaking, the first act of the receptive intellect whereby it forms within itself the inner word or concept as it is informed by the intelligible species.

8. Judgment is the second or complete act of the receptive intellect whereby it understands the nature of its own act, the form by which it is in act, and hence that it is one with the thing of which the form is a likeness.

9. Truth is the known identity of the intellect with its object. Consequently, in its formal sense, as fully known, truth is found only in the second act of understanding, the judgment.

10. The immateriality of the intellective act renders possible a complete, reflective act whereby the intellect is present to itself and thus knows the nature of its own act of understanding, which is precisely that it be one with the object experienced.

11. The act of judging may be defined as the understanding of understanding, for through judgment the intellect understands its own understanding.

12. An existential judgment affirms that something exists.

13. An essential judgment affirms *how* something is or *what* something is.

14. Broadly speaking, the act of reasoning is any activity of intellect by which it strives for, and perhaps attains to, understanding.

15. More properly, reasoning is that activity of intellect whereby it

attains to new knowledge from knowledge it already possesses. Such reasoning is also called syllogistic reasoning.

16. Through reasoning, human knowledge is condensed and ordered and thus brought to a state of greater unity.

17. Metaphysics is the mind's search for the underlying unity within the totality of human experience.

18. Insight and understanding do not ordinarily come easily or automatically but are more frequently the result of a lengthy probing and searching.

19. A proposition differs from judgment in that it is proposed by the intellect as *probably* true, while in judgment truth has been attained.

20. If judgments could of their very nature be erroneous, they would be beyond correction with universal skepticism resulting.

21. The origin of error in the intellective act is ultimately to be assigned to the will which can move the intellect to assent to a proposition with insufficient evidence; that is, without first having obtained a fresh insight into experience.

22. An authentic judgment is true only because it is grounded in the being of the other through insight, while a mere proposition is a statement whose terms have yet to be fused into union through insight.

23. Authentic knowledge is always susceptible of further growth and development because human knowledge deriving through insight into phantasm never fully matches the richness of the intelligibility of that which is known.

24. Every authentic question, since it rests on knowledge already obtained and an awareness that there is still more to be known, derives its validating force from the distinction between judgment and mere affirmation.

8 Language

Speech is the best show man puts on.

Benjamin Lee Whorff

The Language Phenomenon

Language, the human expression of thought in sensible symbol, is perhaps the greatest of all human achievements. Without language the human would not be able to accomplish much of lasting significance. Without language we would not only be incapable of communicating with our fellow humans but we would also be incapable of making anything, for in order to make anything we must communicate thought.

Undoubtedly most of us think of language primarily in terms of its being spoken. Yet language includes all visual and tactile signs; such as, the printed word, sign language, and braille. Since language includes all forms of intelligent human communication, it is unquestionably influential and central to everything humans do.

Most of the ensuing discussion will be focused on the spoken word, simply because it is the first form of language with which most of us become familiar, but the following observations can *mutatis mutandis* be applied to the other forms of human communication as well.

In support of the claim of the unique centrality of language to human existence there are several obvious facts: humans talk a lot, humans talk about everything, and humans simply like to talk. Let us consider each of these in turn.

Humans talk a lot

In its broadest connotation talking is more than verbalizing. It entails listening as well. Talking and listening are correlative terms. We employ language when we listen either to ourselves or someone else speak, or when we listen to the radio, watch television, attend a play, or see a movie. In short, we are engaged in language whether we *send* the word or *receive* it. Similarly, we converse when we read anything. Finally, even when alone with the silence of our own thoughts, we are carrying on a dialogue of sorts with ourselves. Though we are talking to ourselves, we are talking nonetheless. And we are listening. Humans are incessant and hopelessly incorrigible talkers—communicators—for we are talking in some form or other all of our waking time. Some of us even talk in our sleep. Either we have something to say or there is something more we want to hear (learn). The human is naturally loquacious because the human is an intellectual being. Talking is correlative to thinking. It is a commonplace to say that humans think in words.

Humans talk about everything

Not only are we incessant talkers, we are also omniloquent; that is, our topics of conversation cover every imaginable topic and theme. Our interests, our projects, our musings are virtually limitless. Besides, we are capable of thinking about anything that either is, or was, or could be; therefore, our talking is not any more confined to the present than is our thinking, even though our talking, like our thinking, always takes place in the present.

By nature we desire to know everything; there are no built-in barriers to what we want to know. We are continually inquiring into our experiences; seeking out their hidden origins. Little wonder, then, that we are the world's greatest talkers, for we use speech both to communicate our knowledge and to obtain new knowledge. We intellectual beings are *universal talkers* because we are *universal knowers.*

Humans enjoy talking

In all forms of talking we are able to find inner satisfaction, entertainment, and fulfillment. Humans have devised many subtle forms of talking. When we have nothing to talk about, we fabricate and phantasize, or in a sense simply talk about *nothing.* Without conversation of some kind, life assumes the guise of an almost intolerable burden. Surely it is not without its own significance that total isolation and confinement is perhaps for the normal human the worst of all forms of deprivation.

The Nature and Structure of Language

The basic unit of every language is, of course, the *word*, which is a sensible sign or symbol (spoken/written) standing for, or expressing, a concept or idea, and indirectly an inner feeling, a wish, or desire. The word is sensible, because it can activate one of the sensory powers. Thus the spoken word is a sound that can be heard; the written word is a visible mark that can be seen; braille is a figure that can be touched; and a signed word is a gesture that can be seen. Yet beyond being merely sensible, a word conveys meaning; it stands-in for an idea. It is the thought or meaning behind the sound—the signification that has been attributed to it—that constitutes it a word. All sounds have their own *natural* meaning. For example, the drumming of rain dripping from the eaves of the roof tells us something about the properties of water as well as the quality (intensity) of the rain. The sound of rain is a *natural* sign. A word, however, is a sound which has meaning *assigned* to it, and hence as a word its signification is conventional. That the sound of the word which refers to the water dripping from the roof or falling to the ground is *rain* in the English language is a wholly fortuitous occurrence. Just as it is fortuitous that it is *pluie* in French, *pioggia* in Italian, and *ame* in Japanese.

While the word is the primal unit of language, words themselves are grouped together to form sentences in a variety of ways. Sentences, which can be either simple or complex, are highly varied in structure. Some affirm, some question, some command or express a wish or feeling, and all are formed according to a certain order or syntax and must respect the grammatical rules of their particular language. The sentence, which is composed of words that express a complete thought, corresponds to the second act of understanding or judgment, whereas the individual word signifies the concept of the mind expressed in the first or simple act of understanding. The sentence reflects the complexity of judgment by signifying the union grasped in judgment between the intellect and its object. The subject and predicate of the sentence correspond to, and symbolize, this inner union and complexity.

Language as a whole, then, is the total complex of words that has been systematized through syntactical and grammatical rules. The systemization which language confers upon mere *sounds, visible signs or symbols*, and *random touches* makes it possible for us to communicate more clearly and directly with one another. We use the unwritten as well as the written rules of our language's underlying grammatical structure to better express ourselves and we expect to be understood by someone else who knows the same language. As intellective beings we humans can both speak and reflect upon our speaking, and are capable of learning how better to shape and communicate our thoughts.

Through the expression of human language something truly remarkable is accomplished—our abstract, immaterial thought, which we initially derive from our physical, sensible world, is reincorporated into that same world. It is through language that thoughts, imaginings, inner feelings, and desires can be returned to the world as a complex series of sensible, meaningful signs. Our thoughts and consciousness dwell in the world in the forms of language. Language is, therefore, the inverse of insight. Esteeming it as a precious heritage, we pass on our language to succeeding generations.

The Philosophic Significance of Language

Since language is thought clothed in sensible symbols, it can be sensed, although imperfectly. We are able to hear what someone is saying in the sense that our ears pick up the sound waves caused by the movement of the speaker's vocal cords, mouth, and tongue. Yet we are unable to hear the content or meaning of the words spoken. This can only be understood; and for this, insight into phantasm is required, as in the case of any intellective act of knowing.

It is clear that thought does exist in sensible symbols and that we do gain understanding from what is said or from what we read. This, however, is clearly not the case in all instances. What one person is able to understand, another person often cannot, although the words spoken are heard or seen by both individuals with the same level of sensing proficiency. This is demonstrable when one is unfamiliar with a language and is totally incapable of deriving meaning from it in either a spoken or written form.

The phenomenon of speech relates to the material already discussed in the analysis of the active intellect. Thus the human phenomenon of language marvellously teaches us the possibility of an extremely close alignment of thought and matter while at the same time emphasizing their distinction. As an experiential given, language is a forceful rejoinder to every attempt to explain the phenomenon of human knowledge from an exclusively materialist or idealist perspective. Language itself is the product of the union of matter and thought. Consequently, the phenomenon of language is rich in its connotations as regards both the origin of ideas and the very nature of the human.

First, our very use of sensible signs or symbols to give expression to thought reinforces our awareness of our dependency on the material, sensible world, and draws the realms of thought and nature into a dynamic, though stable tension. Language is living thought expressed through sensible symbols. Human language indicates to us, therefore, in a convincing manner that the original source of our ideas was the very sensible world into which we reconvert our ideas through speech. If ideas are not potentially present in the surrounding material world, then language itself is fiction. Yet as a living phenomenon, the existence of language is simply incontrovertible. Indeed it is the meeting place and junction of two worlds, and this reality witnesses to the inadequacy of any theory of knowledge that claims human knowledge is inborn, without an external referant. This reality of language belies the claim of the materialist that matter and thought differ merely in degree.

Finally, language serves to delineate clearly the unique nature of the human as an intellective spirit intimately dwelling within a body. As thought enlivens and gives the shape of meaning to the sensible symbol, so the spirit of the human informs and gives inner shape to the human.

The Ambiguity of Language

Because language is an expression of thought through sensible symbol, it is inherently and unavoidably ambiguous. It is worth focusing on this distinctive characteristic of human language, for it contains several important practical consequences in terms of the nature of human communication.

The phenomenon of the ambiguity of human language is well known and is, in fact, experienced by everyone. Many sounds that are exactly the same often have very different meanings, and hence constitute different words: sea and see; meat and meet, be and bee, by and bye, so and sew. Such words are called homonyms. Contrarily, there are many sounds differing totally from one another which have the same basic meaning. For example, misfortune, adversity, trouble, disaster, mischance, and catastrophe. These are called synonyms. The meanings of each of these words differ in terms of degree, of course, but fundamentally the idea behind these different words is the same—a catastrophe is a *total* misfortune, while a mischance is perhaps best characterised as a *slight* misfortune.

Following up on the idea of ambiguity as a corollary to the nature of human language, it is helpful to recall that it is through language that thought is incorporated into the physical world. Because thought is immaterial it transcends the limitations of singularity and individuality, which means that a perfect expression of thought in sensible symbol is an impossibility. The word-symbol is as incapable of containing the full thrust of thought as a thin copper wire is of transmitting the full electrical charge of a lightning bolt. Consequently, the expression of thought in language is condemned to fall far short of the intellectual reality itself.

In an effort to do the best we can to express ourselves, we multiply words almost without limit and we introduce multiple modifying expressions to indicate the manifold intricacies of our thought world. Also we are forced at times to employ the same or similar spoken or written symbols to convey ideas that are remotely, if at all, related. In some languages such as Latin and Russian the addition of a suffix to nouns serves to indicate the precise function of a word within a sentence, whereas in Japanese this function is served by the use of postpositions, and in English and Italian it is handled in part by prepositions. The differentiation between tenses and moods in verbs is common to almost all languages and is a further illustration of the need to modify the linguistic symbol in order to better express the myriad subtleties of the thought world.

It is little wonder, then, that in speaking we must often grope for the proper word or phrase; repeat what we have said in slightly different words; correct our expression and modify it until we are reasonably satisfied that what we have said more or less corresponds to what we wanted to say. This also accounts for the inadequacy we often feel regarding our ability to tell it like it is, to say precisely what we intended to say. When our inner experience is simply too overpowering, we end up exclaiming, "I just can't put it into words"; "I can't give you any real idea of what it is that I have experienced." What we mean is that we do not have the ability to express what we would like to.

An interesting and practical result of the inherent ambiguity of language and our inability to always express ourselves with accuracy, is that human communication is a phenomenon fraught with the constant peril of misunderstanding. It should, then, be no cause for wonderment that on the level of human communication, frequent misunderstandings arise. The complexity and profundity of human thought and feeling is such that it is simply difficult for us to find for it a suitable release in language, and yet it is through language alone that the world of each individual's inner consciousness is made available, not only to the outside world but to other consciousnesses as well. Humans can only communicate with each other through some manifestation of language. Consequently it is not so much the phenomenon of misunderstandings between humans at which we ought to marvel, as the fact that we are able to communicate our thoughts to one another at all.

All of which further underscores the crucial need of language as a component of an individual's education. The cultivation and perfecting of language skills is important to the full development of the individual because language alone affords the person contact with his or her environment. Further reflection on this phenomenon of intersubjective communication will be found in the chapter on the human person and personality, where it is discussed in terms of the development of personal consciousness.

The Phenomenon of the Plurality of Language

Among the more intriguing phenomena regarding human communication is that of the existence of many distinct human languages. All in all there are approximately 3,000 different spoken languages.

This vast number can be broken down into a comparatively small number of language families. Depending on the criteria employed in making this classification, the precise number of language families will vary from perhaps ten to four. Linguistic scholars have shown that it is not vocabulary which is the more basic indicator of commonality among languages but rather the similarity or dissimilarity found in the syntactical, morphological, and grammatical practices of languages. The arrangement of words within the sentence, and the manner of employing them has been found to provide the more reliable norms for fixing upon the mutual relationship of languages.

The fact of the plurality of human language is undeniable. The reasons for such a remarkable diversity in languages and how they evolved are questions for which linguistic scholars have no answers, and to which they may never be able to provide us with answers. The origin of human language simply trails off into prehistory, and since language in its written form is a recent development within the time frame of the history of the human race, there seems little hope that any discoveries can be made that will throw much light on this intriguing human phenomenon.

Yet none of these questions need be settled before one can fix upon a very significant characteristic of all human languages regardless of how diverse they may be; for despite the divergencies, all languages are translatable one into the other. This phenomenon of the *intertranslatability* of human languages is of the greatest significance philosophically. What this indicates is that all of these languages have a common root, namely thought itself, and this reinforces the analysis we have made above of language as the incorporation of thought into matter.

It is owing to the commonality of human thought that all languages communicate through sensible signs the same fundamental consciousness of human beings. Further, all languages follow some form of syntactical rules, and employ words in an ordered way. There is found a rule of mind or a basic logic which all languages adhere to. The phenomenon of the intertranslatability of human languages thus provides convincing corroboration of the unity of the human race. Despite differences of culture and language, there is clearly an underlying human unity indicating, from a purely phenomenological standpoint, a sharing in a common nature. In a later chapter we shall have occasion to address ourselves more at length to this common nature of the human.

Written Language

While the remarks made to this point are equally applicable to both the oral and written expression of thought, the latter contains unique elements, which merit special consideration. Further, the far-reaching consequences of the written word in terms of the development of human civilization, are so enormous that no discussion of the meaning of language for the human could be complete without special emphasis being placed on the written tradition.

Writing is a recent development in terms of history. The earliest form of the written communication of thought we have evidence of was done in cuneiform characters about 3200 B.C. Hence, according to the present state of our knowledge, the human has only employed writing for about 5400 years. The alphabet, which represented a giant step forward in the art of human writing, was not discovered until 1500 B.C.

The written word differs from the spoken in that it is etched in clay or stone, or is painted, written, or printed on a suitable surface. The written word has an obvious advantage over the spoken word in that it is relatively permanent. It can be preserved almost indefinitely, if proper care is taken, and provides the means by which a systematic growth in knowledge is made possible; something that is altogether impossible in a culture relying exclusively on oral expression to conserve and transmit its past. Through the written word human memory is inestimably aided. With the development of writing, humans devoted more time to thinking and to speculations about the world. The arts and the sciences have experienced unprecedented development through the use of the written word, and this has led to the useful application of knowledge to the physical world. Advances in modes of transportation, architecture, engineering, commerce, industry, manufacturing, were all heavily dependent upon the successful exploitation of recorded human thought.

Yet such development depended not so much upon our ability to communicate with one another through visual signs, but more especially upon our newly won ability to preserve written records. With a minimum of delay and with the added capability of conveniently preserving communication for posterity, one person's insight, such as that of Archimedes, could become disseminated throughout the world and be preserved for all future ages. It was the monumental discovery of the alphabet that made the inter-epochal communication of complex and even highly abstractive thought a human possibility. It was the alphabet that allowed Europe to spearhead first the industrial revolution and then the atomic age.

The alphabet appears to have been a Semitic discovery. All of the known alphabets presently in use seem to be derivatives of this first alphabet. Its discovery represents one of the most significant of all human inventions. By employing a fixed written symbol for each of the basic sounds the human voice used, a system was devised. Utilizing a very limited set of symbols (26 in the English alphabet), all of the spoken words of any language can be expressed in writing. In English the twenty-six letters of the alphabet are presently calculated to be capable of forming 700,000 words. Moreover, the alphabet provides an unlimited capacity for expanding the language's vocabulary, so that there will never be need for it to be revised or added to.

This is a vast improvement over pictographic or chirographic forms of writing, which use a symbol to stand for a word or syllable rather than for an isolated sound. To learn to read literary Chinese, which employs ideograms or characters to depict through images the thought to be expressed, one needs to commit to memory a minimum of some eight to ten thousand different symbols or characters. Obviously such a proliferation of written symbols causes difficulties for the typesetting process, both in the past, when it depended upon individual moveable letters, and today, when it is largely a computerized keyboard system.

Owing to the marvel of written language, people have been able to record and pass on to posterity much of what they have learned and experienced. Our libraries are living extensions of the human memory and of the human psyche, and make possible the knowledge of human history. Through the books and manuscripts conserved in our libraries, the past is made available to us. Through language we have access not only to what people have physically accomplished, but to what they have thought as well. Writing gives us entree to the very mind and heart of the human race, opening up to us the intimate thoughts, aspirations, imaginings, frustrations, and disappointments of other humans to whom we can relate. Through written language we come to a better awareness of who we are as humans, for we are allowed to participate in, and learn from, the experiences of those who have preceded us in time.

Civilization itself is truly the accumulation of human insights through the centuries. One era builds upon another. Writing provides the human with a vast thought-storage system, much as the mountains with their glaciers and snow packs provide us with summer water. Through the written word one is able to irrigate the deserts of one's mind.

The impact of the written word on our historical development is thus almost beyond the possibility of exaggeration. With the invention of the printing press in the West by Johannes Gutenberg (c. 1450) and the ensuing proliferation of books and printed materials, the individual became increasingly less dependent on oral communication within the community, and was thus able to live in ever greater solitude and isolation. Private study through reading became the more common way of increasing one's knowledge. It seems unquestionable as Walter Ong has argued in his book, *The Presence of the Word*, that the revolution in philosophy and speculative thinking, typified by the writings of René Descartes, was itself the direct result of the dissemination of the written word.

Through books the human began to turn ever more inward, cultivating the life of the mind and engaging in the inner world of speculation, including mathematics, astronomy, medicine, and the sciences. For centuries after the invention of printing, the written word held the ascendency. Today, however, owing to the more recent inventions of the tape recorder, radio, and television, the spoken language has staged a dramatic comeback. No longer is the written word the sole manner of preserving thought. The spoken word no longer is condemned to die an instantaneous death unless recorded by human memory. Owing to the modern advances of technology, the spoken word can be made quite as permanent as the written, and the modern day emphasis on speech and oral communication is clearly on the rise. If today people give less time to reading and the written word, it is surely in good part because the once unique advantage of the written word—that of preservation—is shared today with the easy preservation of the spoken word. Yet each mode of preservation of human thought—oral or written—has its own advantages, and it is not likely that oral recordings will ever supplant the written word. Whereas the overtones of the spoken word provide a richness, immediacy, and sensuousness that serve to delicately nuance the message, the written word allows for a more reflective intimacy and profundity of communication. It might even be argued that in the silent milieu of the written word we approach more nearly the inner conditions of human thought. The spoken and written words are surely not to be viewed as rivals, therefore, but treasured as complementary and equally priceless modes of human expression.

The Human as a Universal Speaker

The human, through language, has access to the past, to that which *no longer exists*, and to concerns about the world of the future, to that *which might come into existence.* Since human language is a sensible expression of the inner world of understanding, which transcends the limits of time and space, we find that, as a matter of course, the human speaks about the natures and hidden qualities of things as well as about the more easily accessible sensible qualities. As humans our speech is not constricted to what is merely present, for our mind is capable of rising above all temporal limitation. Ideas themselves are a-temporal.

Thus, in addition to an everyday level of conversation, when the more commonplace happenings of our lives are discussed, the human also spends a sizeable portion of time engaged in what might be termed mythic speech: reading fiction, watching television, attending the movies, attending or participating in games, and reading or writing poetry. The enormous flexibility and variety of the modes and genres of human speech and writing serve to emphasize the intellective dimension of the human and clearly set us apart as an animal that lives beyond the limitations of what we see and hear, transcending the world of time and space. We humans are continually striving to express through language the inner workings of the mind and spirit. We are concerned with exploring the farthest reaches of our own inner being. Thus we engage in what we commonly call philosophical inquiry, seeking to articulate through language the very meaning of our own thinking and the underlying structure of our language and our modes of communication.

A transcendental and universal knower, the human being is also a transcendental and universal speaker. Seeking to uncover the nature and causes of this transcendentality, the human being becomes a philosopher. It is this transcendental and philosophic quality of our speech that most clearly sets us apart from the modes of communication employed by the brute animal.

In comparison with human speech patterns, the "speech" of animals is very limited, and it is, moreover, inborn. For example, each species of bird has its own unique limited repertoire of bird songs, which are made by a limited number of notes. This has been proved by conducting extensive experimentation with the aid of tape recorders and other modern equipment. The song sparrow will produce an all but normal song even when canary foster parents have hatched the egg, and the sparrow has been allowed to hear only the canary song, which differs appreciably in pattern and structure from the sparrow song. In similar experiments the domestic fowl and the European cuckoo also were not influenced by the songs of their foster parents. Experience does not apparently play a role in the development of the specific vocalizations of these species of birds. The human child, however, is capable of acquiring the phonetic characteristics of any language to which it is "regularly and fully exposed" (Thorpe 1974, p. 113).

Similar observations seem justifiable with regard to the call signals of other species of animals; for example, the barking of dogs, the sonar language of whales and porpoises, the buzzing of insects, etc. Among these there is no observable evidence of change or advancement in their modes of communication. Their speech patterns lack adaptation and flexibility. Moreover, "animal language" is in no way intertranslatable from one species to another, but each is found to be permanently confined to individual species. Animal "languages" are not learned but are instinctual.

Of a somewhat more ambivalent nature is the recent speech experimentation with chimpanzees. Claims have been made that several of these very humanlike primates have been taught to employ a primitive form of sign language. From the reports of these experiments it is difficult to assess just what precisely these chimps have learned. There have been critical accounts of the claims made by those conducting the experiments, even suggesting that the experimenters had allowed their own personal bias regarding the equality of human and animal intelligence to influence the reporting of their findings. How ever this may be, the learning capabilities of the chimpanzee are simply not commensurate with those of the human child.

By marked contrast the individual human is inherently capable of learning any of the 3,000 languages that humans speak. Further, the topics for human conversation are as broad and unlimited as the scope of our intellects, and we are continually acquiring new vocabulary, new expressions, and new modes of articulation—advancing ourselves toward greater accomplishments both in understanding and in communication.

The more developed is our command of language, the more ably and accurately are we able to speak our mind. Thinking and speaking go, as it were, hand-in-hand. There is a profound truth underlying the statement made by the German existentialist Martin Heidegger, one of the more original thinkers of this century, who referred to language as the *House of Being*, since it is in and through language that thoughts inhabit the earth.

Art and Technology as Language

Language, like thought, is not an end in itself. It is ultimately aimed at action. As thought is translated into words, so words are translated into deeds. Human action unfolds in two directions. It may aim either at producing something or at an activity, which of itself is not calculated to produce a tangible result; such as, walking, singing, imagining, thinking. It is to the first of these aims of action; namely, that which is ordered to the production of something, that we now turn our attention.

Because of our power of intellective insight, we are able to grasp the relations between objects, relations that remain altogether hidden to mere sensory perception. Thus, while the sense of sight is quite capable of *seeing* a particular apple, it does not see it as an *apple* but merely as an object that is, perhaps, round and red. But through intellective insight an apple can be known for what it is, an apple. Knowing *what* this object is, the intellect can understand something of its potentiality and thus can envision various uses to which it can be put—the human can view apples as a source of cider, as material suitable for baking a pie, or as an ingredient for bread.

It is, then, through our intellective ability—being able to envisage ends and goals to which objects experienced can be ordered—that we are able to transform our environment. We can manufacture tools of all kinds, plan and construct buildings, engineer highways and bridges, assemble huge industrial complexes and shopping centers, etc. By doing such things we restructure the world around us according to the inner patterns of our own thought. Just as through language thought is symbolically expressed orally and aurally, so through the creative activity of making and producing, thought finds expression in the physical world of material things.

Thus by the injection of our thoughts and ideas into the world which environs us, we are truly humanizing the world. We order it according to the inner vision of our own thought world. By virtue of our insightful penetration into the intellective relations between things, we are capable of uncovering the laws of things and of reordering them in a new manner. It is in this sense that the human, the maker of things, is truly creative. What we fashion and construct becomes a new creation whenever our intellective power makes it possible for physical matter to exist and function in a manner not possible without the intervention of our intellective power.

Great inventions, such as, the electric light bulb, the radio, air conditioning, refrigeration, television, nuclear power, the airplane, the submarine, etc., are all the result of the human's ingenious manipulation of the world's natural elements and forces. Without human intellective input nature alone would never have been able to organize itself in this manner. As a technician in the broadest sense of the word, the human is literally "putting ideas to work" and is transforming the environment with patterns of the mind. This insemination process is the inverse of that of insight, for through technology we can give back to the world something in exchange for what the world has given us.

Consequently, just as it is through language that intelligence is found in the sensible symbol, so, too, it is through creative making that intelligence can inhabit the manufactured product. It is precisely this presence of diverse "ideas" in material things that permits us to differentiate between them. Thus we distinguish a thermometer from a barometer by *what* the instrument is capable of doing. Its function depends totally on how the materials of which it was constructed are ordered.

What has been said above about products which are calculated to function in a specific manner is proportionately true about human artistic accomplishments. Works of art differ from other humanly-made artifacts in that their primary function, at least, is to cause pleasure rather than to serve some useful purpose. Of course art is often employed to embellish and beautify functional structures and objects, such as buildings and halls. The human, it seems, clearly wishes to avoid living in a world that is merely functional. We have need of art if only to humanize our world by reflecting our own image of an intelligence that transcends the merely useful, physical world, and opens out to the wider world of beauty and truth.

The human being is the supreme artist and craftsman. Our intelligence permits us to stand back from our world, take its measure, and reconstitute it according to our own image. The humanization of the world is one with its civilization.

The same marked contrast noted earlier with regard to language is found here also in the area of technology. Thus the human has unlimited possibilities for productive creativity, while the animal is tightly circumscribed in what it can accomplish. Animals are capable, as seen earlier, of remarkable accomplishments in the area of making, but we note the invariant, limited nature of their work. The often very complex techniques which they must employ to accomplish their species-related tasks are not acquired, because they are not based on individual insight. Rather they are instinctual and inborn. As a worker the animal displays none of the creative and flexible ingenuity of the human artist or craftsman, and, unless the skills required have already been inherited, the animal is incapable of transforming its environment, even when this might be necessary for survival.

The human alone is the transcendental maker and artist, for through our intellectual prowess we can accomplish an "inner reading" of the nature of things; we envisage thereby the complex series of interrelationships and interdependancies of those natures, and reassemble and transform them in the manner best suited to our needs and to our desires. Through what we make and create, we humans speak a form of manual language, leaving through our action the clear imprint of mind upon things. Thus it is that a flint arrowhead shaped with a primitive stone axe and found among common surface rubble on a desolate Arabian coast is easily distinguishable from other pieces of flint lying in the vicinity by its unique traces of intelligent workmanship. Only in this way is a human artifact distinguishable from the myriad inventions of nature.

At its profoundest level language is an environmentalization of thought, and thus it serves as a bridge between the world of the mind and the world that that mind encounters in experience. Through language and through doing we can humanize our world, enriching the source of our own experience. As a being-speaker the human has an unlimited capacity for conversation. We never tire of speaking and doing because we never tire of knowing.

A unique being-speaker (*Seinssprecher*), whose conversational repertoire is limited in its actual attainments but unlimited in its capabilities, we humans can focus attention on the inner nature of our thought and on our capacity for speaking. In our unrestricted desire to know, we are slowly yet ineluctably led to examine the very wonders of our own ability to explore the ultimate meaning of ourself and of our world.

The human thus wishes to know and to speak about the meaning of "to sense," "to know," "to understand," "to judge," "to create." We are even curious about the phenomenon of language itself, its nature, its origin, its significance. In short, our inner longing for conversation on all levels inevitably leads us to recognize ourselves as *beings* who are involved in the very *language of being.*

In pursuing philosophic conversation, we grope for the unity of all things as well as for the meaning of the totality of our own experience. We seek to uncover the life-principle embodied in the very philosophic language we employ. Our language is unavoidably philosophic. Since we are intelligent beings we need to talk about everything and we can do this only if our language is the language of everything that is. That is why the *authentic language* of the human is *being.*

Summary

In this chapter we have discussed the phenomenon of human language. Language has been understood here in the broadest sense as including all forms and manners of communication. It was observed that during our conscious hours we are constantly *speaking* in some form or another, that we talk about everything, and that we enjoy talking.

The *word* was seen to be the basic structural unit of language and to be a sensible sign (sound or written mark) to which a particular meaning is attached. Language as a whole is the total complex of words employed in speech, including the system and hierarchical organization of syntactical and grammatical rules. Language, a sensible expression of thought, is the inverse of insight, since it returns thought to the world.

The philosophic significance of language consists primarily in the fact that the language phenomenon reinforces the analysis previously made of the intellective process. As a sensible datum, the linguistic phenomenon itself is testimony to the fact that knowledge can be derived from the sensible world. If intelligibility is not hidden within the material world, it seems incongruous to grant that language can be a source of knowledge, since it is no less a material reality than is the physical object sensed. Thus language is a living argument that matter and meaning are somehow compatible, and it is a refutation as well of the idealist view of the world.

The ambiguity of language was next discussed. It was seen that language is inherently ambiguous precisely because it is an expression of thought through sensible symbol. One direct consequence of the radical ambiguity of language was seen to be the need continually to multiply words and expressions through incessant speech.

The phenomenon of the plurality of languages and their mutual intertranslatability was found to be of significance philosophically in that it clearly emphasizes the unity of the human race, since understanding and insight are the common elements of every human language.

The written language was seen to amount to an extension of the human memory, since it serves as an exterior repository of thought.

The language of the human was contrasted with the so-called language of animals. It was seen that the human is the universal speaker precisely because our world of consciousness is the world of being, which includes all things. The human is seen to be the transcendental speaker.

Finally, we reflected on the manner in which both art and technology may be viewed as a form of language and how, through both, the human is able to give an outward expression of the inner self and world.

Definitions and Conclusions

1. A word is a sensible symbol containing meaning.

2. Language is the hierarchical organization of words through syntactical and grammatical rules.

3. Language is the inverse of insight.

4. Philosophically, the primal significance of language is found in the fact that it strongly supports the original derivation of all knowledge from sensation.

5. Language itself is the product of the union of thought and matter.

6. Language is inherently ambiguous because no material symbol can adequately carry the full load of meaning which thought thrusts upon it.

7. The multiplication of words and the human's endless involvement with language is the direct result of the ambivalent nature of language and the material origins of human thought.

8. The phenomenon of the intertranslatability of languages is of the greatest significance for it indicates that all language has a common source—human understanding—and hence points to the original unity of the human race.

9. The consequences of the discovery of the written word are incalculable in terms of the development of human civilization.

10. The written word serves us as an external repository of human thought, thus vastly facilitating the collective growth and development of human knowledge.

11. An intellective being, the human is a universal and transcendental speaker. Our proper inner or mute language is the language of being itself.

12. Because all of the world's 3,000 diverse languages are so many variations of the language of being and move within its ambience, the human is capable of grasping any of them.

13. Because we have an ability to envisage ends and goals toward which objects and experiences can be ordered, we humans are supreme artists and makers.

14. Through art and technology, which are forms of language, we humans learn to return to the world in a transformed condition that which we have drawn from it.

15. Civilization is the humanization of the world.

16. We humans are transcendental makers and artists.

9 Willing and Choosing

Ideas have consequences.

Richard M. Weaver

From Understanding to Willing

The preceding chapters deal chiefly with the cognoscitive act—the realities of sensation, perception, and the three phases of intellection: understanding, judging, and reasoning. The chapter on language and communication focuses on these activities as a symbolic manifestation of thought and idea.

There is, however, another fundamental component of human experience, that of appetition. Twice before, our study actually involved aspects of the appetitive act, but without requiring a formal consideration of it. Mention of it first occurred in the discussion of the evaluating act in the animal, where we learned that appetition follows perception and is essential to the animal's need to suitably react to environmental conditions. It was referred to a second time in consideration of the phenomenon of action as a twofold division of human activity: *doing* and *making*.

Human activity can also be approached from the standpoint of its purposefulness and from the aspect of its freedom. These considerations have been postponed until now, not because they are of lesser importance but because a systematic study of them requires some grasp of the various knowledge-related problems mentioned earlier. Even a brief reflection on our human experience informs us that our knowing acts are not ends in themselves. Rather, knowledge usually points to something further. In short, ideas have consequences; they are a preparation for action. This is as true for the animal as it is for the human. We have already observed that sensation is essential to the animal for its survival and well-being. Unquestionably the knowing acts of the animal are highly functional. They serve an important purpose by apprising the animal of its immediate surroundings and permitting it to act in a manner that is beneficial to its own survival. Thus, for example, a thirsty deer moves toward a stream it has scented. On the other hand, it turns and flees from a wolf if the deer senses that the wolf is an immediate threat. It is obvious that the deer's moving toward the stream but away from the wolf are actions the deer takes as a result of information it receives through its sensory acts.

The knowing acts of the human are likewise purposeful in that there is a clear relation between what we experience and what we do; for our activity follows, and is dependent upon, a prior cognoscitive act. The common term used to refer to all types of such activity is *appetition*. The term itself derives from the Latin word *ad-petere*, which means "to seek after." An appetitive act, therefore, is an act that follows cognition and seeks after that which is cognized. If the seeking after follows a sensory act of cognition, it is referred to as an act of *sensory* appetition. If, however, it follows an intellective act, it is referred to as *volitional* (voluntary) appetition. The following remarks refer to the volitional acts only. However, at the end of the chapter we will devote some space to a comparison of the two basic categories of appetitive acts—sensory and intellective.

The Problem of Volition

Volition is one of the most actively discussed problems in philosophy, and it is likewise one of the most difficult questions that the philosopher must face. The problem is not precisely whether or not we humans perform volitional acts, but rather what the nature of these acts is. More exactly, the problem revolves around the question as to whether or not the human volitional act is *free*.

It is commonly agreed that we humans do feel, or experience, an attraction toward objects themselves or toward acting in a particular way. Philosophers have agreed to call this fundamental attraction toward something or toward a particular course of action, the volitional act. What the precise nature of this attraction is, however, constitutes a question over which philosophers have long been divided. The reasons for this division are not hard to find, for they reflect the different positions of philosophers on the nature of human cognition.

If one assumes a materialist view with regard to human cognition, then one denies a basic difference between sensation and intellection, and it follows that one assumes there is no fundamental difference between sensory and intellective appetition. If this position is taken, one must likewise deny that the human appetitive act differs in any significant way from the appetition of animals. In other words, the materialist, if consistent, must reject the notion of freedom and accept the premise that human behavior is controlled not by the individual but by circumstances beyond his control.

The consequences of such a denial of freedom in the human are far reaching; for one thing, personal responsibility becomes a mere word. This means that one cannot truly be held accountable for his or her behavior. Laws, commands, rewards, and punishments are drained of their meaning, and it likewise becomes impossible to speak of love (in any sense other than that of physical desire) or of justice, guilt, or meritorious behavior. Thus the entire category of moral behavior loses its meaning and to say that someone is a *good* person or that someone behaves well is at bottom similar to saying that Jasper is a good dog, or that a horse is a good jumper. In short, the word *good* merely describes a physical quality or a mode of behavior which someone else finds useful or pleasing. If the human is not free to control his own behavior in any significant way, his behavior is not truly distinctive from that of the animal, and we would have to conclude that moral discourse is an idle pastime.

Human Freedom: The Determinist View

Philosophically, one who denies that the human is free is a determinist. The determinists reason that every human action is a definite, determined act; that since the act of choice is determined, it is clearly caused, not free. Every determinist argument, therefore, rests on the premise that an act is an unavoidable response to a stimulus. The true cause of our actions may not always be clear to us;

it may be hidden from our consciousness. In the determinist's view, what we normally call choices are firmly controlled by factors that lie beyond the individual's control.

If the controlling factor is physiological in nature, then the determinism is hereditary, or genetic, which means that through certain inherited characteristics, one is led to choose and to behave unalterably the way one does. If the controlling factor is one's past patterns of behavior and one's fundamental mind-set, then the determinism is psychological. If the controlling factor is the cultural climate— one's upbringing and one's educational background—then the determinism is environmental. Finally, one can distinguish a theological form of determinism. According to this view the human will is totally subject to the divine will or heavenly bodies. In other words, the human is only able to choose that which God, or the stars, or some cosmic force allows.

It is clear that in some instances, at least, we do not seem to be able to choose freely. It is further clear that when we choose we always do so for a reason, and this seems to indicate that the act was indeed caused. On the face of it, it does perhaps seem reasonable to conclude, as the determinist does, that, since human choice is truly caused, it is *free* in name only; that freedom is a term incorrectly applied to human behavior. Rather than being free, the determinist argues, we are victimized by our past and by our present situation; although we appear to act freely, our actions are shaped and controlled by *foreign* elements from within or from without.

A corollary of the determinist position is the need to acknowledge that the human is not possessed of inborn rights, for these can only be the result of a position acknowledging true freedom of behavior. Yet it is not uncommon for determinists to invoke their basic rights, as though the existence of the latter did not constitute an authentic counterposition to their refusal to acknowledge the only possible basis of those rights; namely, freedom of choice in the human. The determinist position has often proved attractive to those who are prepared to relinquish their freedom, provided they are no longer to be held accountable for their behavior. This is, however, a rather awesome price to pay for the freedom to do as one wishes.

Today many contemporary determinists are to be found among the ranks of psychologists and social scientists who strive to approach the study of the human person by employing a strictly empirical method. In practice this means that no aspect of human experience will be considered valid or authentic which cannot be verified through sensory observation or measured in a quantified or statistical manner. Such a method excludes on purely a priori grounds the possibility of any aspect of our human behavior to transcend the merely physical and measurable—to be a free human act. The circularity of this method seems generally to have escaped the notice of determinists.

Some philosophers assume a determinist stance for what would seem to be semantic reasons. These thinkers, who realize that the free act is truly determined in that it is a limited, specified act, fail to distinguish between the various levels of causes; therefore, they conclude that human choice is not free but caused. In order to clarify the manner in which the act of choice is both free and caused and how this can be held consistently, a careful and detailed analysis of the nature and characteristics of the act of choice is necessary. It seems not unlikely that a considerable number of those who consider themselves determinists of one type or another do so because they have been unable to find any of the proffered explanations of free choice satisfactory. In such instances it may well be true that often a denial of freedom in the human comes to little more than an expression of frustration at being unable to understand not *that* they are but *how* they are free.

An Anatomy of the Human Free Act

Unquestionably, the problem of human freedom is one of the most difficult and elusive with which the human mind is faced. It may help if we begin by focussing our attention on a very common and obvious aspect of our experience—there seems to be no limit to the number and kinds of things to which we humans experience an attraction. This unique and intriguing phenomenon is only to be explained by the fact that we are intellective beings. Because we can understand everything that *is*, there is no limit to the *kinds* of things that we can understand. But in our understanding things we necessarily see some good, or value, in them; to this extent they can be viewed as somehow desirable. Consequently, we note a correspondence and complementarity between our power to understand everything and our power to feel an attraction toward whatever is understood; hence, actively to *incline* toward anything whatsoever. The act of free choice is nothing but the intellective appetite's *positively* inclining toward something that has been understood in some manner, however imperfectly.

It is because we are intellective beings, then, that our range of willing or choosing things extends far beyond the appetitive range of the animal, which is restricted in that it can desire only what it is able to sense. We can desire, however, whatever we understand, and we can direct our understanding not only to the observable present but to the past and future as well. Thus it is possible for us to be attracted by things that are not sensible or tangible, but that can somehow be viewed as *good*, or possessed of value. Humans, therefore, can be attracted not only to something that is immediately sensed, such as a freshly baked pie but to something that is sensibly absent or even wholly insensible; such as, studying, acquiring new knowledge and skills, reflecting upon the past, planning for the future.

The intellective appetite, because it follows upon the activity of the intellect, is as open and unrestricted in its desiring as the intellect is in its knowing. The intellect has as the ambit of its activity, *being* itself, while the will has as the ambit of its activity the *good* itself, that is, *being* as *good*.

It is important to point out at this stage of our inquiry that the good to which we here refer is that *good* which is an inseparable property of whatever is. It is thus simply *being* as related to will. It is not identical, therefore, with moral good, which is one of the subdivisions of good. Aristotle remarked more than two thousand years ago that we are able to view something as good for three basic reasons. We can consider something good because it is pleasureable, or because it is useful, or because it is befitting and proper. We are referring here to the good in its most fundamental and basic sense, which includes all of the above meanings. Good is simply *being* that is *desired*. As Aristotle remarked, the good is that which all men desire.

The will, capable of inclining toward being (inasmuch as it is good in this most basic sense) may be defined as the appetite whose object is the good; that is, the *general*, or *universal*, good. As the intellect has as its horizon of activity *being* in the unrestricted sense, so, similarly, the will moves itself within the broad range of the good. It cannot act otherwise; therefore, whatever it inclines toward must somehow be viewed as good by the intellect. Expressing this same thought in a terminology more in keeping with everyday usage, one would simply say that the object of the will is happiness. Whatever the will chooses or inclines toward, it does so because the object of its desire is viewed as good. Employing the technical vocabulary used earlier with regard to the sensory and intellective powers, one would say that the formal object of the will is the good taken generally or without qualification; that is, the *universal good.*

It should be clear from the foregoing that the question of freedom of the will does not refer to the *formal object* of the will. The good in general is that toward which the will *essentially* inclines, and it is thus necessarily attracted toward it. The will, therefore, does not choose the universal good, or happiness; rather it unerringly is drawn in the direction of the good in its every act.

Where, however, the question of freedom of the will does find application is in its inclination to any *particular* or limited good, or value. In every act of choice the will inclines positively toward, or selects, a particular good; that is, an object that in some way is viewed as good. The question naturally arises as to why the will inclines to this particular value. Why was this particular choice made?

If one recalls what was said regarding the basic thrust of the will toward the universal good, it can be seen why it is that each act of choice is indeed an act that is freely made. Since in choosing, the will moves toward a particular, or limited, good, it cannot be necessitated to that good precisely because that good is limited. That is, as a particular, or limited, good the object desired is seen to be not only good but also not good. As a limited good it lacks some good that other objects possess. Thus, when a limited good is chosen, one cannot look for the ultimate reason for such a choice in the good found in the object itself. Rather, the ultimate source of the choice can only be found in the will which voluntarily, or freely, inclined toward this particular good. In short, the will chooses *this good*, or value, because it wants to. It freely accepts the good, or value, which the intellect views in the object as its own good.

Free Choice as Self-Determination: Moderate Determinism

One can always supply a reason for the choice one has made. One says, for example, "I choose to act in this manner because. . . ." This indicates that the act of choice is truly *caused*, inasmuch as the value I choose does move my will; but of course only because I choose or allow it to do so. In the act of choosing, the will is actually accepting a particular value by which it is shaped. Yet this determination was not forced on the will, because the object chosen is of a *limited value*. The only value toward which the will is *necessitated* is the universal good.

Thus as regards the universal good the will is necessitated but not *determined, or caused*, since determination must always come from the side of limitation. On the other hand, in the act of choice the will is determined but not *necessitated*, since the will is actualized by a limited value it has accepted as its own. This actualization is controlled by the will itself, since it could have chosen to be actualized by some other value.

In choosing a particular good the will is determined, but, since this determination is not necessitated, the act of choosing is an act of *self-determination*. This is also why this account of the free act can aptly be described as one with a moderate determinist position. What underlies this explanation and what is seldom clearly understood by those advocating an unrestricted determinist position with regard to the will is the distinction between formal and efficient causality. Only by carefully distinguishing between these two modes of causality can the apparent paradox of free choice be satisfactorily resolved. The value itself which is chosen is the *formal cause* of the choice, and it moves the will, therefore, not as an efficient, but as a formal and final cause. It explains *what* it is that is chosen.

The efficient cause of the act of choosing, however, is the will itself which is primordially in act with regard to the universal good, and thus does not require an additional efficient cause to move it toward its object. All that is required is the presence of a limited value toward which it can actually move itself. This limited value is presented to it by the intellect. Of itself the will is a blind faculty. It does not understand the good but wills it.

The preceding analysis should make clear, therefore, the source of the confusion that has led the determinist to deny that the will acts freely. Correctly recognizing that in the act of choice, determination is actually present, the determinist concludes that the will is thereby caused and hence is not free. The determinist has failed to distinguish between the efficient and the formal causal factors in the choosing process, and thus has been unable to see how an act that is formally determined may nonetheless be self-determined and hence free. The relevant question to be asked is not whether or not the act of choosing is a determinate or limited act, but rather from whence this determination arises and why. To repeat what has been stated above, the will cannot be necessitated by any limited good. Yet all beings presented to it are limited; consequently, they can be viewed as limited and in some respect not good. As long as the intellect is able to discover in the object understood some dimension of negativity and limitation, it can be viewed as non-attractive, or not good, and as such, cannot compel acceptance by the will.

Because, then, the act of choice is an act of self-determination, one can always provide a reason *why* one chose in the manner one did. One is aware that the nature of the act—what one did—was within one's own control. One therefore experiences a sense of ownership and responsibility toward the action freely chosen, and is thus able to say: I did that, or I decided that. . . . In choosing, one has controlled the value that shapes one's will. One has determined the very determination by which one is determined. In short, one has made that determination one's own. A specific value has been allowed to enter into one's being, to become a part of one's self. It was one's own decision.

It should be noted, however, that, although one can supply a reason for the choice one has made, one is unable to give a wholly satisfactory explanation as to why one has chosen as one has. This seems utterly paradoxical, but it is an unavoidable corollary of the free act itself. The free act, because it is free, escapes total intelligibility. I am unable to assign a necessary reason as to why I chose as I did. I am only able to provide the reason or value for the reason of my choice, but I cannot ultimately explain why I chose that reason or value. All I am able to say is that I did so because I wanted to. And again, this is why the act of choice is said to be free.

The Role of Deliberation in the Free Act

The foregoing discussion concerning the nature of the free act of choice has repeatedly emphasized the relationship between the will and the intellect. At this point we wish to explore somewhat in depth this important relationship between understanding and willing.

The term *deliberation* refers to an intellective act that is ordered to an act of choice. Deliberation is always aimed, therefore, at doing, or acting. It is an act of intellect which is pragmatically oriented. As the term itself suggests, "de-liberation" (*deliberare*) simply means *to free from.* Thus the purpose of the deliberative act is to permit one to make a wise choice, freeing one from the shortcomings that a hasty, poorly thought-out decision can occasion. Nonetheless, the deliberative act as such precedes the act of free choice and is not a constitutive part of it. Deliberation is a form of thinking. When I am deliberating, I am thinking about what I am going to do; calculating about what would be the best course to follow.

During the act of deliberating, the mind is reflecting on various possible alternatives. One evaluates the situation first from one standpoint, then from another. The various consequences of a certain course of action are mentally projected and weighed against the consequences of other equally possible actions. Each alternative has a limited value; from one aspect it seems advantageous; from another, disadvantageous. It is impossible for the intellect to uncover any alternative that is absolutely advantageous. Consequently, the intellect in presenting the various alternatives to the will for a decision is unable to do so with an unqualified recommendation. Rather it affirms, "This course of action would be best if. . .", but "This other course of action would be best if. . . ." In short, the intellect can only evaluate; it does not make a decision. That is the work of the will, which selects one of the alternatives.

This brings us to the fundamental question with regard to the free act of choice; namely, why does the will select this particular alternative over others? No definitive response can be given. If one could, the will would not be free; and if the will were not free in choosing, there would be no need for the deliberative act. Through the deliberative process the intellect can present to the will values on various levels. Thus, one course of action would be preferable if *pleasure* is to be the maximum consideration. On the other hand, if *practical utility* is the major concern, then another decision would be best. If you wish to do what is *morally right*, there would be still another manner in which you might act. All of these *bests* are limited to aspects of a total situation. They are not absolutely good—good from every aspect; hence, the will is not irresistibly drawn toward any one of them. Which value the will actually inclines toward or accepts as its own can be neither predetermined nor predicted infallibly, for there is no compelling or necessitating reason *why* the will should select one value over another. The will itself controls the direction of its choice and selects one of the values presented to it. This is why the act of choice is said to be self-determining and is precisely why the will is free to choose its value.

As indicated previously, the free act is not *uncaused*, for the value which successfully attracts the will is truly a cause of the choice. Yet this cause is on the level of *form*, and not on the level of *act* itself, for the will alone moves itself to accept this limited value and informs itself with this particular good, or value. This it can do— move itself toward a limited good, because the will is already in act with regard to the *universal good*. Thus by its very nature the will is empowered to move toward any limited good. In other words, it is the nature of the will to be able to choose anything at all, which is what is meant by saying that its object is the good taken generally.

It is the *value* chosen by the will that constitutes the content of the free act of choice. It answers to the twofold question: What did you decide and why? *What* was decided was the value you chose. *Why* it was chosen indicates the value you placed in that value. As already mentioned in the previous section, it is always possible to give a reason for our choices.

Several final considerations are in order with regard to the deliberative act and the act of choice. The first is that the deliberative act itself is the result of an act of choice. When I am deliberating about the course of action I wish to follow, I am doing so precisely because I want to; that is, because I see a value in carefully thinking over the situation before deciding whether to accept that value as my own. I do not need to deliberate; I can proceed to decide immediately without further reflection, if I *want* to. The fact that I do not is only because I have chosen not to do so. Thus deliberation itself is the result of a free choice.

Second, the deliberative process is without term; that is, without its own built-in cut-off point. Indeed, that is precisely what a decision is, a cutting off of the deliberative process, and the selection of one value over all others.

A further consequence of the free nature of choice is that prior to choice, *what* one will choose and *when* one will make a particular choice is wholly unpredictable. One cannot know what a future choice will be, because prior to choice the will is undetermined and is uninformed by the value of the future choice. In such an indeterminate state the will is simply unknowable. Hence, although certain probable predictions can be made as to what one will likely choose, it is impossible for anyone to affirm this with certainty until the choice itself is actually made.

Lastly, it should be pointed out that the will is always in a determined state. It is always determined in some way by a limited value which it freely inclines toward. This does not mean that it is always making a fresh choice, but rather that it is always actively inclined toward a limited value which previously it accepted as its own and which it continues to choose.

The foregoing explanation of the free act of choice and its relation to the deliberative act of the intellect indicates that the act of the will is truly reflective. As the intellect is aware of its own act and hence understands its understanding, so the will wills its own act, and it does this precisely because it controls its own determination, and hence is self-determining or free. Thus in every free act, as remarked above, we are able to mention the reason or reasons which led us to act or choose as we did. It is thus psychologically impossible to say that we did something for absolutely no reason at all. The reason which causes us to choose is ordinarily referred to as the *motive* of our choice. Although it clearly is not an agent or efficient cause, a motive is truly a final, or purpose, cause. It moves the will to act, not by force from without, as it were, but rather by acting internally, attracting the will according to its own nature, which is to incline toward the good.

The intellective and volitional acts are intimately intertwined and inseparably related. The intellect moves the will just as the formal cause determines or shapes matter, and the will moves the intellect just as the efficient cause moves its object. Though there are two principles involved, there is but one act. Thus there is no act of understanding without willing to understand, and there is no act of willing without willing what is somehow understood. The act of choice, which belongs most properly to the will, is an intelligent act in that intellective consciousness is its essential prerequisite. It is only for this reason that the human is capable of analyzing their behavior and of voicing their responsibility for a given action. Only because we are free can we say: "I did that. I understand my choosing; I know why I chose what I did, and thus I am able to say that I did this because . . ." To say that I am free simply means that I am the authentic source of an activity, that I am a subject.

Love and the Will

The term *love*, therefore, has many meanings for us. For example, we say that we love warm weather, or that we love fresh salmon, or that we love to ski, etc. The inclination of the will toward the good even in its most basic and fundamental sense is what Thomas Aquinas refers to as love. But the meaning of love, more significant to a study of the human, is love that is intersubjective and mutual. Authentic love refers to a relationship between two or more persons. Here, love in its truest form is love with a will to promotion, whereby the other person is loved for what they are as persons, not for what they possess. The contemporary mode of expressing this, made popular by certain psychologists, is that authentic love consists in viewing another not as an object but as a person. In this manner one seeks to promote the happiness and well-being of the beloved. In other words, authentic love is not selfish. Traditionally, this form of love was called love of benevolence. We shall have occasion to return to this theme briefly in discussing justice and love in the chapter on habits.

At this point it is important to recognize that the universal good which constitutes the formal object of the will is not identifiable with the Supreme Good. Hence, when it is affirmed, as it was earlier, that the will necessarily inclines to the universal and general good, this is not to say that the will necessarily inclines toward God. The basis for the distinction between the general good and God is that the will derives its object from the intellect, which, as seen, knows only through an abstractive process. Consequently, since God cannot be known directly as He is in Himself, He cannot be known in the sense of being fully comprehended as infinitely good, but only imperfectly as reflected through those things caused by Him. Thus the will, whose object is the unrestricted good, does not necessarily incline toward God as He is in Himself; for, since He is not adequately known, God cannot be presented to the will as a value to be chosen that is good in every respect. Yet, as already seen, the will is free in choosing, precisely because the objects presented to it in some aspect or another for assent fall short of the good in the unrestricted sense. If, then, the will does incline toward God, it does so freely. Aquinas adds, however, that in the next life when God is known fully as He is, the will necessarily adheres to Him, since He cannot then be known in any way but as the fullness of being and hence as goodness itself.

The Indeterminist View

The indeterminist does not, like the determinist, deny the freedom of the will; rather he exalts it to the highest degree possible. This position is, therefore, the exact contrary of that of the determinist. Assuming an exalted and unrestricted notion of freedom, the indeterminist holds that the will cannot in any way be determined by the object of its desire, if one is to affirm that the will is free. The term *indeterminism* suggests this very meaning. What the indeterminist claims is that, in the moment of the act of choice, the will remains totally aloof from its object, rejecting the view we have presented earlier that the will is determined by the very object, or value, toward which it inclines.

The indeterminist conceives of freedom as totally unrestricted; that is, as an absolute. Consequently, any admission that the will becomes determined in choosing, amounts, in this view, to a denial of freedom itself. In this sense, then, the determinist and indeterminist, while assuming opposite positions regarding the free act, are totally in agreement with regard to the fundamental principle involved. The determinist has rejected freedom for the same reason that the indeterminist has rejected a determinist position. Because the determinist is unable to uncover any human act which is not in some way determined, and hence limited, he simply denies outright the reality of freedom. Similarly, the indeterminist, ascribing to the same principle that no act can be free, if it is determined, takes the view that, in the human act of choice, the will (the person) must be totally free and undetermined.

The indeterminist position in its essential form can be traced back to Immanuel Kant. Since this eighteenth-century German idealist was convinced that no speculative analysis of human intellection and volition was possible, there was for him no other manner of affirming the freedom of man save through a postulate of practical reason. Kant's basic emphasis has endured down to our contemporary era and finds acceptance in a modified form among certain twentieth-century thinkers, particularly the existentialists. Jean Paul Sartre, for example, espouses an indeterminist position, so exalting the freedom of man that he employs it as the very ground of his atheism. God cannot exist, Sartre argues, if man is free. If God existed, man would then be subordinate to Him, and hence could not be free. This mode of argumentation clearly illustrates the absolutist terms in which Sartre conceived of human freedom.

According to the indeterminist position, therefore, no reason can be given for a choice, since to give a reason is to deny that the act is free. Thus the indeterminist does not admit to the reality of the determinative function of the object willed in the act of choice, and makes no distinction between active and formal causes as we did during our previous explanation of the free human act.

Despite the inadequacy of the indeterminist view and its failure to introduce the nuances necessary to provide a viable explanation for the human act of free choice, the indeterminist position remains attractive to some thinkers and serves at least to emphasize an important element of human behavior. Thus it is surely a valid claim that in some sense the will does genuinely transcend the object desired, for the natural or formal object of the will as a dynamic power is precisely the good in general, or the unrestricted good.

If this is what the indeterminist means as a solution to the problem of freedom, one can only agree, for this transcending of the will over all limited objects is the very basis for affirming that the act of choice is authentically free. Yet, it is not enough to satisfy the exigencies of our experience to emphasize this point unless we also recognize that the will, at the moment of choice, is truly determined by the object.

This determination is not, of course, irrevocable, precisely for the reasons outlined above, since the will itself transcends all limited values and remains free to move itself to another value, and thus to reshape itself through another choice. The will always retains the power of repudiating the choices it has made, because, though it is determined by the value it accepts, it is not controlled by that value but retains the power to move away from it and claim some other value as its own. By making a choice it does not lose its own radical power of self-determination; it simply exercises it in a limited and restricted way. In this sense, even when determined in the act of choice, the will can be said to remain undetermined, if by that is meant that it still retains the ability to move itself from one act of determination to another. Though not absolute, human freedom is yet authentic and real.

Motivating Factors and Freedom

In shaping our argument to meet the objections of the determinist, who opposes the notion of self-determination of the will, we have thus far given scant attention to the function of motivating factors in our discussion of the act of free choice. To remedy this omission we turn our attention to those dimensions of experience which in some manner influence the choices we make.

While it is true that no limited value can impose itself on the will so that the will necessarily inclines toward it, it is also true that numerous factors are present at the time of choice which can and do exert an influence on the manner in which we choose. Among such influences can be numbered habitual behavioral patterns, past experiences, emotions, personal outlook, and past decisions. All of these factors serve to concentrate and focus the mind's attention on various aspects of the alternatives available for choice, either emphasizing or lessening them; thus modifying the manner in which they are viewed and presented to the will as values to be chosen.

There can be no question that these factors do exert a profound influence over the manner in which a situation is analyzed, predisposing one to choose in a manner consonant with one's previous behavior patterns and experience. Yet such a predisposition is not to be confused with a necessitating cause, although it appears that this is precisely how the whole question of free choice is viewed by the determinist.

It is understandable that if the determinists define freedom as total and without influences of any kind, they should deny such freedom to the will. At least it appears to be the case that the determinists, not unlike the indeterminists, have often assumed an antifreedom position precisely because they have defined freedom in an artificial and absolutist sense, allowing them to grant freedom to the human only if our choices are made without the presence of influences of any kind. As we have sought to demonstrate in the pages that preceded, such a view of freedom is by no means necessary for one consistently to explain the freedom of the human act against the full backdrop of human experience. As humans, we are not of course absolutely free, but we are free.

The point is, therefore, that the presence of strong influences and motivating factors, although definitely worthy of consideration in attempting to determine the reason for a particular choice or, more importantly, to help predict the choice that one might make, never necessitates a choice, for no object can be viewed as good from every aspect. It would appear that many of the arguments offered by the determinists in support of this contention are traceable to their failing to distinguish between motivating factors and necessitating causes. Many forms of psychological determinism certainly rest upon just this oversight.

Sensory Appetites

The intellective appetite is not the only appetitive power found in the human. Thus in concluding this chapter on willing and choosing, we turn our attention to the sensory appetite which follows upon sensory perception. As remarked earlier, appetition is complementary to cognition and consists in a purposive response to what is known. It is characterized by an inner motion either of attraction toward an object cognized or of aversion from it. Consequently, in the human there are two levels of appetition, since there are, as seen, two levels of cognition, namely, intellective and sensory.

In our discussion of the sensory act it was earlier stated that sensation was purposive; that is, ordered toward a goal. Not being an end in itself, sensation has as its goal the perfection of the subject which senses. Consequently, the inner attraction toward, or aversion from, that which is apprehended or sensed either as pleasant or unpleasant, or as useful or harmful, is precisely the activity which is designated by the term *sensory appetition*. Appetition is thus distinguished from cognition in that the latter is characterized by the object's becoming intentionally one with the sensory or intellective power, while appetition is precisely the subject's response to what is sensed or understood. It is thus essential to appetition that the object cognized be somehow grasped either as pleasant or unpleasant, useful or harmful.

In order to better grasp individually the two levels of human appetitive activity, it is helpful first to focus our attention on the appetitive life of the animal. It is a matter of simple observation that animals do react to what they perceive; that there is a direct correlation between their perceptions and their behavior. A deer, for example, will move toward a stream it has scented; a fish will swim toward a baited hook, a cat will stalk a chirping robin. In all three instances—the waters of the stream, the baited hook, the chirping robin—something is first sensed and then favorably evaluated by the sensing animal. Only then does the inner appetitive motion of attraction toward the sensed object occur. (This appetitive motion is not to be confused with locomotion, the actual physical motion by which the animal approaches what it is sensing, which is a subsequent effect of the appetition.) Thus, in the first instance, the flowing water is perceived and evaluated as pleasant and useful for satisfying the deer's thirst. Similarly, the worm on the hook and the chirping bird are viewed as the potential source of a satisfying meal by the trout and the cat, respectively.

As already indicated at the beginning of this section on sensory appetition, however, animals do respond to what they perceive in a fashion other than that displayed by the preceding examples; that is, not all sensory appetition is a response to what the sensing organism might perceive as either pleasant or unpleasant. On occasion the animal will either exert great effort to achieve a difficult goal or will expose itself to great danger, even risking death, in defending its territory or its young. For example, a herd of moose will run to the point of exhaustion to escape a pack of hungry wolves; an antelope will flee from marauding lions. On occasion, too, an animal, rather than fleeing when faced with a dangerous aggressor, will itself become aggressive, stand its ground, and risk serious injury and even death. Thus a she-bear will defend its cubs against a mountain lion. It also happens that certain animals will undertake exhausting and arduous tasks in order to provide for themselves, to propagate, or to protect their own kind. Salmon will fight their way upstream against incredible odds to reach safe spawning grounds; beavers will toil endless hours constructing their dams which serve both as homes and as a defense against predators; in the fall geese will fly many thousands of miles south in search of more favorable feeding grounds. Such actions are undeniably physically demanding and are undertaken not because they are pleasurable but because they are useful or even necessary for survival of the individual animal or its group.

Sensory appetition is observed to be dual in nature, for two distinctly separate objects or goals are involved in the activity that ensues from sensory perception. On the one hand some acts have as their formal object the pleasant or the unpleasant (painful); on the other hand, some acts have as their formal object the useful and the arduous, whether it be to achieve a difficult objective or to ward off impending danger.

Because powers are known in their acts and distinguished by their formal objects, it is clear that the sensory appetite consists of two distinct powers, since the formal objects of pleasant and difficult are irreducible one to the other. The first of these powers is called the concupiscible appetite (from the Latin *concupiscere*, meaning "to desire"), since it inclines to what is apprehended as pleasant or enjoyable. Some authors have referred to it as the *desiderative* appetite. A more contemporary psychological term for it is the *pleasure drive.*

The appetite that inclines toward the useful or difficult good is traditionally called the *irascible* or *anger* appetite (from the Latin *ira*, meaning "anger.") It is also referred to as the *aggressive* appetite, or more simply as the *aggressive drive.* Its specific function is to overcome obstacles that stand in the way of the achievement of that which is pleasurable or fulfilling. From this it can be seen that the irascible appetite stands in a subordinate position with regard to the concupiscible, or pleasure appetite, since its role is to assist the latter to achieve its goal by rendering present what is desired but absent, or by eliminating or minimizing a present or future danger.

The twofold sensory appetite observed in the animal is also present in the human. This ought to come as no surprise, since humans experience sensory activities comparable to those of the animal. There is an obvious difference, of course, since in the human there are higher operations as well, specifically the intellectual and volitional, which permit humans a much wider range of activities and enlarge their vision and their options to encompass an unlimited horizon.

Essentially, the existence in the human of two sets of appetitive powers—the intellective and the sensory—is an advantage, but it would be naive to conclude that this advantage, entailing as it does an added complexity vis-à-vis the animal, does not provide the human with added challenges. Since the intellective and sensory appetites each has its own distinctive goal, they provide the possibility for a fundamental, internal division within the human psyche. The reality of an appetitive duality within the human carries with it no guarantee that the two levels of appetite will function in a coordinated and harmonious fashion on all occasions. It is precisely this division deep within the human psyche that provides the potential for internal tension as the two levels of appetite struggle to gain the ascendancy one over the other. Thus the whole world of emotional tension becomes both creditable to us and understandable as a human phenomenon when we recognize its source in the dual structure of the appetitive powers.

In short, because the same experienced object can be viewed as pleasurable or unpleasurable; useful or not useful; befitting or unbefitting or any feasible combination of these contrary pairings, it is frequently impossible for the human to opt for a particular value without of necessity abandoning or rejecting values or goals at another level.

Thus, to consider an obvious example, taking what belongs to another may have certain advantages on one level, and yet be clearly disadvantageous on another. Another's property, an automobile or sailboat, might be viewed by one as a useful acquisition and as a possible source of considerable enjoyment, and consequently could be desired and even unlawfully taken. Yet, since it is unlawful to take what belongs to another, the theft of such property also entails certain consequences of a thoroughly undesirable nature. Little reflection is needed to recognize that few human decisions of any import can be thought of which do not require the subordination of one perceived value to another. There is no cause for surprise, then, that a suppressed desire should result in the buildup of tension in one form or another. If pleasure is sacrificed for a higher value, that desire must be sublimated in some way if tension is to be avoided. Contrarily, the pursuit of what is pleasurable at the expense of known higher values results in a tension of a somewhat different quality, readily identifiable as guilt or remorse.

Further, through the human's ability to make plans and to project into the future, the human psyche is presented with unlimited options and values from among which it can choose. Clearly this constant process of weighing personal values, together with implementing chosen priorities, constitutes the essence of the human's interior struggle for the good life. As self-reflecting subjects conscious of themselves and their own willing, humans emerge as responsible beings who cannot escape their enduring awareness of themselves as responsible.

Summary

In this chapter we have discussed human appetition. We have seen in what sense the act of appetition is a corollary of the cognitive act and why in humans there is an appetitive activity corresponding to intellection. We further explored the nature of this appetition, examining at some length the act of free choice and the manner in which it is simultaneously determined and undetermined. The views of the determinist and indeterminist were also examined, and reasons were presented for the inadequacy of these alleged explanations of human behavior. The deliberative act was analyzed and the mutual dependence of the intellective and volitional acts considered. Finally, the division of the human appetitive activity into intellective and sensory, and the further division of the sensory into the concupiscible and irascible appetites was examined. Consequences for the human of this appetitive pluralism in terms of psychic tension were also considered.

Definitions and Conclusions

1. In general, an *appetitive* act is one which follows an act of cognition, inclining toward the known object.

2. *Sensory appetition* is an internal movement or inclination toward, or away from, an object perceived by a sensory power.

3. The *concupiscible appetite* has as its object that which is sen-

sibly perceived as pleasant or unpleasant.

4. The *irascible appetite* has as its object that which is sensibly perceived either as difficult or useful.

5. *Intellective appetition* (willing) is an inclination either toward, or away from, an object known by the intellective power.

6. *Determinism*, as it relates to the question of freedom, denies that the intellective appetite freely inclines toward its object.

7. *Indeterminism*, as it relates to the question of freedom, affirms that the intellective appetite (will) is totally free in its willing; that freedom is absolute.

8. *Moderate determinism*, as it relates to the question of freedom, affirms that in the act of choice the will is both free and determined; determined in that it is shaped by the value chosen, yet free in that the value which formally determines the will is selected by the will itself.

9. The *will* as an intellective appetite necessarily inclines toward the general or universal good.

10. The will is free only in inclining toward a limited good; that is, toward a good that is inherently limited, or toward an unlimited good (God) that is but imperfectly known.

11. Since the will is free in selecting the good or value toward which it positively inclines, no reason can be given as to why the will chooses a particular good, other than that it wants to.

12. The *deliberative* act is an act of intellect by which the intellect reflects on the various means or values available for the attainment of a specific goal, presenting them to the will for its ultimate choice.

13. The purpose of the deliberative act is to permit one to make a better, more reasoned choice.

14. Since every option for choice presented by the intellect to the will is merely a limited good or value possessing also its dark or negative side, the will is never forced to accept a judgment of the intellect that "this is what should be chosen."

10 Emotions and Feelings

Comic discovery is paradox stated—
Scientific discovery is paradox resolved.

Arthur Koestler

The Phenomenon of Emotions

Everyone experiences joy, sadness, irritation or anger, fear, affection, etc. These emotions and feelings are taken for granted by everyone as an integral part of the human condition. It is difficult for us to imagine a human society without emotional experiences; such a society of individuals would not seem to us to be a society of humans. Individuals who were not able to experience emotions would seem to us to suffer from a serious inherent defect.

The human emotional experience is so prized that we seek it. In fact, the cultivation of the emotions is a highly developed art, and we have established professions whose chief purpose is to provide the occasion for a contrived experience of emotions. We actively cultivate the arts of music, drama, dance, painting, etc., because they evoke and stimulate a deep personal experience of emotions.

The adventuresome spirit of the human is a further indication of this interesting phenomenon of the world of emotion. We are intrigued and enticed by the prospect of adventure. The thrills we experience in auto racing, sky-diving, rock climbing, white water rafting, high-wire acrobatics, etc., are clear evidence of the strong claim the experience of risk has for the human both as a participant and as a spectator. Risk and adventure are attractive, it appears, because they lead to the thrill of a profound or even violent emotional experience. Athletic events are similarly linked to our need for adventure.

Mystery novels and horror movies, another source of emotional stimulation, seem to exercise an attraction for wide audiences precisely because they hold out the prospect of a vicarious experience of terror and fright.

Toward the Definition of Emotions

While the foregoing reflections clearly underscore how central the emotional experience is to the human condition, they do little to clarify the true nature of this phenomenon. Integral as emotions and feelings are to human life, they remain, nonetheless, as elusive as they are engrossing. What is an emotion?

First, it is to be noted that in the discussion that follows no differentiation will be made in any systematic way between emotions and feelings. They differ, after all, in degree and not in kind. The stronger the feeling (emotion), the easier it is to identify and study.

Emotions are not to be identified with ordinary acts of sensation, whether these be sensory acts of the special senses or the interior senses or any combination of these. This does not mean, however, that they are not intimately related. The reason for the above claim is the common enough observation that we are able to sense things without the slightest trace of an accompanying emotional experience. I may, for example, observe that the lawn has been freshly mowed or that a commercial airliner is flying overhead without experiencing joy, sadness, fear, or any other particular emotion. Likewise, the emotional experience is not to be identified with the intellective act, for it is possible to understand something without feeling any emotion.

Yet, as I analyze the phenomenon of emotional experience and seek to trace it to its source, I am able to detect that no emotion occurs in a vacuum, but rather that it is always accompanied by an act of awareness. Indeed, I am able to observe that an emotion is the *result* of an awareness; that a psychic awareness of something is an integral part of the emotional experience. It is impossible to experience fear without first understanding that somehow I am in a dangerous situation. My life might actually be in jeopardy, but unless I am *aware* of the danger, normally I would not be fearful. For example, without the slightest fear I might enter a building in which a bomb had been planted, provided I was completely oblivious of the presence of the bomb. As soon as I became aware of the bomb's existence, however, I would experience a sense of fear. Or as another example, I might receive a letter containing good news, but only after opening the letter and reading its contents could I be transported from a normal attitude of calm to one of joy and great enthusiasm. The letter, unopened, would not convey to me the reason for joy it contained.

Such an experience of fear or joy or of any of the emotions involves a somatic or bodily component which is altogether inseparable from the emotional experience itself. Fear may induce bodily transformations; such as, an increased heartbeat, a tensing of the muscles, a change in facial coloration, a dilation of the eyes, increased physical strength and so on.

Consequently, our analysis makes clear that there are at least two underlying components of the emotional experience—a mental awareness and a bodily response to that awareness. Yet it is important to note that the emotional experience also contains an appetitive element that mediates the union between the psychic awareness and the bodily response.

Following upon the psychic awareness that includes an evaluation of the experienced situation in terms of the well-being of the individual subject, there is an affective response according to whether the situation is pleasant or unpleasant, reassuring or dangerous, terrible or joyful, etc. The affective response, located in the sensory appetites, mediates appetitively the psychic awareness and communicates it to the body. Thus the emotional experience is composed of three constituent elements; namely, a psychic awareness, an affective response, and a somatic sharing in that response.

The emotional experience, then, cannot be any one of these elements, but must consist of a unified composite made up of all three. If any one of the above elements be lacking, it is not possible to have an emotional experience. Thus, if one were to think of a being as possessing knowledge but as lacking the dimension of body (an angel, for example) one would not attribute to it an emotional experience. In such a case, the somatic response to the psychic or intellective awareness would be lacking. On the other hand, a being possessing body but lacking psychic consciousness, such as a plant or a tree, would not be capable of emotional experience. Although the leaves of the tree might tremble, this would be a response to a breeze or some other external cause; this would not be an emotional response.

Hence we may define an emotion as *a complex, internal activity consisting of an intense, spontaneous affective and somatic response to a psychic awareness.* This definition is supported by the etymology of the term *emotion.* The Latin verb from which it derives, *emovere,* simply means "to move out from." As already noted, in an emotional experience a somatic response is first caused and elicited by a psychic awareness which in turn is followed by a mediating affective response; that is, the emotional experience involves a bodily reaction that results from, and is initiated by, a mental awareness. We have here in an analogous sense an extension of the theme already emphasized in the chapters on language and on free choice; namely, that ideas have consequences.

Should we wish to probe further the nature of the somatic response as an integral part of the emotion, we would do well to fix our attention on the sensory appetites. These powers respond to what is sensed and to what is understood. What is affectively experienced in an emotion is the sensory appetite that responds in a rather violent manner to the good or evil that is perceived to be present. These appetitive powers, then, truly constitute the seat of the emotional experience in its somatic dimension; for, being sensory, they are intimately related to body and can thus directly and forcefully influence it. Hence, through the reception of very favorable news, one can break into exclamations of joy and otherwise manifest in a highly visible manner the internally lived experience we commonly refer to as emotional.

The Significance of Emotional Experience

What does the existence of emotional experience tell us about ourselves as human beings? What are the conditions for the occurrence of such a phenomenon?

An emotion exhibits our acceptance or nonacceptance of some manner of conscious experience, and this acceptance or nonacceptance is manifested in a somatic or physical way. What the presence of emotions within the human clearly indicates is the intimate alliance between human consciousness and the body; the same kind of alliance as that referred to in our discussion of insight—a pivot between the concrete and the abstract—and in our discussion of language—a sensible symbolization of thought.

Through emotion we are in effect taught that the human is a unity of mind and body, both of which are so intimately in accord with, and attuned to, each other that something of each is shared in the activity of the other. In an emotional experience the body is rather mysteriously sharing in the consciousness of the mind. Our joy that is externally exhibited has as its source our inner awareness. Thus, in some sense one can truly say that in an emotional experience the body is, after its own manner, living the life of the mind or soul. Emotion is a kind of language in that it involves an affective incorporation of thought, thus paralleling the cognitive symbol of spoken language. It is, further, highly interesting to note that both the cognitive and appetitional languages can be united in one complex language expression. Thus it is possible for the human to give expression to his or her thoughts and emotions conjunctively and simultaneously, either through spoken or written language. Rhythm, tone, inflection, choice of words, and rhetorical structure all assist in revealing the affective experience. There is ample justification, therefore, to view the emotional experience as a form of intellective residue that, affectively expressed, allows the body to share in a life that is superior to it, but to which it is nonetheless intimately conjoined. As a primitive form of body language the emotions do permit us to communicate, though in imperfect form, our thoughts to others. Emotional communication is always imperfect because it is vague, inexact, and non-cognitive in expression. Though I can determine with reasonable certainty that another is either sad or joyful, fearful or angered, from his or her outward appearance—manner of speaking, gestures, facial movements, etc.—these sensible manifestations themselves are totally inadequate to communicate to me the *thought* that they indirectly manifest. Thus, though it may be readily apparent that my friend is in a jovial mood, my awareness of the emotion he or she is exhibiting is of no real help toward my learning the reason for such exuberance. I might, of course, attempt to guess the reason, if I happen to know the person well, but this effort can produce nothing more than a tentative result. Alone, the emotional manifestation is insufficient to indicate to me its precise cause; considerably more information is necessary. If I am really to learn the cause, my friend must inform me.

The fact that the body is, after its own manner, able to share in the act of understanding and to live out an idea, seems to strengthen the view that the world of material bodies is indeed the original source of the very ideas that the mind possesses. It seems fitting that the body, which first shared in the appropriation of ideas, should also have a part in their actuation and fulfillment. Further, the whole of the emotional phenomenon would clearly seem to fit in with the claim made in a previous chapter that all knowledge is ordered ultimately to the promotion of an activity. As we shall have occasion to elaborate on shortly, the emotions also perform valuable functions in the area of human activity, although it is also true that they can unquestionably influence it adversely.

The Cultivation of Emotions

Doubtless it has already occurred to the perceptive reader that the emotional experience is not limited to the human. Animals also manifest an experience that in many ways strongly resembles the emotional experience of the human. Animals are clearly capable of manifesting joy, fear, anger, affection, and sadness, all of which are evidently bodily responses to a perceptive awareness. But the range of animal emotions is notably limited in contrast to the range of the human's. Its bodily response is restricted to sensory cognition and its elicitation and spontaneity are controlled instinctually.

Thus, while there is an identifiable behavioral commonality between the human and the brute animal as regards the emotional response, the differences in this area are noteworthy and remarkable. In the animal the sensory experience is the sole stimulus of the emotions; whereas in the human, intellective awareness plays the central, although not exclusive, role. In the human, consequently, emotions can be aroused simply as a result of thought, a fact that is strikingly illustrated through the arresting power of language. By the use of words alone, whether oral or written, profound physiological changes can be noted as the message is first received and then grasped. Language can evoke a range of feelings from anger to joy.

Further, through our unique ability of total self-reflection, we are able to turn our attention to the emotional experience itself. Only the human is capable of analyzing his emotions; isolating them in thought; inquiring into their nature and their origin. As a result of this reflective ability, the human is able to study the emotion of sadness even when experiencing joy or can reflect on the nature of anger when totally calm. An emotional experience, which is no longer present in actuality, can be recalled through the power of intellective memory. Thus the human can know sadness without at that moment being sad and can know the meaning of joy and happiness when experiencing the most cruel disappointment.

Through this unique ability to bring the past into the present and to stand before oneself in reflective self-consciousness, the human is able to view any emotional experience as a value and to desire it. Because of our transcending intellective and volitional powers, we are able to consciously cultivate emotional experiences and to refine and regulate them. In this way, they may be experienced often and with increased enjoyment. Our pursuit of what are commonly referred to as the fine arts represent the culmination of our achievment in this area. The cultivation of literature, drama, music, painting, sculpture, and architecture, wonderfully attest to the creative genius of the human and to his pursuit of the beautiful and the sublime. Through the arts we seek to replicate in an external manifold the richness and haunting profundity of our own humanness, which then becomes a living, continuing dialogue between matter and spirit.

It may be noted, somewhat parenthetically, that one of the ever recurring themes of music, drama, and literature is the tragic dimension of life. Conscious of our own finitude and of our constant dependence on the other for both mental and volitional growth, as well as simple survival, we seem inevitably drawn to tell our own story as it truly is, with all its setbacks and limitations. Thus we are drawn often to relate our story to others essentially as it unfolded, in order to bear authentic witness to our real self. Sadness and disappointment, loneliness and rejection, fear and remorse, all find their place in the songs we sing, the poetry we write, the music we compose, the stories we relate. It would seem that we are drawn to the vicarious experience of the tragic much as a moth is to the flame, for it resonates to something within us that we find inescapably and profoundly true.

Living consciously on the edge of nothingness, we humans are aware of our own nothingness, or finitude—a theme central to much of the writings of existentialist philosophers Martin Heidegger and Jean Paul Sartre. This self-awareness accounts for our being an *anxious animal*, one who lives in a state of tension, anxiety, and even dread.

In the fleeting light of the present, not only are we able to reflect about the past but we are also able to project our thoughts into the vast uncertainty of the future. Faced with an infinite possibility of events made available to us in consciousness by our intellective vision, and empowered by our self-determining choice, we are never in total repose.

Controlling the Emotions

As an expression of the body's sharing in the intellective and volitional world of the human, the emotions themselves have no built-in control. If left unchecked, they easily become destructive of the very force which initially occasioned them. If they are to prove truly beneficial to the individual, the emotions need to be controlled and channeled. It is particularly in the fine arts where this emotional control becomes most manifest, where the vicarious experiences of feelings and emotions provide us with a temporal pleasure and release from the tensions of life's everyday problems. This is merely another way of saying that the emotions must be intellectualized, which, of course, is not the same as saying that they should be suppressed. To speak of the intellectualization of the emotions is merely a technical, philosophical way of saying that order and harmony must be allowed to extend from the human's world of intellectual consciousness to the human's world of sensible, emotional experience.

A person in an emotionally agitated state is in a disadvantageous position to apply himself or herself to problems of profound intellectual concern. The function of concentration is to assist one to focus one's attention on a job to be done or a problem to be resolved. Such concentration inevitably requires the conscious exclusion of overt emotional distraction. Hence in situations which naturally tend to engender emotional excitement, the continued application of the mind to a difficult question is all but impossible. This fits in, of course, with the observation made earlier concerning the occurrence of human insight; namely, that significant mental breakthroughs generally occur in a time of rest and repose. The same is true when one needs to deliberate over an important decision to be made. The advisability of postponing such decisions until emotional equilibrium has been achieved or regained is a piece of practical wisdom known to all.

Since a healthy, integrated emotional life is an essential component of both our physical and mental health, it is a prerequisite for significant achievement on practically any level of human endeavor. In order to avoid the destructive forces of continuing internal pressures and tensions, humans require emotional outlets. Toward this end play and leisure fulfill a not insignificant need of every human being.

The Phenomenon of Humor

In concluding this chapter on the emotions it is fitting that our attention be directed toward the phenomenon of humor which so uniquely characterizes the human, and which is all but inseparable from the emotion of joy.

The human smile is exasperatingly difficult to describe, and any attempt to define it exclusively in physical terms falls short of its mark. As a fleeting expression that involves the facial muscles, the mouth, and the eyes, the smile is, like the word, much more than a mere physical phenomenon. While the smile is a universal human sign, common not only to all cultures but to all ages, it retains its elusive, Mona-Lisa-like characteristics because it is a human phenomenon of the human psyche itself. The smile, despite our untiring efforts to analyze it and place it in its proper category, remains elusive simply because it is an expression of the free thought of humans. It cannot, therefore, escape the law of inherent ambiguity to which all physical expression of idea is subject.

The nature of humor appears to be as elusive as the cause of the smile. The human is the only animal that indulges in humor beyond the level of playful, physical gestures, such as we might witness in the play of the puppy or the otter. Indeed, for the human, most calculated humor is a matter of language, and this is certainly true of jokes, where the intent of the communication is to cause others to smile or to laugh. Yet there clearly is an element of understanding behind the smile, which is indicative of intelligence. We cannot authentically laugh or smile unless we have first understood something. If someone tells a joke and we find nothing funny in it, we say that we do not "get the point." Humor is truly a form of intellectual play. Thus, the clever storyteller or jokester builds up to a suspenseful moment when understanding occurs suddenly and in a wholly unexpected way. It is because we are "caught by surprise" that we are amused by the recounting, and the inevitable physiological reaction of the smile or laugh follows. That is why we do not think that even a very good joke is so funny the second time we hear it. The spontaneous groan let out by the audience, as an unrehearsed response to the query, "have you heard this one before?" is a clear indication that familiarity quickly transforms what was once found to be humorous into the decidedly ordinary and mediocre. Surprise is essential to humor; if this dimension is absent, we fail to see anything funny in what was said.

In addition to the qualities of intelligence and surprise, humor also involves the grasp of the incongruous. What strikes us as funny involves the juxtaposition of two notions that we would not normally dream of associating. Thus the element of surprise derives from this sudden, instantaneous grasp of the incongruous. In all humor there is the *double entendre* or the "bisociative" dimension, as Arthur Koestler refers to it (Koestler 1967, p.85). Thus we are caused to smile or laugh when we are somehow fooled. We had been following a train of thought down a certain path only to experience unexpectedly a reversal of direction. Led to anticipate one set of events, we are astonished to find another unfolding right before our eyes, and in a manner that somehow makes sense in terms of what had preceded. One needs to do more than be awake in order to grasp the incongruous, one needs also to be alert. Humor has always been a favorite pastime of intelligent people.

The pun or the play on words is perhaps the most common form of humor. Two British newspaper headlines, one from the *Manchester Guardian* and the other from the *London Observer,* provide two examples of the pun. The headline from the *Manchester Guardian* for an item about a woman who was evicted from a pub because she used her space at the bar to do her knitting, simply asked, "Knit Picking?" The headline from *The London Observer* for a story about movie stars in India who were running for Parliament was "Film Stars Want to Lead Castes of Millions."

Slips of the tongue can also prove amusing, particularly when the effect is to say in a perfectly intelligent manner exactly the opposite of what one intended. A recent instance of this occurred on national television when the moderator of a prestigious panel program signed off by announcing that the panel was grateful for the letters they had received from listeners. He concluded, "We are not able to read all of the letters submitted, but we do answer them all."

Humor is employed for various reasons. Sometimes it is used as a harmless form of entertainment, but it can also take the form of satire, a witticism that is basically critical of something. For example, the following definitions are humorous attacks on what they pretend to define.

"What is Psychoanalysis?"

"Psychoanalysis is the malady for which it pretends to have the cure."

"What is Philosophy?"

"Philosophy is the systematic misuse of a terminology specially designed for that purpose."

Whatever the reason for which humor is employed and whatever the manner in which it is expressed, it always involves a playful use of language made possible in turn by the fact that human language is unavoidably ambivalent. The symbols and signs employed in language often have more than one meaning, and, in addition, language-meaning is often modified by the context in which it appears. All of this adds up to the presence of hidden and unforeseen meanings in language. At bottom, humor flows from the mind's sudden grasp of the incongruous.

There is a hidden meaning in the following story that made the rounds some years ago in Eastern European countries.

"Comrade, what is your definition of capitalism?"
"Capitalism is the exploitation of man by man."
"And how do you define Communism?"
"The reverse!"

Words are never quite able to measure up to the burden placed on them of giving precise expression to the intangible, transcending world of ideas. And it is largely this radical poverty of language that creates the possibility of the expression of humor, for humor rests primarily on the ambiguity of language, which accounts for any sudden shift in the anticipation of insight and the consequent experience of surprise.

Surprise, the dashing of raised expectations, and the sudden grasp of the absurd, all contribute to the human world of humor. That is why having a sense of humor is not far removed from being in tune with the real; for in order to laugh, one must recognize one's limitations, and accept oneself as one is. It is interesting that in the idiom of everyday speech a person with a sense of humor is viewed as one who is human.

It was noted in a preceding chapter how insight comes suddenly and without warning; how it brings about release from any tension that may have been built up in the course of inquiry. The phenomenon of humor is a by-product of insight. Within the broad field of human experience it is in its release of accumulated tension and frustration that humor plays a significant role. It serves as a point of confluence of two main streams of the human condition; namely, the human's intellective prowess on the one hand and the awareness of his profound limitations on the other. As a self-conscious knower—the only animal that knows both its own considerable capabilities and its own limitations—we humans can appreciate and understand the underlying reasons for our own anxieties and our own frustrations. Viewing ourselves against the backdrop of unlimited being and our unrestricted desire to know, we are capable of grasping the incongruity of our own limited efforts to achieve what in fact is unachievable.

Traced back to its primal roots, humor reveals itself as a corollary of an ontological humility that allows one to accept oneself as one is—a human being. People who take themselves too seriously habitually find nothing to laugh at, and life, rather than being a comedy in Dante's sense, is for them a tragedy. Authentic laughter is an outward expression of humility, which is certainly the reason some students of humor view it as always including as one of its points of reference the very person who is laughing. In short, when one laughs, one is in fact also laughing at oneself.

This seems to explain why it is that much humor is directed toward the foibles and limitations of human nature and why we are generally amused when comedians poke fun either at their own or someone else's stupidity. In these instances we are laughing, however gently, at ourselves, for we recognize that the occasional breakdowns in intelligent behavior we witness in others provide us with a mirrored image of ourselves. In a sense, misery does love company and in laughing at the *faux pas* of others we rather happily recognize that we are not alone, for others make mistakes and do stupid things too. As a univeral social phenomenon humor is witness to the finitude of humans.

Clearly, humor has a central role to play in human experience. It is, further, a truly universal phenomenon. Humor is found to exist among all races and all cultures and in all historical periods. Much of world literature centers around humorous themes, and many contemporary plots are adaptations of stories well known to the ancient Greeks and Romans.

In addition, humor can be seen as an essential component of the normal and well-balanced emotional life. Serving as a soothing analgesic to psychic pain, it takes one's attention away from an unhealthy fixation on self, tempering the sometimes corroding influences of the stronger emotions, particularly those of anger and hostility. A humorous word will often turn away wrath, to paraphrase scripture. Humor can also provide a welcome outlet from nervous and physical fatigue, and in this manner performs nobly as a marvellous restorative of depleted creative energies.

In recent years psychological studies have made us increasingly aware of just how key the role of humor is in the fashioning of human behavior and how truly essential it is for the maintenance of mental health, especially on the contemporary urban scene. It is significant that emotionally disturbed people generally lack a sense of humor.

As humans we require the outlets for relaxation that humor provides. Further, it can be suggested that the pursuit of hobbies, sports, and leisure itself are phenomena which are closely allied to the interesting and intriguing questions we have considered pertaining to humor—its nature, its significance, and its causes.

Throughout this chapter we have spoken of emotions and their significance within the broad context of the human condition. We have concentrated on the emotional experience because of the ease with which it can, at least superficially, be identified. Yet most of the comments made are applicable, with some slight modification, to the entire world of human affectivity, which includes the phenomenon of the feeling state in general. As noted earlier, feelings differ from emotions more in degree than in kind, being a somewhat weakened and faint affective response to a psychic awareness.

Emotions may be distinguished from *mood*, in that the latter is more permanent, and, for that reason, less intense; although, like feelings, the mood is an affective state resulting from some form of cognitive awareness, even though it may be vague and difficult to identify. *Temperament* may be viewed as a habitual personality characteristic that reflects the manner in which a person ordinarily responds emotionally and affectively to all levels of human experience.

These brief reflections have focussed on the significance of the emotional and affective experience as it relates to the human condition. The more subtle and detailed questions touching on the relationship of the emotions to the affective states of feeling, mood, and temperament, can best be left to the psychologists.

Summary

In this chapter on emotions we have analyzed the human emotional experience, observing that it is an intense, spontaneous appetitive and somatic response to some form of psychic awareness. We have reflected also on the significance of the emotional experience in terms of an overall definition of the human person, emphasizing that it clearly indicates that body and mind are inseparably united in one human nature. We touched briefly on the role of the emotions in human development and the need for their cultivation, channeling, and control. We have also discussed the phenomenon of humor and have examined its relation both to human intelligence and to the human somatic nature. Lastly, we have briefly alluded to the other common forms of affective states such as those of feeling, mood, and temperament.

Definitions and Conclusions

1. The experience of emotions is a universally human phenomenon common to people of all eras and cultures.

2. An emotional experience is a complex internal activity involving an intense and spontaneous appetitive and somatic response to a psychic awareness.

3. The principal philosophical significance of the emotional experience is the positive reinforcement it lends to the view that an intimate union exists between idea and matter, spirit and body; an emphasis already made in both the chapter on insight and that on language.

4. In the emotional experience, the body reflectively shares in the consciousness of the mind.

5. It is fitting that the body should somehow share in the conscious awareness of the mind since the body initially serves as an instrument for the mind's acquisition of knowledge.

6. Emotional expression is rightly viewed as a kind of body language.

7. Though the higher animals share the emotional phenomenon with the human, the latter alone consciously pursues emotional experience as a value through a wide variety of activities.

8. Because of the human's unique ability to presentiate the past and to "stand before oneself" in reflective self-consciousness, the human alone is able to understand the origin and significance of the emotional experience as well as to control and to channel it.

9. Though in themselves a valued dimension of the human scene, the emotions, precisely because they lack an internal system of controls, can become a destructive force within the individual if they are allowed to run their course without direction and intelligent restraint.

10. An integrated emotional life is an essential component of both physical and mental health, a prerequisite for significant human achievement.

11. Humor is the sudden, unexpected grasp of the incongruous.

12. Like a word, a smile is revelatory of meaning.

13. The philosophical grounding of humor rests primarily on the ambiguity of language and the sudden shift from an anticipated to an unanticipated insight.

11 Habits and Learning

On the human level, spiritually and
intellectually, we all need friendship and love, we
all need a good society to live in, we all need
knowledge and wisdom.

Mortimer Adler

Acquired Operational Structures

We have reached the place in our study of the human person where we are able to address ourselves to second-level questions, questions that are derivative of questions previously discussed. They are not necessarily less profound for that reason, but they are of a somewhat more concrete and practical nature. The first of these involves habits. Most people associate habits with matters of conduct; such as, smoking, scratching one's head, coming late to work or to class, etc. In philosophy, however, the term *habit* actually refers to what can be called *operational structures,* or learning skills.

No other animal is as ill-prepared at birth to provide for itself and its individual development as is the human. Without being provided by nature with protection from a hostile environment and without the ability to secure the necessities of life, the human offspring requires constant attention during its early years and supervision and assistance for approximately one-fourth of its total projected life span, after which the human still has scarcely attained a high level of self-sufficiency.

We humans need to acquire skills and abilities that nature has not provided us with. Without the acquisition of these operative skills, the human cannot survive, let alone develop normally to a state of maturity. Thus it does indeed seem paradoxical that the human organism, which is the only known organism possessed of intellective and volitional capabilities, should be, of all organisms, the one most completely dependent upon others for its survival and development.

Yet, as we scrutinize the situation, the apparent paradox is resolved; for it is the very complexity of the human organism and its high capacity for development and performance that necessitates a comparatively long period of *environmental* gestation. Precisely *because* the human is an intellective being who is open to the vast array of activities identifiable as strictly human, they enter life with no inborn knowledge, no precoded skills, and a highly unspecialized physical structure. This initial state of the human's operational openness contrasts starkly with the animal's inborn instinctive ability to perform all the activities essential to its own survival as well as to the survival of its species.

The highly specialized organism of other animals allows them to perform only a limited number of activities. It is this limitation that makes it possible for them to be equipped with a priori operational structures that are specifically tailored to their limited needs. Their physical structure is also highly specialized and calculated to complement their inner instinctual code in the most amazing manner. Thus, some animals are provided with claws, others with talons, others with paws, others with fins, etc. While the specialized anatomical structure is of great benefit to the individual species of animal, it is so only because its repertoire of activities is extremely limited. As a result, what one animal can do, another cannot, because it not only lacks the physical structure but also it is absolutely incapable of modifying these structures to accommodate other modes of activity. Thus, the serpent, the elephant, the whale, and the cheetah each lives in totally different worlds. Their activity wholly lacks any kind of recognizable, specific commonality.

The human is an animal in the generic sense only, for we come equipped with none of the special capabilities of the other animals. Rather we are characterized by our structural *openness* and extreme flexibility that permit us to adapt to our environment, and where necessary, to adapt our environment to our needs. The human hand perfectly exemplifies this state of openness, which the human anatomy as a whole wonderfully reflects. For this reason Aristotle refers to the human hand as the tool of tools, because it is non-specialized or universal in its structure, and thus can adapt itself to a seemingly unlimited number of highly divergent tasks. What the human hand cannot itself perform it can accomplish through the use of tools or other hands, which it fashions for itself. In this sense, the human can burrow under the earth more proficiently than can the mole; swim under water faster than any fish; fly higher, faster, and farther than any bird; and move on land more swiftly than any other mammal.

Earlier we noted that the human is the world's greatest knower, doer, and speaker. To this list of accomplishments must now be added that of learning, because whatever the human is able to do, is an acquired capacity which may be viewed as an operational residue of past activity. Our ability to learn is, of course, closely tied to our intellective nature, which opens us to the unrestricted world of being. Indeed, it is precisely because we are intellective beings that we are, as it were, condemned to learn. The same radical openness to the world that our intellect grants us also prevents us from being, like the brute animal, preprogrammed through instinctual operative structures. Because, in short, we humans are able to do *everything*, we can accomplish nothing without first acquiring a singular capacity for any specific kind of activity.

The Nature of Habits

It is the human's acquired capacity for these varied forms of activity that we presently intend to focus on. The sensory and intellective powers, both cognitive and appetitive, are essential for human activity, and provide us with our root operational capacity. Yet, they do not suffice of themselves. They must be completed and reinforced, as it were, by permanent characteristics that enable one to perform specific kinds of activities and to perform them well. The term *habit,* or *acquired operational structure,* refers to these added capacities and not to the sensory or intellective powers themselves.

It should also be noted that an acquired capacity is to be distinguished from the activity toward which it is ordered. Possessing the ability to do something does not imply that one is always doing it. Thus, we refer to someone as a musician, a skier, or a mathematician, without intending to suggest that that person is presently playing a musical instrument, or skiing down the slopes, or pondering over a mathematical problem. What we obviously mean by these expressions is that this person has the ability to play a certain musical instrument, or to ski, or to solve mathematical problems.

A habit may be defined as an acquired operational structure that permits one to act in a certain way quickly and with comparative ease and proficiency. The habit, then, lies midway between the operational power itself and the activity toward which it is ordered. As a perfection of the power in which it inheres, it is relatively permanent, though it always remains open to further development. If not made use of, the habit is subject to deterioration and in some instances it can be lost. For example, one can lose the ability to play a musical instrument or to speak a foreign language. This acquired habit, or skill, may thus be viewed as a kind of superstructure added to the basic structure of the power itself, through which the root capacity of each power is channeled toward a specific operation. The habit permits the power to perform an activity, which the power could not otherwise accomplish.

If, then, we consider the habit in relation to the power in which it inheres, it can be seen to be a partial actualization of that power, and it is thus related to the latter as act is related to potency. If, however, we consider the habit as facing toward the activity for which it provides the ability, the habit is seen to be related to the activity as potency is related to act. That is, the habit is a capacity for activity; it is not identical with the activity itself. Thus, one does not have to be singing in order to be called a singer, although one does need to possess the ability to sing.

Hence, through the acquisition of habits, or skills, the individual is gradually moving from a state of potentiality to one of actuality. This means that one's being is taking on a new quiet dynamism by which one will be able to accomplish unobtrusively and at a moment's notice highly complex tasks. Through the presence of habits, or acquired skills, we can transpose ourselves from a state of repose to a state of dynamic action almost instantaneously and perform multiple tasks in a relatively skilled and proficient manner. Habits, then, provide for the human the same capacity that instincts provide for the animal. Because, however, there is no limit to the actual proliferation of such acquired human skills, the human comes to possess a repertoire of activities and a flexibility for action that exceeds that of the animal. There is a universality in the level of tasks we can perform that matches the expansiveness of our intellective horizon and our ability to provide our own behavioral programming by selecting from an unlimited array of values those values we adopt as our own.

Habits and Traits

From the foregoing one can appreciate the importance of distinguishing the acquired operational structures we term habits from a mere repetition of acts. Although it is true that many habits are acquired only through a frequent repetition of acts, they are clearly distinct from the activity itself, since they abide within the power long after the activity itself ceases. As previously suggested, the acquired habit can be described as a kind of operational residue if it is understood in a dynamic and active sense, for the human habit is acquired consciously and is directly related to insight and free choice. Habits do not come at random or as a matter of course; neither do they occur involuntarily.

Habit as it is used here should not be confused with what is more properly referred to as a mere trait or mannerism. It is true that we often refer to one's having, for example, the habit of speaking rapidly, or of humming to oneself, or of scratching one's head. Yet, more properly, these are idiosyncratic traits or mannerisms that involve no real skill, were not acquired consciously, and do not fit the definition of habit as presented in the second section of this chapter. The term habit is also used to refer to other common actions simply because they are repeatedly performed; such as, cigarette smoking, overeating, getting up late, procrastinating, etc. These are habitual modes of acting, but a habit in the full philosophic sense provides one with a capacity of performing a specific activity with relative ease and facility. It is thus a consciously acquired capability which positively enhances the operative capacity of the individual human.

The Value of Habits

Habits are much more than useful acquisitions. For the human they are absolutely essential. As already indicated, we are totally dependent upon the acquisition of operative habits precisely because we are not equipped with instinctual or inborn knowledge. Thus our behavior is not preprogrammed or precoded.

Habits, then, can be looked upon as a type of fueling up of the tanks of human capability. They provide us with the energy we can draw on to permit a quick transition from an inactive to an active state over a wide range of activities. In addition, habits serve a directional purpose as well, for they contain a definite program for action specially designed to accomplish specific tasks. Thus habits also provide a dimension of balance and consistency to an individual's activity, enabling one to repeatedly perform intricate and difficult actions at a reasonably high level of proficiency with minimal effort or fresh preparation. For example, one who has mastered the intricacies of a musical instrument, such as the violin, is capable of playing that instrument whenever he or she wishes.

Through the presence of habit within a power, therefore, we humans remain in readiness to act in countlessly different ways. Habits enable us to conserve energies expended in the past and to profit from our past experience. With the increase of habits, our capacity for activity and accomplishment increases in something like a geometric proportion. This capacity for growth through the acquisition of operational structures is commonly referred to as learning. We humans are the world's greatest learners, thanks to our intellective capabilities.

The Division of Habits

Up till now we have spoken of habits in general without attempting to distinguish between the different kinds. That there are different classifications of habits should be clear from the previous comments regarding the habit as a further determination of our operative powers. As we have seen, all of the powers of the human hitherto considered fall into one of two generic classes; namely, cognitive or appetitive. Consequently, the first division of habits is between those that are cognitive and those that are appetitive. In the following sections, we shall consider each of these divisions of habits separately, including their major subdivisions. Since some of these considerations are normally taken up in a philosophical course on ethics, we shall confine our reflections to a general overview of the range of acquired habits and emphasize principally the manner in which they differ one from another, as well as the goal at which each habit aims.

Intellective Habits

Although we may not be accustomed to viewing knowledge as a form of habit, it does accurately fit the definition of habit, for it is a permanent operative quality enabling us to act in a certain way with relative ease and proficiency. Through the intellective habits the intellect is able to understand more quickly, to repeat almost instantaneously acts of understanding that have previously occurred. This was the case with regard to Archimedes and his famous insight in the Baths of Syracuse, for what he discovered passed into the habitual texture of his mind. The problem he had worked so hard to resolve seemed absurdly simple once he had understood its solution. Thus, all learning is really identical with the acquisition of habits, which involves a retention of past understanding. Through knowledge the root capacities of the intellective power are actualized.

Like Aristotle, St. Thomas Aquinas divides the intellective habits into those that are *speculative* and those that are *practical*. The speculative habits are concerned with knowledge for its own sake; the practical habits aim at the performance of some activity.

Speculative Habits

Speculative habits are divided by Aristotle and Aquinas into three categories: *intellectus, science,* and *wisdom.* The habit of intellectus, or understanding, is not an *acquired* habit in the strictest sense of that term, for it is considered a habit of the active intellect. Precisely because it is by nature ever in act, the active intellect does not require the addition of other operative abilities to perform its function of the illumination of phantasm. In fact it is called an active power precisely because it is in act by nature and does not require the addition of further actualizations to move from a state of capacity to that of action.

The habit of understanding is also known as the habit of first principles. These include the principle of *non-contradiction*, which simply states that something cannot be in act and potency at the same time and in the same respect; the principle of *identity*, by which a thing is simply what it is; and the principle of *causality*, by which a thing that comes to be in some way, comes to be through the activity of another. These principles are a priori, because they are not learned in the ordinary sense. They could not be learned, because all knowledge presupposes their existence. Consequently, if they were not known from the very beginning, no knowledge at all would be possible.

While these principles are indeed first principles of knowledge for the reason just given, Aquinas even more properly calls them first principles of being, since they find universal application in reality and are the bases of whatever is, knowledge included. While the habit of understanding, which includes these principles, is a priori in that it is contained within the agent intellect itself, Aquinas adds the qualification that these principles are not known prior to insight into phantasm. Indeed even then they are first known only *implicitly*, for they are individually instantiated in the knowledge of whatever is first known. They become known *explicitly* as principles and in the form given above only through reflection in which they can be isolated from the manifold of the concrete knowing act and recognized as the underlying ground of whatever is. In short, these principles are the principles of reality itself. Such explicit knowledge of these principles is evidently on the metaphysical level, and it is not necessary to have such a knowledge for knowledge actually to occur.

In addition to the habit of understanding there are found to be two fundamental habits present in the receptive intellect, those of science and wisdom. The habit of science enables the intellect to reason from certain and universal premises to certain and universal conclusions, and would, for example, include all major branches of mathematics. Science in this sense differs from the habit of understanding in that the latter consists merely of a single judgment, the truth of which is known as soon as the meaning of the terms of the judgment are understood; whereas the habit of science always involves three judgments, the third of which is known to be true once the truth of the other two judgments—and their interlocking relationship—is known. It is important to note, therefore, that the term science, as it applies to this habit of the intellect, is used in a considerably more restrictive sense than is commonly the case in dealing with a non-homogenous body of knowledge, much of which is merely hypothetically true, as in the case of the natural sciences.

The third speculative habit is that of wisdom, which enables the intellect to judge of all things inasmuch as they are beings and to draw conclusions about the first and ultimate causes. From the first of these perspectives this habit of wisdom is referred to as metaphysics, and from the latter, as first philosophy. Aquinas is careful to insist that metaphysics studies concrete, material reality, but always from the aspect of a thing's being. Thus for Aquinas there is no sense whatever in which the subject of metaphysics is God or any transphysical being, for its proper subject is the singular material thing from the aspect of its being. This is what he means by saying that the subject of metaphysics is *being as being*, or common being. It is, unfortunately, the notion of a metaphysics isolated from the concrete world of existents that has often been taken for the authentic notion of metaphysics. Such a metaphysics would be totally a priori and thus would be altogether indistinguishable from our understanding of academic logic and would be able to tell us nothing of the real world. This sense of metaphysics has been rightly repudiated by Immanuel Kant and others.

Practical Intellective Habits

There are two habits of the practical intellect, by which the intellect is ordered toward an activity other than thinking; namely, *art* and *prudence*. As a practical habit of intellect, *art enables it to judge properly about things to be made*. Art, therefore, deals with the right manner of making things, and involves the harmonious coordination of thought with matter, or, in other words, the incorporation of idea within the physical world. Thus in the most fundamental sense of the term, everyone is an artist who is adept at making or doing something well. This includes craftsmen of all kinds. For example, shipbuilders are artists, who in constructing a ship must know the materials with which they are working and incorporate within them a design that is in accord with the basic laws of hydro- and aero- dynamics. Similar observations could be made regarding engineers, architects, culinary artists, and industrial workers of all kinds. At the highest level of artistic achievement are the poets, the musicians, the painters, the dramatists, the sculptors, etc., who possess the ability to communicate thought itself through its incorporation in matter.

The practical habit of *prudence* is a permanent intellectual quality that enables one to be able to judge and calculate properly about actions to be taken. It follows, therefore, that this habit is directly related to acts of choice that are ordered to the performance of an action but are not of themselves ordered to making. Prudence, then, enables one to judge correctly regarding the rightness and wrongness of actions. Prudence is one of the four cardinal or moral virtues and constitutes the core of the study of ethics, which itself is the science of the rightness or wrongness of human actions. Through the habit of prudence one is possessed of the ability to deliberate clearly and with relative ease about the fittingness of various courses of action. What, precisely, the criteria for the determination of befitting or proper behavior are, is itself one of the principal tasks of the ethicist.

There are numerous subdivisions of the habit of prudence, all of which are oriented toward the courses of action to be taken. Jurisprudence, which treats of obligations deriving from the civil law, is a branch of prudence, and constitutes the domain of the profession of law. Thus one consults a lawyer to obtain advice about how to proceed in order to fulfill the requirements of the law, or how to avoid the penalty if one has in some way contravened the letter of the law. Similarly, all forms of counseling and advising make use of a specific branch of the habit of prudence. There are, consequently, a significant number of professions—the tax specialist, the real estate broker, the investment banker, the consulting engineer, the architect, the academic advisor, the family counselor, the health care specialist, the clinical psychologist, the physician, the industrial consultant, the travel agent, etc.—that draw on some form of this habit.

The practical intellective habits of art and prudence are directly concerned with the deliberative act. Thus both art and prudence provide us with the ability to think through wisely and readily problems that arise with regard to the implementation of thought in the surrounding physical world. These habits, particularly that of prudence, are important to our attaining a state of maturity.

Appetitive Habits

The remaining habits pertain to the appetitive powers; that is, the rational appetite and sensory appetites. In each of the appetitive powers there is found to be one fundamental habit, each of which correspondingly has numerous subdivisions. Let us first consider the rational appetite, the will.

It was pointed out in chapter nine that the formal object of the will is the general, or universal good, and that the will is thus internally and irrevocably ordered toward the good taken in the unqualified, or unrestricted sense. It was also pointed out that the will is free in its inclination toward any limited good. Thus it is possible for the will to choose anything whatsoever that is presented to it in some manner as having value. The value presented to it, however, need not be an authentically befitting value, but may be merely a pleasureable or utilitarian value.

Moreover, it may be a value that is viewed merely from the perspective of the individual self. This possibility underscores the need for a habit within the will to permit it to choose according to the enlightened and prudential directives of the practical intellect, rather than solely from the perspective of its own personal interest. The habit that enables the will to choose values that view the self in communion with other selves—in a manner that recognizes others as the subjects of rights and hence as persons—is the habit of justice. Justice, then, is the volitional habit by which the will is facilitated in choosing its values in an unselfish manner, providing for its own needs while at the same time respecting the needs and rights of others. Through the virtue of justice one is able to give to another that which is their due. Note, however, that giving to another what is their due is not the equivalent of giving to another what they might desire.

The reason such a habit is needed is precisely because the will itself is not *a priori* ordered to seek the authentic or unselfish good but rather to seek any good or value whatsoever. Wherefore, if it is to choose its value within the parameters of a social context, it requires an habitual ordering and disposition to facilitate its choosing only those goods which are humanly, and not merely individually, befitting. From this it may be seen how basic and fundamental justice is to the full and mature development of the human person; for to say that a person possesses the virtue of justice is really another way of saying that that person is unselfish. In other words, the self is not one's world. Again, the need for such a virtue or habit is directly owing to the fact that the will can choose any value presented it by the intellect, so that, without the restraining influence exerted by the habit of justice, the will possesses the raw capability of choosing whatever it wants, without being influenced by the consideration of the needs of others.

From this it may also be seen that justice is the most fundamental and basic of all the social virtues, and that it thus constitutes the absolutely essential basis of human society itself. Clearly, any authentic form of society must be based on justice, and this in turn requires a general consensus among the individual populace as to what constitutes just behavior. Toward this end, every society formulates laws, directives, and rules, whereby the concept of justice is concretely defined, and the means of its implementation carefully articulated.

Also, it is important to recognize the intimate relationship between justice and love. In the popular view the two are often considered as unrelated or even opposed. However, justice is a form of love since it wills the well-being of another by according him or her their due. Thus, there can be no authentically human love where justice is not present. This is not to say, however, that love and justice are identical. In the Christian sense, love goes beyond justice and seeks to accord to one's neighbor not merely what is his or her due but all that one has and is. Total availability is, then, the unique mark of Christian love, which is most properly identified as charity. It should thus be emphasized that charity is not one with justice, since it goes beyond it, although it does necessarily include it. It would thus be impossible for one to act charitably without at the same time being just, although, contrarily, one could be just without being charitable, positively.

We turn now to the sensory appetites where the two remaining cardinal or moral virtues find their proper habitat; namely, the concupiscible and the irascible appetites. We have noted previously in the chapter on willing and choosing that the formal object of the concupiscible appetite is the pleasureable good. Of itself, in the order of that which pleases, this appetite, or drive, is absolute. The concupiscible appetite necessarily inclines to what is perceived, or sensed, as pleasureable. It possesses no built-in restraints and is activated directly by an infinite sweep of intellective awareness. Consequently, the restraining influence on the concupiscible power can only be acquired and can thus only be a habit or a permanent disposition of that power. The habit that exercises this function is the habit of temperance. As a permanent quality of the concupiscible appetite, temperance facilitates measure and control in that appetite's pursuit of the pleasureable good.

The other sensory appetite, the irascible, also requires the support of an operative habit to facilitate it. However, the specific reason for the need of such a habit is the inverse of that cited above with regard to the concupiscible appetite. The irascible appetite, since it has as its object the difficult or arduous good, requires encouragement rather than restraint in the pursuit of its proper function. The habit that provides this added strength necessary for the power to move forward in the face of difficulty and danger is the habit of *fortitude*. This habit enables one, then, to proceed calmly and with presence of mind in the face of imminent danger and to strive to overcome opposition when it is proper and appropriate to do so. Patience in the face of trial, determination in the face of a difficult undertaking, perseverance in fulfilling a long-term commitment, bravery in the face of danger, are all aspects of the habit of fortitude.

The function of the irascible appetite is ultimately subordinated to that of the concupiscible, since its goal is either the acquisition or the retention of that which is desirable.

Habits and Education

The acquisition of habits is clearly essential to the development of the human person and is a direct consequence of the finitude of the human condition. Our investigation of the phenomenon of the human learning process has shown how the acquiring of habits manifestly complements the human's dependence on the sensory world. It is because our knowledge originates through insight into phantasm that the human cognoscitive and appetitive powers are so entirely beholden to further actualities, which enhance their overall dynamism and enable them to move quickly and competently from a passive to an active state.

The acquisition of habits by the various operative powers of the human is roughly analogous to the activity of the memory, for the habits themselves may be looked upon as a kind of ontological memory. Through the habit, past actions are in part retained, and the past is somehow *made present*. Through the retention and conservation of past actions, a gradual build-up of operative resources, which are at the constant disposal of the human person for instantaneous deployment, takes place. Thus it is through the acquisition and build-up of habits that we humans can individually free ourselves from the existential inertia imposed upon us by the exigencies of our natural condition, allowing us increasingly greater options for activity, thus broadening the range of our influence, and improving the quality of our achievement.

It becomes clear, then, that achieving maturity and self-liberation is one with the acquisition and development of operative habits. In short, the ordered acquisition of operative habits on all levels is precisely what is meant by saying that one is educated, for the educated person is one who has achieved that level of independence whereby he is able to carry out his hopes and legitimate aspirations, having acquired the ability to order things according to an inner plan, and of thus imposing his mind and will in some way on his world and his environment.

Thus, besides being the world's greatest knower and speaker, the human is also the world's greatest learner. Indeed, because of our unlimited ability to know as an intellective being, we have an unlimited ability to learn and are thus perpetually learning. Paradoxically, we can never completely achieve what we understand to be achievable, for we are limited both in terms of time and space and in the manner in which we must acquire the habits that lead to our mature development.

As the noted psychologist Jaime Castiello has written, education and the acquisition of habits are inseparable realities, so that the true definition of the authentically educated person is one who has achieved a harmonious development of all of his or her operative powers. As is clear, too, from what has preceded, the harmonious development of the operative powers only comes about through the acquisition and development of habits.

Unquestionably, all education is a highly personal achievement, since the acquisition of habits rests so completely on insight, understanding, and personal choice. No one ever *becomes* educated, if by that is meant that one *receives* an education in the literal sense. Ultimately, we must educate ourselves. Others may assist and encourage us, but each individual must perform the activities essential to the attainment of those operative habits needed for self-fulfillment and maturity.

In order to provide individuals with such assistance, the institution of the school was originally established. Any school's primary function should be to provide a learning atmosphere in a reasonably controlled environment, so that the individual student might pursue in an orderly and intelligent manner those intellective skills essential to his or her overall human development. The planned curriculum is the means by which learning can take place with a minimum of repetition. The student is encouraged to advance along the path of his or her own self-development and the most important task of the educational institution and its curriculum is to provide whatever assistance is required to aid the student to educate himself or herself.

The ability to self-educate is the true goal of a liberal education, which, as the term itself indicates, is a freeing or liberating form of education. The central aim of a liberal education, therefore, is the making available to the student the fundamental and essential abilities which human nature itself requires, if one is to progress to true human maturity. Thus, the liberally educated person is one who has learned how to learn, possessing the fundamental skills that are indispensable to all learning. This includes, surely, the ability to communicate effectively, both in writing and speaking, and the ability to think clearly, logically, and profoundly. It also entails an awareness of the nature of the human person. Toward this end philosophy, history, literature, art, and the sciences play a key role. That is why no one who is wholly ignorant of these areas can legitimately lay claim to being liberally educated.

Professional studies, which aim—and laudably so—at the acquisition of those special skills necessary for the achievement of particular and well-defined tasks, are complementary to, rather than antithetical to, the true goals of a liberal education. Therefore, they may not be substituted for the liberalizing dimensions of the humanities. Since they are not calculated to provide one with an overall vision or understanding of the nature and meaning of human life itself, they cannot of themselves constitute an authentic education. Though they provide us with the means of getting things done, they do not give us the slightest idea of what is worth doing. For this, professional studies need to be fully complemented by studies in the humanities.

As a discipline in its own right, philosophy aims at making a person more present to himself and thus more available to others. It seeks to accomplish this by uncovering for him the nature of his activities, abilities, and powers, particularly those of understanding, judging, and willing, which uniquely set him off from all other organisms. B. J. Lonergan has aptly termed this performance one of "self-appropriation."

Habits and Freedom

The question has often arisen as to whether or not the acquisition of habits does not diminish our freedom, for through habits we are predisposed to act in a certain way. Indeed this does seem to be a currently popular prejudice, but it is one which can be seen to have no actual basis in the authentic sense of habits.

Rather, if we learn to use our intellect, our freedom is enhanced, for the horizons of our free choice will have been greatly expanded. Knowledge, therefore, increases our freedom, for it enlarges our range of choices. Further, it refines the quality of the deliberative process, thereby enabling us to make better decisions, ones which will, in the long run at least, contribute toward our well-being. To accomplish this is to enhance our freedom, for it enables us to make good use of it.

On the other hand, a person with few developed habits is hemmed in, as it were, by the fences of everydayness and, much like a cork bobbing on the surface of the water, is mercilessly subjected to the moods and changes of an environment that is often alien to the human mind and will. One who is uneducated in this fundamental sense, therefore, is mired in a state of immobility, as he finds all complex tasks difficult and distasteful, since they require uncommon effort to realize. Without the acquisition of operational habits, our true freedom is, in fact, actually minimized. Without a panoply of habits, we engage in activities at the level of animals that lack creative dynamism, being condemned to the boredom of an endless series of repetitive acts.

It is of course true that habits predispose one to follow certain courses of behavior, but, since freedom itself has as its goal the charting of a determinate course leading toward fulfillment on the level of our *total* humanity, such a predisposition can be highly favorable to our freedom, for it facilitates the repetition of those very choices that inherently lead to the authentic development of the human person. Further, habits create an atmosphere conducive to the creative engendering of new, enriched choices and decisions, which only serve to accelerate the pace of development toward yet higher levels of maturity and human accomplishment both on the individual and the collective level.

Habits and Technology

A final word is in order regarding the relation between the development of operative skills in the human and the domain of technology. Technology simply means the "science of making"; that is, the *right way* of making things. As mentioned earlier, all forms of making consist in a transference of order and idea to the world of material things, thus imposing structure on the environing world. Let us hastily acknowledge that the animal is also capable of a *technological performance* in the broad sense of that term. Yet, we should also recognize that the animal does so without full consciousness of what it is doing; its activities are the result of a genetic encodement that rigidly controls and limits its specific tasks.

The structures imparted to the world by the human, however, are thoroughly human structures, in that they are the result of human ingenuity and insight; they are implemented through human choice. Thus, even that which the human employs as an instrument, is truly an incorporation of an idea in the physical world. As such, the tool or machine, which is truly nothing more than a sophisticated tool, is an extension of the human mind. The tool is in reality an extrinsic repository of human thought. Thus it is not surprising that through a study of what any human has confected, other humans may uncover the idea that was "breathed" into it; that is, come to understand what another human has done, and be capable of imitating and replicating that work.

These reflections permit us, then, to consider the tool as a form of habit that is extrinsic to the human subject. The tool extends and perfects our ability to act in innumerable ways, contributing to our overall operative dynamism and power. Through the deployment of tools and machines we are able to perform these diverse tasks with a minimum of effort and with a marvelous proficiency. As workers, in a truly profound sense we are not any better than the tools we employ; the tools are but an extension of our intellect and our body.

Summary

In this chapter we have considered the phenomenon of habits, finding them to be permanent operative qualities residing within the various powers, enabling us to perform specific operations with ease and proficiency.

Habits, are, therefore, a perfection of the power in which they reside, and they are distinct both from that power and from the operations to which the powers are ordered.

Further, we investigated the reasons behind the existence of habits in the human and found them to be the consequence of the human's intellective nature, whose operative horizon is open to the entire world of being. It is this openness that precludes the possibility of the human's activity being rigidly channelled and controlled by an inborn instinctual codification. Thus, although the habit performs a function in the human analogous to that of instincts in the animal, it is acquired only through the human's free interface with the world.

The division and classification of habits were next considered. Habits were first classified according to the different subjects in which they resided, and this provided the broad distinction between *cognoscitive* and *appetitive* habits. The cognoscitive habits were then further divided into *speculative* and *practical* and the major subdivisions of each of these were individually considered. Similarly the appetitive habits were divided into *volitional* and *sensory* and each of these was briefly studied.

We next considered the relation of habits to the education of the human, and to our deployment of freedom. This last consideration led us to a recognition of the tool and the machine as a kind of repository of human thought and insight, and thus as a form of extrinsic habit permitting the human a yet greater operational dynamism. It was noted that, far from diminishing human freedom, the acquisition of habits enhances our ability to choose well and adroitly.

Finally, with regard to education, it was seen that the educated person is precisely the one who has acquired those minimal and basic operational structures permitting him or her to act in a mature and fully humane manner. Toward accomplishing this end, the singular importance of habits commonly associated with a liberal education was underlined, for such an education aims not at preparing the student to perform specific tasks well, but rather at enabling him or her to fulfill the larger task of living as an authentic human being. It was noted in this regard that in education, philosophy plays a unique role in that it seeks, in the most fundamental manner possible, to assist a person to achieve an appropriation of his or her own inherent capabilities and powers by uncovering to them the infinite, unlimited horizon of human knowing and willing by which the human becomes not only the world's greatest knower and lover but also the world's greatest speaker and learner.

Definitions and Conclusions

1. Without the acquisition of operative skills the human cannot survive, let alone develop to full maturity.

2. The human, the most gifted and the most advanced of all mammals, begins life in a state of total dependency.

3. The human is characterized by a structural openness and extreme flexibility to adapt to the environment and, where necessary, to adapt the environment to human needs.

4. The human is condemned to learn precisely because the human is an intellective being. The radical openness to the world which our intellect grants us prevents our being preprogrammed instinctually after the manner of the animal.

5. A habit is distinct from the power that it actualizes and from the act toward which it is ordered.

6. A habit is an acquired operational structure that permits us to act in a certain way quickly, with comparative ease and proficiency.

7. Habits provide for the human a capacity similar to that which instincts provide for the animal.

8. Through the acquisition of habits we humans provide ourselves with our own behavioral programming.

9. The acquisition of habits is precisely what we mean by learning.

10. *Intellectus* is the speculative habit of first principles whereby the intellect understands whatever it understands.

11. *Science* is the speculative habit of intellect whereby it draws certain conclusions from knowledge already possessed.

12. *Wisdom* is a speculative habit of the intellect enabling us to judge things on the level of being.

13. *Art* is a practical habit of the intellect enabling one to judge correctly regarding things to be made.

14. *Prudence* is a practical habit of the intellect enabling one to judge correctly regarding actions to be performed.

15. *Justice* is a habit of the intellective appetite (the will) that facilitates its inclining toward the good of another.

16. *Temperance* is a habit of the concupiscible appetite which facilitates moderation in the pursuit of what is pleasurable.

17. *Fortitude* is a habit of the irascible appetite which facilitates the pursuit of what is useful but unpleasant and difficult.

18. The achieving of maturity and self-liberation is one with the acquisition and development of suitable operative habits.

19. The educated person is one who has achieved an ordered, harmonious union of habits at all the basic operative levels of human endeavor.

20. The tool, inasmuch as it is a repository of human ingenuity and design, is correctly viewed as an extended operative habit.

12 The Human Person

*Person signifies that which is the most perfect in
all of nature.*

St. Thomas Aquinas

The Human as an Individual

It has already been noted in the previous chapter that we refer to
people according to our knowledge of their abilities, or skills. For
example, we refer to someone as a musician; another as a painter;
another as a polyglot, on the basis that the first is able to play an instrument; the second, to paint a landscape; and the third, to speak
in several languages, each with notable ease and proficiency. Furthermore, it is not only when we witness someone in the performance of their skills that we apply the appropriate appellations, for
what we refer to is the person's *habit* or *ability*—a relatively permanent and stabilizing disposition by which one is able to perform in
a certain way.

Yet habits themselves are acquired, and although they qualify the
individual in a certain way, they do not constitute the individual.
Rather, habits are perfections of powers that predate the existence
of habits. Just as activities are actualizations of habits, so habits are
actualizations of powers. It is, then, the individual who performs the
activities, and it is the individual who is the recipient or subject of
the various habits which are acquired. It is not true to say that the
individual is *constituted* of habits and associated activities, but rath-

er that the individual is *in possession* of them. The activities and habits are ascribed to the individual, so we say that Gina sings; that Einstein is a mathematician, etc. Consequently, the individual is the ultimate subject of all acquired habits and activities. The latter does not possess the individual; rather the individual possesses them; that is, we are perfected and qualified by the activities and habits we possess, but we are not constituted an individual by them.

The Human as a Person

The human individual differs from other individual things— whether they be animal, plant, or inorganic matter—on the basis of human intellective and volitional activities, which permit us to reflect in consciousness upon our individual selves and our own activities, and to become aware of them as activities. We humans sense as the animal does, but we humans also understand and are reflectively conscious of our own sensing. Not only do we control our own behavior through choice and decision, but we are aware of this control and give witness to this awareness when we indicate *why* we act as we do.

The human individual is designated, therefore, by a special term that is exclusively applicable to the human individual and to none other. Among all beings directly experienced through sensation, only humans are honored with the term *person*. A special dignity attaches to this term, for it is reserved to those individuals who, possessed of an intellective and volitional nature, are consequently conscious not only of their own activities but also of themselves as individuals. Only a person knows who he or she is, for only a person is capable of the complete reflective act whereby the nature and source of the act itself is present in consciousness to the one knowing. Only the human is able to trace its activity back through reflection to its very ground, to the subject from which the activity originates and in which it inheres.

It is through this dual self-consciousness, whereby we humans are aware both of our individuality and of our being the ultimate subject of the act of our understanding and willing that the notion of the *I* emerges. The use of the word *I* (or its equivalent) which every conscious human employs to identify the self as the ultimate ground of individual activity, is in and of itself an infallible sign of our self-consciousness.

As an identity sign of the individual, therefore, the word *I* designates the ultimate subject of all of our activities and habits. The *I* says, "I did this," and "I did that," etc., because all of our activities belong to it and are rightfully its possession. *I* refers to the self that is permanent. Activities come and go; habits are acquired, but the *I* does not exist one moment and cease to exist the next; nor does the *I* grow and develop as do habits; for were there no ultimate subject, there could be neither activities nor habits. Note, then, that the *I* is not a mere flowing stream of consciousness; it is not a mere series of activities, nor is it the full spectrum of learned habits. Rather it is the underlying reality to which all activities and habits are attributable.

Since the *I*, therefore, refers to the invariant and stable structure of the individual, it does not of itself change. This permanency of the *I*, or conscious subject, permits the individual person to claim identity not only between itself and the activity that it may presently be performing but also between itself and activities that may have been performed in the past or may be performed in the future. The *I*, then, grounds the continuity between the present and the past and makes it possible for one to say, "I did such and such a year ago," and also permits one to say, "I am the same person today as I was ten or twenty years ago." Further, it is the underlying reality of personhood that permits one to speak of the future and to say, "I plan to do this," or "I intend to go there." Only the perduring subject to whom the actions belong (but who does not belong to the actions) renders comprehensible the phenomenon of experience itself. It is the person who experiences, not the activity.

Personhood and Personality

From what has been said, then, it should be clear that the *I* transcends the ordinary events of time and space. In a sense, it preceded the present, and even made the present itself a possibility. Further, the *I* is that which survives the past. It is the enduring reality that is the center and source of personal progress. It is the ultimate ground of all activities and habits. It is this *I* that we refer to as *the person*. We may note, then, that *I* is not directly perceivable; rather, it is merely capable of being understood, for it itself is inherently self-reflective and self-conscious. The self-consciousness of the *I* is only made possible through its self-presence, and self-presence is the result of its spiritual intellective nature. The animal is not self-present to itself simply because it is not intellective and thus does not know *who* it is. Consequently it cannot think in the idiom of the *I* as all humans do.

The elusive and impalpable structure of the *I* is connoted by the very word *person* itself. Derived from the Latin, person is composed of two words, *sonare*, which means "to give a sound," and *per*, which means "through." Thus, etymologically, a person is one who "sounds or speaks through." The reference here is to the Greek and Roman theater, where the *personae* spoke through masks, which served to hide or disguise the actor's own identity so that the player's assigned part, represented by the mask, might be played with greater realism. Though the performer's voice spoke through an aperture in the mask, the inner character of the performer remained hidden. Similarly, through language the inner person, or *I* is unveiled; but it is unveiled incompletely and indirectly, for the language itself is merely a symbolic expression of the *I* it refers to.

It is important that one recognize the twofold meaning of the word *I*, for we employ it not only to refer to the basic structure of the individual, which underlies all activity and is properly the *I* of the person, but also to refer to those permanent acquisitions which are the result of all levels of human activity. This second meaning of *I*, commonly used in everyday speech, is the *I* of *personality*. This personality-I refers not to the invariant structure of personhood but to the growth and development aspect of a person. It does not answer the question, "What are you?" for you are a human being, but rather "Who are you? What kind of a human being are you?" The I-of-personality refers to the special kind of human being one is; the I-of-personhood is the ultimate reality controlling the kind of being the human person is. The *I-of-personhood* is only indirectly conscious, but the *I-of-personality* is conscious at least in part since it is composed of the totality of the individual person's experiences.

The I-of-personhood is the ground and foundation of one's personality, which is the acquired possession of the person. We reflect this important, fundamental distinction, when we make such comments as, "I see," "I am thinking," "I am a musician," for in such statements we are acknowledging that the person is the ultimate subject of all activity of the individual as well as the ground of every attribution made regarding it. A person possesses a personality but nothing possesses a person. Personhood, therefore, is something all individual humans share in common, but persons differ markedly from one another in the expression of personality. The importance of the distinction between person and personality is profound and far-reaching, and it is often through the obscuring of this distinction that some contemporary philosophers and psychologists have been led to support utterly incompatible claims regarding the human person.

We attach a profound dignity to the term *person* because, as suggested above, we perceive in the human an activity center that transcends the world of sensible things. Possessed of an intellective and volitional nature, we humans, in a sense, float free from the world in which we are immersed. Though we make use of the physical world that environs us and depend upon it as the source of our knowledge, we remain nonetheless fundamentally unencumbered by it and are free to control the quality and direction of our own activity.

As an intellective being, then, the human person is open to *being*; that is, to all that is, and it is precisely this openness that sets the human apart from all other material beings. Because of this special orientation toward being, we acknowledge the human's unique worth and dignity. Through intellective knowledge and love, the human person is a dynamic center for union with all that is. As a consequence of our root capacity to become one with whatever is, we humans cannot be claimed as an object or as a possession and can never become a part of something else. Thus, though open to everything, we humans belong to nothing; while capable of communicating with all things, we can never relinquish this radical quality of communicability itself. In the profoundest recesses of our own personhood we humans remain incommunicable.

One *is* a person, but one can only be said to *have* a personality, since the latter is an acquisition of the person. Personality is constituted by what one *does*; it is the *product* of one's free activity. The basic reality behind personality is *habit*; not this or that habit, but the integrated and harmonized union of all of one's consciously acquired habits. Personality can be likened to an operational residue of past activity, melded into a dynamic unity which provides a semi-permanent base for activities of all kinds. In this sense personality depends upon what one has done in the past, although its inner shape does not emerge automatically from the mere raw collectivity of individual actions, but is molded by the more basic free decisions. The power of these decisions hierarchically organizes the welter of human experiences and confers on them purpose and direction.

One's personality, then, is the entire network of habits that one has purposefully acquired. This points up the fact of the uniqueness of each personality, for each personality is forged, as it were, in the furnace of the responsible free act, by which each person responds and reacts to situations in his or her own way. It is freedom that is the root cause of the discrepancies between personalities, which are individually constituted of a unique, integrated totality of consciously acquired habits.

In consequence of the above and as a corollary to our previous discussion on human freedom, the personality may be viewed as a kind of *second nature*, consciously and freely acquired by the individual person. It is not a product of hereditary and environmental factors, obtained mechanistically; although heredity and environment do play an important role in personality development. Similarly, one's racial, cultural, and educational backgrounds function as significant influences on the kinds of decisions one will make, but they do not *determine* these decisions, nor is their influence ultimately decisive. The crucial determinative factor in the development of one's personality is ultimately the individual person *per se*. We are, in short, precisely who we *wanted* to be.

In concluding this section on the concepts of person and personality, it should be pointed out that, while personality is the end product of the individual's use of freedom, not all decisions play an equally important role in the shaping of a personality. It is the more broadly based and far-reaching decisions that bear this responsibility. Such decisions may be termed *master decisions*, since numerous other decisions are subordinated to them and cluster about them for both continuity and support. Examples of such master decisions are: to enter college; to marry; to pursue a particular profession; to devote a portion of one's life to aiding the disadvantaged. If we wish to understand the true nature of anyone's personality, preferably we should direct our attention to such master decisions, for they best unveil the true scope and purpose according to which a person has used and is using their freedom.

Consequences of the Distinction between Personhood and Personality

Owing to the distinction between personhood and personality discussed in the previous section, we are able to speak of inalienable human rights. These rights are clearly not dependent upon the nature of one's personality; if they were, they could not possibly be universal rights. Rather, these basic rights, or freedoms, rest securely on the intellective and volitional nature of the human person. Since one is a person because of what he or she *is* and not because of what he or she *has done*, and since these rights derive from one's personhood itself, they are unqualifiedly universal in application. The consequences of this for moral as well as for social and political philosophy are abundantly clear. Unless the term *person* as such is inseparably united with the individual human, human dignity cannot be viewed as an inalienable quality, which means that we could not claim any inalienable rights for ourselves. If the special dignity commonly attached to the human person were merely a derivative of one's personality, it is plain that all laws would, by definition, become a matter of arbitrariness and caprice, subject to the whimsical manipulation of unscrupulous lawmakers.

Historically, the failure to recognize the all-important distinction between personhood and personality has led to a frequent justification of slavery, of caste systems within society and, today, to the legal toleration of abortion. In all instances these institutional practices are defended on the grounds that certain individuals are, or are not to be, recognized as authentic human persons who are possessed of certain inalienable rights.

Knowing Other Persons

So far we have discussed the notion of personhood, its relation to personality, as well as the singular import of this distinction. We now turn our attention to an intriguing and difficult—though seemingly easy—question, which stems directly from what has already been said about the nature of the human person. Namely, we now address ourselves to the manner in which one person comes to have knowledge of the personhood of another; how, in short, do we know that there are persons other than ourselves?

It might seem, superficially at least, that this is a pseudo problem, since it is obvious that other persons do exist. But we are not actually calling the fact of the existence of other human persons into question. What we are inquiring into is simply the manner in which we *know* that there are other humans. What we have previously said about the nature of personhood is precisely what makes the knowledge of other persons a subtle and interesting problem. It is clear that the question is not sufficiently answered by replying that we know that there are other persons because we can *see* them, because we have already discussed how one's personhood is not a tangible or sensible quality. It is, rather, the underlying structure of an intellective being; as such, personhood transcends the sensory act and cannot be reached by it. This problem of the knowledge of the existence of humans other than ourselves is one that has received considerable attention by certain contemporary phenomenologists, who often refer to it as the *problem of intersubjectivity.*

It is clear that the unique avenue of approach whereby we can come to know that other humans exist is through our being able to identify in them exclusively human activities that we ourselves possess; namely, understanding and willing. I can fully recognize that an individual is a human person only if I grasp that an individual is, like me, a center of activity that radically transcends the world of physical reality. Yet, since powers and abilities are known only in their acts, I can know that another has the ability to understand only if I actually experience that other in an act of understanding.

Understanding That Another Understands: A Phenomenology of "Yes"

How does one person come to the realization that another person is actually understanding? One might at first reply that we can tell when another understands by some facial expression. Yet this is ultimately to no avail, since it is only through a relatively extended experience that we first learn how to "read" the expression of another. Only after we have come to associate a certain facial expression with intelligence (understanding) can we justly surmise that such an expression is a sign of intelligence. But this does not explain the association in the first place and, hence, from the philosophical standpoint, cannot provide us with the answer we seek.

Since the intellective act is internal and of itself is not directly sensible, it is only through the medium of signs that I am able to come to an awareness of the reality of someone else's actual understanding. Since all knowledge begins with the senses, I am capable of detecting understanding in another only if that person is able to communicate to me his or her act of understanding through symbol. This can be accomplished either through language or through the performance of an activity that clearly manifests intelligence, by which I am able to grasp that there exists another intelligent subject like myself who is able to understand and to incorporate his or her understanding into our physical world. Because of this incorporation, I judge that subject to be intelligent.

I am able to understand that another understands if the other first gives expression to thought in the physical, symbolic expression of language. Then I in turn must hear (presuming a spoken language) what has been said, and I must understand the meaning of the words. If indeed I do understand, we may then note that, though there are two individuals understanding, there is but one act of understanding, inasmuch as both of us understand the same thing. Numerically, there are two acts of understanding, but in terms of content there is but one.

At this point, then, I am able to say, "I understand what you understand," only because the acts of two individuals have been melded together into one act of understanding—we both understand the same thing; we both have had a similar insight. In this manner two separate knowing subjects are brought together into an intimate, interior union of understanding, and that union is given its linguistic expression through the word *yes* or its equivalent. *Yes* symbolizes the unity of understanding between two or more knowing subjects and indicates at the same time the self-transcending nature of understanding. That is, *yes* clearly manifests that the union taking place between the two knowers is a union and identification with something that is not themselves; namely, the *content* of their several acts of understanding, which reflects the object that is known.

In this manner, then, yes involves a candid admission on the part of the one uttering it that knowledge is not a wholly private matter, even though it takes place within the inner realm of one's own person. Intellective knowledge is always *de se*; it is, of itself, a public act that is inherently shareable with other persons. We refer here, of course, only to intellective acts that can be responded to with a yes, for there are indeed certain acts of inner awareness that cannot be shared in this manner simply because their evidence is noncommunicable. Thus, should one say that he or she has a headache, it would be pointless for anyone to respond by saying yes.

Through the expression of *yes*, then, we signify that a mutual act of understanding takes place between at least two knowing subjects, and it is in this way that we come to the deepest possible realization of the existence of other humans besides ourselves. It is the intellective act of the human that sets him apart from all other sensing organisms, and it is thus through understanding that another understands that I am most fully aware of that which actually manifests and constitutes him or her a person.

The above reflections reinforce much of what was said earlier in the chapter on language and communication. Since thought and understanding are immaterial operations, there is no way that I can come to know what the other person understands, nor is he able to understand what I understand, unless each of us has recourse to the phenomenon of a shared language. Through language our thought is reintroduced into the material world of symbol and then disengaged once again from those symbolic conditions, as the understanding present in one mind is communicated to the mind of the other.

Toward a Phenomenology of "No"

What has been said above about our employment of the word *yes* applies equally to the word *no* with one significant difference—the word no denies that an act of understanding has taken place. If to a factual statement (and this qualification is important) another replies no, the no-sayer is saying far more than merely denying that they have understood what was said, or even indeed that they simply do not agree with what was said. What the no actually implies is, "I am unable to understand what you said because what you said was not understandable." Such a reply implies that the person making the statement could not have understood what they claimed to have understood; that they have used language fraudulently by maintaining that they understood something, which, in fact, they did not.

To illustrate the foregoing, it may be helpful to take a simple arithmetical example. Let us suppose that a child says to you, "Seven times seven is seventy-seven." Knowing the rudiments of arithmetic, you know that what the child has uttered is simply false. You immediately understand that the child could not possibly have *understood* that seven sevens are equal to the number of seventy-seven, unless it were actually the case. Indeed, whenever anyone makes such an incorrect assertion, ourselves included, it is usually a simple enough matter for someone else to call to their attention the error they have made and why what they have said is incorrect. Once the person in error recognizes the error, they are aware that it is indeed true that beforehand they had no authentic understanding of what they had earlier claimed to have known. They can then doubtless discover some flaw or oversight in their thinking and recognize that somehow in their haste they glossed over a point in their reflections that merited further scrutiny.

It is important to emphasize that the preceding analysis concerns itself exclusively with factual statements. We have scrupulously excluded from these reflections any statements that inquire into the area of one's wants or desires, feeling states, mere opinions, or statements that deal with the future. In such instances no firm claim is made by the one uttering them that they are actually grounded in an act of understanding, and hence the preceding analysis would be inapplicable without the addition of the appropriate nuances.

For example, if someone should say, "It will probably snow tomorrow," they are not claiming that it is absolutely certain that it will snow. Hence, a yes or no response would, within this limited context, not mean you are right or you are wrong, but merely I believe that you are right or I believe that you are mistaken. In a similar vein, should someone remark that they feel chilled, it would make no sense for me to reply, "I agree. You are right." Or, "No, that is not true." In these instances we lack a *common* experience, without which we cannot enter into one act of understanding.

As explained in the discussion of habits, any product or artifact resulting from some form of human endeavor is an extension of the human mind and can be considered an extrinsic habit. Also it was noted in the discussion of language that a tool or machine or anything that is fabricated by the human is in truth a form of language, for it reveals that an act of understanding has taken place.

According to Aristotle, it is the function of human intelligence to order and organize things; to insert intellective vision in the world of sensible objects. It is likewise our ability to detect intellective activity in the world that makes it possible, in a restricted way at least, for us to become one with it by understanding what others both intended and achieved. This form of union of one mind with another does not require the actual presence of the maker. In our recognition of an Indian arrowhead, a Cretian mixing bowl, an Egyptian hieroglyph, the ruins of an ancient Assyrian city, a pagan temple, an ancient burial ground, we share, however imperfectly, in the intellective workings of the minds of individuals who at some time in the past planned and made these things. If we happen upon a circle of small stones rimming a deposit of wood ash or encounter a foot bridge spanning a small creek, we immediately conclude that these were the works of other humans and can guess at their significance. A trace of intellective activity has been left behind enabling us to reconstruct the human acts of understanding and to become one with those we have not met.

Such indirect recognition of other minds genuinely serves to constitute a union of minds and to form a human community that spans centuries. To understand that an object is a human artifact is to recognize that it is a product of human intelligence. This means that we can understand what someone strove to achieve because we are capable of sharing their intelligence.

The Human Person and the Community

The earlier discussions relating to the uses of yes and no serve to bring out the communitarian dimension of the human person. As a subject open to the world of being, the person is capable of entering into intimate union with others in a manner wholly denied to the brute animal. We have already dwelt upon this community inasmuch as it is grounded in a shared act of understanding. We ought not to omit mentioning, however, that such community also includes the act of willing, which involves the higher community that the human is capable of as a person—the community of love. For love is, in its fullest sense, the union of two wills in a common act of willing. This is accomplished, just as in the case of understanding, when the wills of two or more incline to and accept as their good, or value, one and the same object. Stated most succinctly, therefore, love is a *union of wills*. Persons are brought into union by willing the same object, which again, as in the case of understanding, cannot be initially identified with either will; otherwise it could not be shared by both. Consequently, love in the authentic sense is always self-transcending.

This dimension of the self-transcendence of love is clearly shown by a simple reflection on any act of agreement whereby two or more persons accept a common value as their own. Thus, when one person makes a proposal or a suggestion that a certain decision be made or a specific project be pursued together, the second party announces his or her acceptance by some such expression as "I agree." The agreement clearly concerns a value that both parties understand as worthwhile and that both freely accept as their own; it is a value that is distinct from either of the two parties willing it. It may readily be recognized that such is the nature of all agreements, whether of a very personal or of a purely business nature. Thus contracts on all levels are, if honestly and authentically entered into, expressions of an interior union of wills regarding some good, or value, to be accomplished mutually by some designated means.

In opening out to the world through understanding and willing, the human person is a social being par excellence. No other creature excels the human in the capacity for community, so that we come to grasp at length that the *I* of the person-subject always remains incomplete if left to itself and can find fulfillment only within the community of other persons. This means, in effect, that the human *I* cannot stand alone in isolation but is oriented toward other consciousnesses—other *I*s. An *I* that is not oneself is a *thou*, or *you*, viewed as distinct from oneself. Yet in the union with another, in the agreement of wills, there is a melding of *I*s. These melded *I*s then become *We*. (These notions have been developed at great length by two prominent twentieth-century philosophers, Martin Buber and Alfred Schütz.)

The social nature of the human is grounded on the "other-orientedness" of the human person, and all succeeding levels of society are but a natural development of this inherent capacity and longing for association with others, not merely on the physical and biological plane but also on the intellective and volitional plane. The human person's radical openness to whatever *is* makes him the most authentically social of all animals, for as a person he is open to the higher community of the mind and the spirit, of understanding and of love.

The Human Person and Loneliness

Without wishing to minimize in any way the communitarian dimension of the human person, but indeed rather to exploit its richness and further bring into focus the special quality of intersubjective union, we turn briefly to a consideration of the human phenomenon of loneliness. Loneliness is an emotion that is poignantly experienced by all at almost all periods of their lives; it is a stranger to none. Much, of course, has been written on this topic from the psychological standpoint. What we wish to do here is reflect philosophically on the loneliness phenomenon in the human and to seek to coordinate our experience of it within the paradoxical context of our social nature.

We have just explored, however briefly, the human person's inherent thrust and leaning toward community. In seeking to emphasize this extremely valid dimension of the human person and of human personality, we naturally concentrated our attention on its positive aspects. But if we turn our attention to the experience of loneliness, we are forced to recognize the imperfect and deficient manner by which human persons are able to reach a state of union one with another.

Although we humans can express ourselves in language and come to an understanding of other persons and enter into agreement with them, what was earlier said concerning human language must be borne in mind here. The sensibly symbolic expression of thought that constitutes language can never adequately present the full sweep and depth of the thought of the mind. As a consequence, the individual human person never quite succeeds in expressing himself or herself adequately, and hence is at length forced to acknowledge that much of what constitutes their inner life and spirit must ever remain locked within.

In this sense, each human is "condemned" to live his or her life alone, for one has neither the ability nor the time to uncover the full riches of one's personal experiences to the outside world, eager as it might be to receive them. Indeed, it is even true that one remains in some sense a stranger to oneself, for not all that one experiences can be either adequately articulated or carefully integrated into a coherent whole. One is aware of mere partial understandings and graspings of one's thoughts and motivations, of one's volitions and decisions.

To render matters worse, one is forever haunted by the gnawing action of forgetfulness, which continually threatens to consume the substance of one's experience. One is thus left quite alone with one's past and with the awareness that much of that is now forgotten. This general or cosmic forgetfulness tends indeed to isolate oneself from one's very self. It is to protect oneself against a total internal collapse of conscience that one seeks out a world, or a philosophic, view. This sense of estrangement and loneliness is further fed by the fact that the human person is open to the vastness of being itself. Perfectly aware that we humans are questioners, that we always need to know more, and that we can never truly exhaust the capabilities our own nature has provided us with, we cannot help experiencing a certain feeling of emptiness. Estranged from the being that we require if we are to uncover and unveil ourselves to ourselves, the human inescapably feels nostalgic and alone.

As suggested earlier in the discussion of habits and learning, the human is, as the world's greatest learner, continually in search of further knowledge in a quest for the true human self. All of the perennial themes of literature, music, and the visual arts; all building and making, are an expression of our human search for our lost horizon, the full meaning of our lives. The German philosopher Martin Heidegger suggests that the loneliness we experience is first made possible by a primordially antecedent togetherness.

Our loneliness also derives from the fact of our sexual differentiation, according to the Russian existentialist philosopher Nicholas Berdyaev. The sexual division between the male and the female means that *biologically* neither the woman nor the man is completely human. Rather, each depends upon the other for the achievement of biological fullness. Just as no individual human can claim, "I am humanity," so no individual man or woman can say, "I am biologically fully human," for each of us lacks the perfection and capabilities of those individual humans of the other sex.

This biological incompleteness serves to promote and enhance our awareness of solitude, for it brings to the surface in a very tangible way a sense of our cosmic dependency and finitude. It seems, then, as Berdyaev has argued, that sexual differentiation is a fertile source of the human experience of aloneness and estrangement, which, though it can be modified and assuaged by union, can never be wholly overcome.

As human persons, we are oriented toward being and, indeed, are the very house of being. Paradoxically, however, we are simultaneously very close to being and far removed from it. That is why only humans experience a profound sense of loneliness, an estrangement from a total self; for only we possess a consciousness of our inner self and reflectively can know who we are. Only we humans know that our full self lies beyond us; in every act of willing and knowing, we experience, however obliquely, our own self-transcendence. The early Greek philosophers, who realized these singularly profound depths of humankind, encourage us to turn our gaze within."O Man, know thyself!"

Yet we humans ever remain our own transcendental mystery. No creature is more present to self than we are, but none is further removed from self than we are. We alone speak the language of being; consequently, we alone are capable of recognizing the distance that lies between what we are and what we might be. Thus despite our multitudinous and complex relations with the physical world and with the beings that populate it (including other persons), we remain the *social solitary.* We borrow this felicitous expression of Professor Jacob Bronowski's even though he intended it to have perhaps a different connotation. Even in the midst of what the poet Thomas Gray called "the madding crowd," we remain ever alone.

Self-Knowledge and Ethics

Before concluding this chapter on the study of the human person, it may prove helpful to point out the connection between what has been said regarding the nature of the human person and how this can be applied to the study of ethics. Since ethics is a special branch of philosophy and is thus treated separately in another course, it will suffice here to confine our remarks to the bare essentials, indicating merely the continuity obtaining between our self-knowledge and the meaning of our human responsibility.

We have already seen how the human person is a singularly self-conscious being. We humans are authentically and really present to ourselves reflectively within the dynamism of our own activity. This self-presence, which is also a conscious presence, enables us to analyze and study the nature of our act of understanding and willing, thus, to understand our own free activity. Consequently, the human stands in a position to calculate both the direction and the effects of that activity and behavior. In short, we human persons can know *what* it is we are doing and *why.*

Through this remarkable ability of reflective consciousness, which no other animal possesses, the human is permitted to raise questions regarding that very activity, to scrutinize its nature, and to search out its ground. All of this is, of course, a corollary to our self-knowledge.

The Human Person and Religion

The considerations of these last sections on loneliness and the ethical dimension of human life bring us perhaps as far as the human mind is able to venture on its own. Indeed, the history of human thought seems in many ways to be little more than an open acknowledgment of such. Thus, it would seem that, at the very moment it reaches its own zenith, philosophy leaves us with an opening into which the religious dimension of human inquiry may enter. History does seem to teach us that only through religion have the highest human aspirations and the profoundest hopes been realized. As much of contemporary philosophy dramatically illustrates, philosophy—left to its own devices—can do little more than lead its devotees to the edge of sadness. It seems incapable of offering a total solution to the profound paradox in the human condition. Often it seems capable only of proclaiming the absurdity of life, of asking finally the eternal, tormenting question *Why?* This seems to approximate the state of mind St. Augustine was in when he struggled to understand the meaning of his life. In the sixth book of his *Confessions* he writes:

> Hope of mine from my youth, where were you and where had you gone from me? Was it not you who had created me and distinguished me from the beasts of the field and made me wiser than the birds of the air? Yet I walked through shadows and on slippery ways, and I searched for you outside me and did not find the God of my heart. I had come to the depths of the sea, and I had no confidence or hope of discovering the truth.

Summary

In this chapter we have considered the human person. We have discussed in what personhood consists, how it is related to personality, and how we know other persons. In reflecting on the complex problems of intersubjective communication, we gave special attention to: the human as a social being who seeks union with others in a free sharing of values; the meaning of the "yes" of agreement; the meaning of the "no" of disagreement. In the final sections we explored the phenomenon of human loneliness and solitariness, seeking to divine its nature and its causes. We discussed the human person as a being who is self-present, and we sought to show how such self-presence constitutes the ground of ethical theory. Lastly, we touched briefly on the relation between philosophy and religion.

Definitions and Conclusions

1. The individual is the ultimate subject of all activities and habits and the ground of all positive attributions.

2. *I* is used in two distinct but related ways. It can refer either to the person or to the person's personality.

3. The I-of-personhood refers to the invariant underlying reality of the individual.

4. The I-of-personality refers to the manifold of acquired behavioral characteristics of the individual person.

5. A person differs from things in that the person is radically open to the full sweep of being.

6. One *is* a person but *has* a personality.

7. Personality is similar to a second nature, yet is consciously and freely acquired by the individual person.

8. The distinction between personhood and personality is essential to a consistent defense of the inherent dignity of the human and the grounding of inalienable human rights.

9. I come to an awareness of the existence of another human being by experiencing that person actually understanding.

10. Interpersonal communication is always mediated by language.

11. "Yes" indicates that two or more persons are united in one act of understanding.

12. Intellective knowledge is self-transcending; since it can be shared, it is by nature public.

13. "No" is a denial that another person has understood what he has claimed to understand.

14. Love is a union of wills in one act of willing. Although there are two (or more) willings, there is but one willed.

15. Because of the limitations of linguistic expression, the individual can never adequately communicate his or her inner world to others.

16. We humans are social by nature because we are intellective beings.

17. Precisely because we are intelligent, we experience loneliness, for we can reflectively recognize that there is more for us to know and to achieve.

18. The differentiation of the sexes among humans contributes to the individual human's experience of loneliness and isolation, since, biologically, neither the man nor the woman is fully human.

19. The human being is a moral being because the human is capable of calculating the relationship of human behavior to itself, to others, and to the world.

20. Ethics is the study of human voluntary behavior inasmuch as it is voluntary and to the extent that it is right or wrong.

13 The Human as a Living Being

All men are philosophers, because in one way or other all take up an attitude toward life and death.

Karl R. Popper

What Is Life?

Since the human is clearly a living being, an investigation of the meaning of life is in order. Precisely what do we mean when we say that something is living, and what is it that is responsible for life within living beings. These questions are, of course, raised by biologists and other students of the life sciences, but they are at bottom philosophical questions and cannot be adequately considered by the experimental sciences alone. What is needed in addition are the grounds for a philosophy of biology.

Following the method of Aristotle, let us begin our investigation by attempting to isolate from our everyday experience those elements commonly associated with the phenomenon of life. To begin with, clearly there are things that we recognize as being alive and others that we recognize as being nonliving. What, then, makes the difference?

Surely the most prominent characteristic of living things is that they are capable of motion; that is, they are able to move about. The motion in question is, of course, a kind of self-motion. Fallen leaves blown about by the wind are not considered to be alive, for the motion observed in them is accounted for by their environment. The leaves are more properly said *to be moved* than to move, since they do not move themselves. We do not say that something is living simply because it is in motion; its motion must be centered within the living thing itself. Thus animals are said to be living because the animal itself is the source of the motion we observe in it. The bird we see flying is said to be a living thing because it provides the power for, and controls the direction of, its flight. Spacial motion originating from a moving subject provides the most obvious sign of life. This is not to say that every living thing possesses locomotion, but that everything with the capability of spacial self-movement is alive.

When one speaks of the living waters of a stream or the voices of the wind or the rhythmic dance of the waves upon the shore, one is speaking metaphorically. The waters and the wind are not considered to be alive since their motion is explainable purely in terms of the physical laws of nature. Many physical things can display movement of some kind, but only those capable of moving themselves can be said to be living. There are, however, other life-indicators besides that of self-induced spacial motion.

Growth, repair, and reproduction or self-replication are also incontrovertible signs of life that provide the biologist with basic criteria for differentiating between the living and the nonliving. Growth is an activity whereby the living thing moves itself toward a state of physical perfection or maturity. Although the growth of an organism is not possible without the taking in of food, the process of growth is orchestrated wholly from within, regardless of what it takes in as its food. Hence two entirely different organisms will convert identical food, each through its own metabolic process, into its own particular living tissue and substance.

The growth process of living things is easily distinguishable from other natural phenomena that superficially appear to involve a kind of growth. Crystals, icicles, and stalactites might seem to grow, but the increase in their size results not from metabolic change but from accretion. The genuine growth process, by contrast, is truly an activity of self-motion, for the living thing provides its own dynamism and the direction for the development that takes place within it.

In repairing itself an organism performs a vital act as well. A broken tool or machine is incapable of restoring or repairing the broken part, while a pruned bush or shrub will quickly replace the parts excised. This restorative act is a vital one, since its goal is to restore to integrity the very subject of which it is an act. The shrub or bush moves itself toward this activity; it acts but is not acted upon.

What has been said about growth (self-movement in process) and repair (self-movement in equilibrium) can also be said about the reproduction process, for an organism produces the genes that render possible its replicating its own species.

In addition to local motion, growth, and reproduction, as manifestations of self-movement, we can also add the activities originating within the being itself. While both the sensory and the intellective powers are dependent upon the reception of a sensible and intelligible form respectively in order that they may move from a state of "can see" and "can understand" to actual seeing and actual understanding, these activities are, all the same, truly life-acts, for through them a kind of growth does take place.

We may note, then, that the term *life* can be used to refer to three main categories of action, each of which can be considered as analogous to the other two. These acts reflect three levels of activity: the vegetative which includes growth, repair, and reproduction; the sensory which includes the acts of the special and internal senses, and the intellective which includes understanding, judging, reasoning, willing, and choosing. Plants exist at the vegetative level and animals exist at both the vegetative and sensory levels. Only the human exists at all three levels of activity, for the human is capable not only of vegetative activities similar to those of the plants, and of sensory activities similar to those of the animals but also of a uniquely human intellective activity as well.

Each level of activity involves some kind of change for the living organism; but no such change is total change. Through any growth the living organism becomes somehow different from what it was, but it retains its underlying identity. It is still the same individual thing it was before the growth took place. Were this not the case, we could not speak of it as having grown since it would be totally different from what it was previously. In short, a living thing, through its varied growth activities, undergoes change, but at the same time, it continues to be substantially the same living thing.

The above definition of living things as self-moving is a suitable one because it is applicable to all those things we ordinarily consider to be living, and it accords as well with the more recent advances in the life sciences. For example, the eminent English zoologist W. H. Thorpe states: "Living organisms can be defined with much cogency as self-reproducing and self-programming systems which store and organize information." (Ayala and Dobzhansky, 1974, p.118) These self-reproducing and self-programming systems are self-movement activities.

The Unity of Living Things

The convergence of the activities of living things toward the support and development of the total organism is a natural phenomenon which never ceases to elicit wonder in one contemplating it. Within the past few decades, developments in genetics and microbiology alone have led us to the realization of undreamt-of complexities existing within the living organism. For example, it is now known that there are approximately 100 trillion cells within the human body, and each of the cells, far from being a simple organism, has been likened to a highly organized society within a walled city. Each cell contains "factories" for the manufacture of proteins and amino acids, a highly complex communications system, and molecules that act as sentries by monitoring the cells' "outside world," supervising the importation of needed chemicals into the cell. In addition, a disciplined biological "militia" stands ready to fend off invaders; within the cellular city, order is maintained by a highly centralized government.

While the human cell and its organelles, or interior parts, still contain many unlocked secrets, more and more of its wondrous activity is being brought to light. The master blueprint within each cell which strictly monitors and governs its activities is the recently discovered deoxyribonucleic acid, more popularly known as the DNA molecule. The complexity of this molecule alone is of truly staggering proportions. Its complex architecture was discovered by Crick and Watson in 1953 and since that time the progress made in the area of microbiology has been nothing less than breathtaking.

Crick and Watson established that the DNA molecule, the master molecule of life, has the shape of a double helix like two twisted threads. This single molecule, and it is but one of 200 trillion others in the human cell, is composed of 46 chromosomes which in turn contain as many as 100,000 human genes, or genetic bits of information. The DNA molecule, present in each of the 100 trillion cells in the adult human body, contains the code or program by which myriad cellular activities are channelled and directed. It contains the code, for example, that permits the manufacture of some seven million different proteins within the cell. The protein in turn is made up of organic chemicals called amino acids, which are essential to human life. According to John Maddox, "intact protein molecules may contain from ten to several thousand amino acids." (Maddox, 1964, p. 58)

The DNA molecule controls the function of the ribosomes, which are protein-building factories with which the cell manufactures new parts and replicates itself. It directs the work of the lysosomes, bags of digestive juices which recycle food into particles for the cell to utilize for its own growth. It controls the traffic of the golgi, mobile pouches which export proteins from the ribosomes to the membrane. It oversees the sentry duty of the membrane which walls off the cell and regulates what enters and what leaves the cell. It regulates the operation of the mitochondria, the sausage-shaped bodies responsible for the manufacture of chemicals providing the cell with its energy. It monitors the messages sent by the microtubules, the long hollow girder-like tubes which give the cell its shape and send signals from the membrane to the nucleus. In regulating these functions and more, the DNA molecule is responsible for how the two million molecules of adenosine triphosphate (ATP), which the cell consumes each second, are utilized.

Compared with what we knew of the cellular activity only a few decades ago, the present state of our knowledge is spectacularly advanced. Yet there is so much more for us to know. As Nobel laureate Christian de Duve of Rockefeller University stated recently, "What we have today is a description of what happens in the cell, not an understanding of how it happens." (*Newsweek,* Aug. 20, 1979. "The Secrets of the Human Cell.") In the same vein the philosopher-biologist Ludwig von Bertalanffy once said that "we presently know the vocabulary of the genetic code, the triplets standing for amino acids; but we do not know its grammar, the meaning of the message as a whole." (Koestler and Smythies, 1969, p. 70.)

Scientists are still looking for the mechanism of cell regulation. Why, for example, do some of the cells in the pancreas produce insulin while others manufacture energy for the muscles and countless other bodily needs? What makes genes turn on and off, and how does the phenomenon of cell differentiation take place? "At a critical moment early in the life of an embryo, identical cells miraculously (no other word will do) begin to take on specialized roles—some forming tissue for the heart, for example, others for that of the liver or skin. Each of these different cells still contains all the original instructions for producing the entire organism, but somehow unneeded genes are switched off. How does this differentiation come about? Do certain genes order up particular proteins that serve as *on* and *off* switches?" ("Genetic Engineering," *Time*, March 9, 1981.) In the world of technology the computer comes closest to resembling in activity the cellular molecule. In a recent article the magazine *Discover* presents an interesting comparison between the silicone microchip and the molecular biochip:

> In place of the usual green plastic boards holding silicone microchips are ultra-thin films of glass crusted over with invisible layers of proteins, linked together in complex crystal patterns not unlike those of the arctic retreat in the movie *Superman*. Within the delicate protein latticework are organic molecules, called biochips, that dance at the touch of an electric current, winding or unwinding, passing hydrogen atoms from one end to the other...

> As they shift position or shapes, the molecules pass along information in the manner of ordinary integrated circuits. But because they are so tiny and so close together, they can perform a calculation in about a millionth the time of today's best chips. One more thing: these molecular diodes, transistors, and wires, as well as the protein architecture that holds everything together, were manufactured by simple E. coli bacteria fashioned to do the job by genetic engineering (May 1982, cover article).

It has been calculated that a bacteriophage, or virus, with a DNA chain, say 200,000 bases long, has in its molecular "instruction book" the equivalent of 60,000 words, which would be roughly thirty pages of an instruction book written in English. The molecular instruction book for a bacterium would be 10 to 1000 times larger than this (Thorpe, 1974, p. 35).

When we seek to calculate the genetic information stored in the human cell, however, the numbers resulting are altogether astronomical. The genetic information stored in the forty-six chromosomes of each somatic cell can hardly be likened to an instruction book at all. Rather, as Thorpe suggests, it is more accurately likened to a large encyclopedia comprised of forty-six volumes, containing about six times 10^9 base pairs, two times 10^9 words and a million pages. Each volume would average about 20,000 pages (Thorpe, 1978, p.23).

Thorpe hastens to add, however, that the above quoted figures do not "specify the detailed positions, actions, and functions of the great hordes of molecules in each cell, still less any question of atomic species and activity."

What then is cause for unceasing wonderment not only in man but in all living organisms is that, despite their seemingly inexhaustible complexity, all components of an organism are hierarchically structured and ordered to the promotion of the organism's wellbeing. Thus all of the activities within the organism fall under the control of a master program, which guides and channels them to the accomplishment of a unified, common goal. The aim of the program encoded within the DNA molecule and found within every cell of the organism is the promotion of the health and overall development of the total organism. When one recalls that within the mature human there are as many as 100 trillion cells, all of which are interconnected by a common network, one has some idea of the magnitude of this task.

The living thing, pulsating with activity, is in a state of dynamic equilibrium, whereby, through the constant internal repair and creation of new cells to replace the old, the organism maintains itself in being. What above all, therefore, is worthy of note is that although many living things are constituted of millions and even trillions of cells, not to mention countless more subcellular structures, the living organism remains an effective, closely knit unity. It is but *one* being, *one* reality. All of the activities observed within it are its very own possession, and all aim at its conservation and further development.

It is the phenomenon of the unity of living things that provides us with the profoundest question of all, How does one account for the dynamic unity of living things? This question is a philosophic one, for it involves us in an extrapolation that carries us beyond the evidential data of direct observation. It is an inquiry into the internal causes of living things.

The Soul: First Principle of Life

The preceding reflections have led us to the basic question about the source of life in living things. In the living organism there is a complexity and a unity, a harmonious balance that is dynamically maintained throughout its incessant exposure to change and adversity. The bark of a tree that has been slashed, and the paw of an animal that has been cut or somehow injured will repair themselves. But marble carved by the sculptor's chisel will not restore itself to its original state, nor will a desk divest itself of the initials boldly scratched upon its surface. The nonliving thing lacks the coordination and organization found in living things, whereby the activities of the latter all aim at the support, renewal, and development of the organism itself.

It was to account for this truly spectacular phenomenon of the unity found within the activity of living things that Aristotle developed his matter-form theory. By introducing a sophisticated dualism into the very center of living things, Aristotle felt he could provide an intelligent and acceptable account of their basic phenomena. The form, or soul, of a living thing is, for Aristotle, the ultimate life principle within the living thing. Conjoined with body, not as two separate and independent entities but as principles, body and soul constitute a living thing with the soul as its principle of life.

When, therefore, Aristotle speaks of the soul as the formal cause of the body and its life principle, what he affirms seems to be clearly in accord with the most recent and advanced findings in modern biology. The recently discovered genetic code, which applies to each cell of any living organism, becomes readily explainable as the effect of the pervasive presence of the first principle of life, the soul. Further, without the presence within the organism of a code that transcends each of its individual cells and organic parts, there is clearly no explanation of the obvious hierarchical control which the organism itself is able to exert over each of its parts. By virtue of the "strict governmental" control that the totality is able to exercise over each of its parts, commands that are handed down to each of the trillions of cells control the manner in which they function—what chemicals they are to manufacture within their own factory systems; where in the organism they are to serve the good of the whole, and in what capacity. For example, if so commanded, some blood cells will produce proteins that convert into heart or liver cells; others, into muscle and sinew cells; still others, into skin, tissue, or brain cells.

This utterly remarkable organizational achievement, observable in all simple organisms but reaching incredible levels of complexity within the human, is accounted for solely through the presence of an organizational principle permeating the entire organism and transcending each of its constitutive parts. Only such a principle could account for the original genetic code found within the cellular structures themselves, as well as for the government and control of the specific programs within that code which are to be followed at any given time.

Singularly illustrative of this functional complexity is the structure of the human brain. The ten billion nerve cells of the human brain communicate with one another over the spaces between the endings of neuron processes, which are called synapses. Each cell is known to send impulses to many thousands of other cells through an individual nerve fiber called an axon; when stimulated, each cell triggers reactions in many hundreds or even thousands of other cells. In short, the human brain is an extensive neuronal network, which in its complexity, is not unlike a vast telephone exchange.

Despite its complexity the human brain is an enormously efficient organ. As Dr. M. Mitchell Waldrop wrote recently, the human brain is beating out the computer even though it functions with neurons that operate about a million times slower than silicone. The reason, according to Dr. Waldrop, is in the wiring. "The neurons are in there doing millions or billions of operations simultaneously. Whereas computers, with a few exceptions, are still based on a serial, one-step-at-a-time architecture" (*New York Times*, Sept. 25, 1984).

What constitutes these cells a neuronal network rather than a vast horde of individual entities, each pursuing its own path to development, can only be a pervading reality that programs the entire organism. The individual cell is fitted out with a program, but it does not control its own destiny. It receives instructions as to what course of action to follow from outside. The cell functions not for its own well-being alone but subordinates its activities and "decisions" to the health of the organism of which it is an infinitesimal part. Borrowing from Professor Bertalanffy's metaphor referred to earlier, we might say that the code contained in the DNA molecule provides the vocabulary and the grammar for cellular activity, but it does not control the word choice or the manner of expression.

What we mean by *soul*, therefore, is simply this first organizational principle. Although it cannot be directly observed or experienced, its effects, which all living things exhibit in their activity and in their being, can be. These effects point to the organizational principle itself. Further, it should be noted that soul, as described above, is present in every living being and at every level—vegetative, sensory, and intellective—within the organism.

Indeed, plants and animals as well as humans possess souls. This is not to say that the plant soul is identical to an animal soul, or even to the vegetative aspects of an animal soul, or that either is identical with a human soul, for as already indicated in this chapter, living forms are analogous, not univocal.

Although all organisms are living things, the intensity and quality of the union of body and soul, as well as the complexity of their organization, differ in a dramatic way. Indeed, so highly organized is the human that, as seen, we have the added capability of modifying our given program and, on the operational level, of creating even new ones. Through our intellective and volitional capabilities, we humans are in part self-programming, which is simply another way of saying that we are free and self-determining.

The Human Soul and Its Relation to Body

In this section we will address the thorny problem of understanding the nature of the human soul and its relation to the human body. Along with the questions involving intellection and human freedom, this problem has perhaps received more attention by philosophers over the course of centuries than any other. It is a watershed problem, in that so much depends upon the manner in which it is resolved. It is intimately related not only to the question of human immortality but also to the question of God's existence and to the whole area of religion. For these reasons it has inevitably attracted considerable interest and attention.

As might be expected, the positions taken by philosophers regarding the problem of the human soul have greatly varied, even though the basic options which are available to them are actually quite limited. Of course, not all philosophers admit to the existence of a human life principle as really distinct from the body. Those scientists or philosophers who do not are deeply influenced by the scientific model, which moves them to seek an explanation of the human life phenomena in merely physico-chemical terms. The scientific bias in this regard has been prevalent in the past, but currently it appears to be yielding in some quarters to a fuller acceptance of a distinction between biology and the physical sciences.

Indeed, the recent discoveries relating to the genetic code have served to cast a lengthy shadow over a narrow, reductionist interpretation of life phenomena. Professor Ludwig von Bertalanffy states that, in the face of recent scientific developments, the mechanist, even in the area of molecular biology, is quite silent. The reason for this silence, Bertalanffy believes, is not simply imperfect knowledge:

> The trouble is rather that the conventional categories, concepts and models of physics and chemistry, do not deal with the organismic aspects that I have mentioned. They seem to leave out just what is specific to living things and life processes; and new categories appear to be required (Koestler and Smythies, 1969, p. 58).

Perhaps what is lacking are not new categories but a new look instead at some old categories viewed from the fresh perspective of recent findings in the area of microbiology.

Aristotle views the body and soul as distinct principles, matter and form, which unite in one essence or nature; whereas, the mechanist considers body and soul to be two distinct terms employed to designate only one identical reality, hence the term *monist* is used to describe such a position.

The mechanist may speak about soul and admit to an existence of organization within living things, but the organization that the mechanist has in mind really turns out to be nothing more than the perceptible configuration of matter. Soul is thus ultimately reduced to body or material particles, and body and soul are indistinguishably one. Such a position may be described as *mechanist* or *materialist monism*.

In contrast to materialist monism is the view that identifies soul and body in the human, but does so in a way that incorporates body within soul and treats the body as an epiphenomenon, or mere projection of mind. This view is also monist, but it is spiritual monism rather than material monism. In the view of a spiritual monist, the human is exclusively mind, or idea.

In neither of these monist positions is a real distinction made between matter and spirit in man. One denies the existence of spirit in man altogether and holds simply that man's nature is ultimately composed of material particles or molecules; the other denies the reality of matter and restricts the nature of man to spirit or mind.

There are, however, variant theories of *dualism* that recognize an important distinction between body and soul. Plato is among those who have exaggerated this distinction, at least if the account of soul in his dialogue, the *Phaedo*, is to be interpreted as presenting his own view. In this work, the body is viewed as a prison of the soul, and Plato suggests that the soul merited being placed in the body because of some misdeed it perpetrated during a prior life. At any rate, Plato's theory of knowledge clearly maximizes the intellectual component, while playing down the sensory, and allows no place for any insight derived from an intellective knowledge that comes to the soul through its contact with the empirical world.

The French philosopher René Descartes, influenced by the views of Plato, clearly opts for a theory of soul-body relationship which strongly emphasizes the distinction between these two. In Descartes's view the human is essentially a soul to which is attached a body. The union of body and soul does not, according to Descartes, mean that the human is a *third thing* which is neither body nor soul, as Aristotle believed, but rather that the human, in possession of a body, is essentially soul, or mind.

The difficulties emanating from such an exaggerated dualist position are grave, as the development of philosophy since the time of Descartes very clearly attests. Since, for Descartes, body and soul are united mainly in the sense that they occupy the same place, and that the soul makes use of the body as its instrument, the manner in which any meaningful collaboration between the two can occur becomes immediately problematical. In addition, the question inevitably surfaces as to why the two ever came to be so united in the first place.

In an attempt to resolve the questions that soon arose regarding Descartes's theory of soul and its relationship to body, the German philosopher Gottfried Leibniz (1646-1716) suggested that the two remain independent of each other in essence but are united in their activity through a preestablished harmony whereby each marvelously anticipates the actions of the other. Leibniz used the example of two clocks ticking synchronously to illustrate his view.

Variations of such exaggerated dualist positions continue to attract the attention of philosophers today. All, however, share the burden of an excessive artificiality that renders the problems of the origin of intellective knowledge, the nature of human language, the emotional experience, and any realist theory of learning and education, not only paradoxical but also insoluble.

According to the theory first espoused by Aristotle and further developed by Thomas Aquinas, the body and soul are distinct, not as entities but as principles, and unite to form one essence which is neither body nor soul taken singly. This view seems to be the only viable option among the various attempts by philosophers to solve the soul/body problem.

In this view, which can be termed a moderate dualist position, the soul is related to body as its form. The form spoken of here, of course, is an internal form, and thus invisible—not at all the same as the visible external shape of the body. The soul is not, therefore, an accidental or secondary form of the body but is its first or most basic form. For this reason it is called the substantial form, for nothing actual within the individual precedes it. This substantial form does not make the body be in *this* or *that* particular physical way, but simply makes it *be what it is,* a human body.

According to the moderate dualist view of Aquinas, the form, or soul, of man is the first principle of life within the human composite, for it is the active, determining cause, internal to the being, which alone accounts for why this individual is a human being. As mentioned earlier, when discussing soul as the first principle of life, we say the soul, or substantial form, is itself the programmization of the total living being, for it is that being's first organizational principle.

The marvelous hierarchical ordering of the internal structure of living things, including the cellular and organic levels, whereby the health, well-being, and activity of an individual are both regulated and maintained, can only be the result of one unique organizing principle within it. Since it is the soul that is this supreme organizing principle, it is clear that there can be only one soul within one being. From this it follows, therefore, that one and the same principle accounts for all of the levels of vital activity found within the human, which includes the vegetative, sensory, and intellective operations.

It further follows, then, that the soul must be present throughout the entire organism and cannot be limited to some special or single organ such as the pineal gland, as Descartes thought, or the heart, or even the brain. Because the soul is omnipresent throughout the body of the living thing, the latter is but one being. Thus, in the case of the human, all members are ensouled in the one organism so that the totality is present even within the parts. This indivisibility of soul within the organism permits one to refer to his finger or nose or foot as his own. The parts are "one with" the whole, so that they are not possessed by it as an object, but rather form a part of one and the same subject, permitting one to say, "I am my foot" or "I am my body"; not in the sense that my foot and I are identical, but in the sense that we are one in being. The being of my foot is an integral part of my being and does not have an existence apart from the being that I am. This means, then, that my body is not an object that I possess such as a coat or sweater. Although such things are *mine*, their being is independent of me; they are not considered a part of me.

Thus the living thing itself, the individual human, composed as it is of myriad parts all spectacularly organized to promote a transcending commonweal surpassing any of the parts taken severally, is much more than the mere sum of its parts. Rather, the individual transcends them all, having being in itself; at the same time the individual is distinct and distinguished from all other individuals.

Finally, it should be noted that, since body and soul unite to constitute the essence of the human, neither the body nor the soul taken separately can be viewed as the total human essence. Thus, in Aquinas's view, the human is not most properly either body or soul but a third thing resulting from the union of body and soul. Consequently, only of the total composite can an unqualified affirmation be made. One makes such an affirmation when one says, "I am a human." I may not *properly* say, "I am a soul" or "I am a body,"

since these are incomplete substances united as principles to constitute a total, complete substance, which alone *I am*. However, it
should be noted that my denying that *I am a body* is not incompatible with affirming that *I am my body*. In the former instance what
is denied is that the human is body alone; what is affirmed in the
second is that the body is an integral part of me.

The Uniqueness of Human Life: Self-Presence

We noted earlier that a living thing is a being that is able to move
itself toward its activity and its fulfillment. Thus, to be alive is *to be*
a certain way. Also we noted that there are three significant levels of
living things; namely, the vegetative, the sensory, and the intellective; that on all three levels we find a dynamic, operational center
but that there is a difference in the scope and quality of the activities
emanating from these centers. At the highest life-level—the intellective, or human—there is a deeper interiority, a reflective self-
consciousness; hence, a more perfect form of self-presence.

It is through their intellective and volitional activity that the
human is in greater self-possession than is either the plant or the animal. Indeed, as already mentioned in the discussions on the problems of understanding, language, and personhood, only we humans
are able to know who we are; that is, each human is able to grasp
his or her own essence within the given of their individual activity
and thus can study not only himself or herself but other things as
well. As an intellective being the human can know *the causes* of
things, can inquire into the organization of living things and the
order and nature of nonliving things, and can inquire into their
many interconnecting relationships.

Further, through free choice, we humans can implement and
augment the programmization with which nature has provided us.
In this manner the human can chart a personal course. Through intellection we are able, much like a solar cell, to charge the batteries
of our being with the energy resources of our environment, procur-
ing for ourselves the energy and enlightenment needed to power
and steer our way. Through reflection we can realize a self-presence
that only a self-conscious activity can achieve. As our own inner life
of consciousness unfolds, we come to know our "self" as the organizational center it truly is. Only in the human is "indwelling" possible. The interiority that characterizes our intellectual life allows us

a sense of independence and security, an experience of at-homeness. The quality of interiority, uniquely characteristic of the intellective life of the human, allows us to transcend the world that surrounds us and at the same time to experience a sense of familiarity within that world, for the reflective process reveals that we are the "house of being." Nothing, that is, no-thing, is alien to us. We understand our role as that of "host" to the world.

All this is in sharp contrast to the conscious experience of the animal world which, unable to transcend mere sensory perception and awareness, is deprived of the higher level of that experience. The animal can never, therefore, complete its reflection upon its own vegetative and sensory activities, and hence is forbidden to return to itself as a dynamic organizational center; that is, as a living, sensing thing. It is a profound paradox that *only humans* know *who* animals are!

The Phenomenon of Death

Inseparable from the phenomenon of life is the experience of death. Since every living thing is subject to its law, it might be helpful to isolate the death phenomenon from life itself and to formulate a descriptive definition of death. As just stated, all living things die. Most trees and all plants, insects, birds, and animals of every species have highly limited life-spans. In terms of the age of the earth and of the universe itself, the endurance of individual living organisms is brief.

Death, of course, is actually nothing more than a type of change, for it is not the same as annihilation. When a living thing dies, it ceases to be what it was, but it does not cease to be without qualification. Something of what once lived continues to be. Substantially it is other than it was. Clearly, death is a term which is properly applied only to living things, and it signifies not a partial but rather a total change. When something living dies, there is a total cessation of its life. The organism is no longer the dynamic organizational center it was, and it is no longer possessed of those activities by which it was previously identifiable as a living thing. It is important to note, then, that something is judged to be dead not simply because it no longer performs its accustomed vital activities, but more precisely because it is perceived to be radically *incapable* of performing those activities. There is, therefore, a profound difference between an animal that hibernates in winter and an animal that is dead; between a tree or plant that is dormant and one that has died. Death, therefore, involves a total or a substantial change in the organism, and it is, indeed, the specific term we employ to designate the occurrence of just such a change.

Phenomenologically, then, a living thing is said to have died when it no longer functions as a source and center of self-movement. If, however, we wish to push our analysis further by inquiring into the very grounds of death and seeking to understand what makes the death phenomenon itself possible, we must return to our earlier reflections regarding the body-soul dualism found in the natures of all living things.

The monist, whether of the materialist or spiritualist persuasion, is faced with a very grave problem in attempting to explain the reality of death and has been unable to provide a convincing account of this experience. The monist does of course trade on the common perception that death occurs. The effects of the phenomenon of death are abundantly obvious; the organism ceases to function in any capacity whatever. Yet how does the monist explain the possibility of death, if the living thing is nothing but body? Body cannot cease to be body. Why, then, does it cease all of its previous functions? And why has this change come about so abruptly? The monist is unable to answer these questions without being entrapped in a circular argument. The same impasse greets the spiritual monist. For him death must be an illusion, for he has no way of explaining the sudden change that has occurred which prevents the living thing from performing any of its observable customary activities. For the moderate dualist, however, a consistent explanation of death is available, for it can be seen as a separation of the two essential principles of the living thing. For Aristotle and Aquinas, therefore, death occurs when the life principle, the soul, no longer informs the body in which it resides. Since the body has life through the soul, it can no longer continue as a living body without the presence of the soul. In this view, then, death consists in the dissolution of the very essence of the living thing.

The reason, therefore, why all living things are subject to death is that their inner structure contains within it the very seeds of its own dissolution. The soul cannot continue to provide life to a body structure that has been radically altered either by age, disease, or accident, and has thus lost its ability to be enlivened. The dualistic theory of man seems absolutely essential for explaining both the reality and the possibility of death.

Human Death and Immortality

All living things must die, but we alone foresee our death. Because of our ability to know ourselves and to reflect upon our own experience, we stand closer to death than any other living organism does. We know that it is appointed one day for us to die; that it is according to our nature that we should die. Finite, we know our own finitude. In the arresting phrase first employed by Martin Heidegger, the being of the human is a *Sein zum Tode,* a "*being* toward death."

Death-awareness pervades our consciousness, not in the sense that we always expressly think about death, but rather in the sense that death is never totally removed from our consciousness. No one would give credence to the view that they are not going to die. The fact of death is certain; what is uncertain is the time, the place, and the circumstance.

Apparently, death has occupied a prominent place in our psyche ever since the dawn of human history. This is attested to by the numerous monuments of earth and stone which people of many cultures and eras have placed over their dead. It is further witnessed to by the visual arts, by music and song, which often dwell on the theme of human finitude and the phenomenon of death, and by its frequent use as a central theme in the performing arts and literature. Indeed, it may well be that the greatest artistic works of the human spirit have been elicited by profound reflections on the significance of death and the transitoriness of human life. Clearly, the true meaning of life can be read only against the all-enveloping, constant awareness of death.

Even on the existential level, then, human death is seen as markedly distinct from the death of other living things. The human, to be sure, is the only living being that *understands* and foresees the reality of death. Our life-consciousness contains within it the fact of death, and as a result, we are able to stand back and apart from death. Thus the human *plans* for death. Life-insurance policies, wills, and last testaments, cemetery plots, funeral plans, etc., all are witness to our conscious grasp of our own finitude.

The singular respect and reverence which humans display toward the dead is yet another experiential phenomenon of human existence. Burial rites and cemeteries, together with the continued honor shown the memory of the dead even years after their decease—in all this we note that the passing of the individual human is distinct from the death of all other living things.

It is not surprising that the human should have shown a profound and continuing interest in the phenomenon of death, particularly in the fact of human death. As an integral part of human life and of the human condition, death serves to set parameters within which the meaning of human life itself is to be evaluated. It is no mere accident that we humans should have exercised a pervading interest in the meaning of human death. Such an interest is clearly recognizable throughout the annals of recorded history. As a phenomenal event, death is not self-explanatory, and its very existence is for the human an occurrence to be explained; for, without an understanding of death, we must realize that we fail in our overall effort to understand ourselves.

For this reason, all serious philosophers have given their closest attention to this central problem, for the questions to which it gives rise are among the most important that we might ask. It avails us little to reflect on our nature and our relation to the world if our questioning stops short of facing up to these final questions regarding our own future. Indeed, our present is necessarily bound up with our future, so that our inability to know our future becomes one with our inability to know our present and who we humans are. In short, if we can know who we are we cannot help knowing who we can be. It is, then, with questions concerned with our future that we now need to deal; such questions as: What is the meaning of life? What is the meaning of death? Does the individual in some manner survive death, or does death simply signify the end? These are questions that occur to every thinking man and woman.

In responding to these and similar questions, Thomas Aquinas concludes that, although the human truly dies, the human soul, or life principle, survives. His argument is simple enough and rests on the analysis previously made regarding the nature of the human intellective and volitional acts. Because the act of human intellection is intrinsically independent of the physical world, owing to its self-reflective nature, it must proceed from a principle that is similarly immaterial in nature and inherently independent of the physical world. The ultimate principle grounding the intellective act is, of course, the first life principle of the human, that is, the soul.

When death occurs, then, the human soul is capable of continuing in being after its separation from the human body because, as intrinsically independent of matter, it does not rely on body for its existence. Aquinas's technical term for describing this characteristic of the human soul is that it is *subsistent*. By this he means that, although the human soul is truly the form of the body and unites with it to form one essence, it directly receives the actuality of being within itself. In this sense, then, the human soul is unique and differs fundamentally from all the other life principles found in plants and animals. These souls are not subsistent, for they do not possess the actuality of being within themselves. Rather, it is the composite of body and soul within these organisms which, properly speaking, has being and exists. Consequently, when death of these organisms brings an end to the union between the body and soul, neither principle is able to survive, since both depend upon each other for the act of being by which they both exist.

Contrarily, however, the human soul subsists within itself; that is, it exists in itself and not in another, or in virtue of its relation to another. Hence, while the soul exists as the form of the body, it does not inherently depend upon body for its existence. Thus it is capable of existing alone even after the separation from body which occurs at the moment of death.

It is, of course, important to note that Aquinas's argument on behalf of the immortality of the human soul does not overlook, much less deny, what we have previously seen to be his position regarding the dependency of intellective acts upon the material world for their content. This dependency, however, is *extrinsic* merely in that the physical world provides the *source* for the intellective ideas. The acts of understanding, immaterial in nature, are intrinsically independent of any material principle.

Let us add one concluding note on Aquinas's argument. He does not base his argument for the human soul's immortal nature on the fact that it is *simple*; that is, not composed of parts, and hence is *de se* incorruptible. He does, of course, agree that the human soul is simple, but this truth in itself provides insufficient grounds for concluding that it can, as a consequence, continue on without the presence of the body.

The reason is that corruptibility is of two kinds, namely, intrinsic and extrinsic. Something is *intrinsically* corruptible if it is composite and thus is capable of an internal breakdown. But no form, according to Aquinas, is corruptible in this sense, since unlike matter it is not composite but simple. If, however, the human soul were incorruptible because of its simplicity alone, it would follow that the souls of animals and plants would also be incorruptible, since they, too, are simple.

Extrinsic corruptibility means that something can cease to be because its existence depends upon the existence of something else. We can use a glass vase as an example of extrinsic corruptibility. The shape of the vase is not identical with the glass of which the vase is made; for the glass need not have received this particular shape. Nonetheless the shape of the vase does depend on the glass for its existence. If the vase is broken, the shape of the vase ceases to be because it cannot exist apart from its subject, the glass in which it resides. It is in this sense, then, that the shape of the vase is said to be extrinsically dependent upon the glass. Such is the case with regard to the forms of the lesser organisms, for these forms depend upon the composite for their existence. When, therefore, Aquinas argues that the human soul is incorruptible because it is subsistent, he is simply denying that it is either intrinsically or extrinsically corruptible, which is the same as affirming that it is immortal.

Aquinas provides another argument for the soul's immortality which is perhaps more frequently heard. He argues that, because our intellect knows being absolutely apart from material conditions, there is a natural desire to exist always. Now such a desire, being natural, would not occur were it not grounded in reality. Accordingly, the human soul, he concludes, will continue to exist after its separation from the body.

As to the manner of the human soul's existence after death, Aquinas has not a great deal to add from the vantage point of human reason alone. He does acknowledge, however, that in its separated state the human soul would be unable to derive knowledge from the sensible world as it previously had done, and hence, any further knowledge it obtained would have to be derived from another source; that is, from intellective beings (separated intellects) or from God, and would consist in some form of infused knowledge. It is interesting that what Aquinas claims for the life condition of the soul *after death* is very much like the position espoused by Berkeley for the human *during this life,* for whom all knowledge derives exclusively from other minds, finite or infinite.

Thomas does insist, however, that the individuality of the human soul would be retained in its separated state, since the soul received its individuation from its union with body. The individuating characteristic would remain, therefore, since it is now the quality of an incorruptible and subsistent form and thus can never be dissociated from it.

Summary

In this chapter we have discussed the problem of life, inquiring first of all into the meaning of life itself. We concluded that a living thing is capable of moving itself to its own proper operation. We then explored the nature and function of the originating principle of life, which we termed soul. Next, the various levels of life were examined as we distinguished human from plant and animal life, and emphasized the salient characteristics of human life as being those of self-presence and self-consciousness, together with the human's ability to provide, on the operational level, its own programmization. Finally, the nature and meaning of death were discussed, together with the question of life after death.

Definitions and Conclusions

1. A living thing is a being capable of moving itself toward activity of some kind.

2. Growth and reproduction are the two most obvious signs of vital activities.

3. The human body contains approximately 100 trillion cells, all hierarchically organized to form one living being.

4. Each cell (human) is an organized society of staggering complexity containing "factories" for the manufacture of proteins and amino acids; a communications system; a defense militia; and a "trade commission" to oversee the importation of needed chemicals and the exporting of finished products.

5. The DNA molecule within each cell of the organism contains the master blueprint whereby all of the activities of the cell, including its own replication, are maintained and governed.

6. The convergence of the activities of each of the cells and organs within living things toward the support and development of the total organism plainly indicates that it is but one being.

7. The soul is the name given to the first or most basic organizing principle within each living thing.

8. Monism is the view that the terms *body* and *soul* refer, ultimately, to the same reality.

9. Dualism, in general, is the view that body and soul are somehow distinct realities.

10. Exaggerated dualism views the body as a mere instrument of the soul, and as incidentally united with it.

11. The moderated dualist views body and soul as two distinct principles, intimately united to form the one essence of the living thing.

12. Among living things the highest level of life is found in the human, for whom a lived self-presence is possible because of the intellective nature of the human soul.

13. Through death the living thing totally ceases to be what it was, having lost all capability of self-movement.

14. Death can be explained as the separation of body and soul.

15. Conscious of their own finitude, the human is the only living creature who lives within the horizon of death.

16. The human soul differs from other life principles in that it alone is subsistent.

17. Owing to its quality of subsistence, the human soul is intrinsically independent of body and, consequently, has the capability of continuing in being after death.

14   The Beginnings of Human Life

By his very nature, man is a metaphysical animal.

Etienne Gilson

The Origin of Human Life: The Problem

The question of human origin concerns the origin of the individual person on one hand and the origin of the first human on the other. Although in recent decades scholars and scientists have discovered much about the origin of the human, it must be acknowledged that the question at its profoundest level still goes unanswered. This situation is, after all, understandable, for newly discovered scientific facts must await interpretation, and interpretation must await insight.

It seems clear that one's response to questions concerning the origin of the human is directly related to the view one has both of the nature of the human person and of the meaning of human life. Indeed, the very direction of one's response is initially conditioned by one's prior commitment as to what it means to be human.

There are, surely, few questions facing the philosopher that provide a greater challenge than those concerning the origin of human life, and it must be granted from the outset that no response can be completely satisfactory. Even so great a thinker as St. Augustine acknowledged that the origin of the individual human person was one of the most difficult and intricate problems to be contemplated.

For the philosopher who also happens to be a religiously committed person, the import of the question of the origin of the individual can scarcely be exaggerated, nor can it be totally divorced from the related issue of life after death. In addition, the relation of these questions to the more complex question of the origin of humankind taken collectively need not be further emphasized. In the inquiry that follows we turn first to the question of the origin of the individual human and second to the larger question concerning the origin of the human race itself.

The Origin of the Human Soul

The question of the origin of the individual human is truly a problem only for the dualist who admits to the immaterial nature of the human soul. It is evident that the materialist philosopher faces no special problem in attempting to account for the origin of the individual human, save that perhaps of determining the moment when a human life actually begins. Yet, even this question is of lesser moment to the materialist, for on principle he denies a true distinction of kind between the human and the animal and sees no real inconsistency in arguing that ultimately all living things derive from what is nonliving. Thus, for the materialist, the problem regarding the individual human's origin can, in effect, be deferred to the question of the origin of the human race, being hardly distinguishable from it in terms of its solution.

Difficult as the question is regarding the origin of the individual human, the options available in resolving it are, nonetheless, rather starkly limited. One can either maintain that the two parents alone provide life to their offspring, or one can hold that, while the parents fashion the body, it is God who is the source of the first principle of life, the soul. It is evident that the materialist will opt for the first alternative, since the materialist's basic philosophic commitments do not admit of the existence of a transcendent Being from whom all things derive.

For the dualists, however, special and serious problems arise, should they seek to explain the origin of the human person on the basis of the parents alone. For, if they grant that the parents are the sufficient cause of the origin of new human life, they must explain the origin of the new individual human soul. It cannot be that the soul of the new individual preexisted within the souls of the parents in an actual state, for then for each offspring there would be two souls rather than one. In addition, such a position brings in its train a whole series of seemingly unanswerable problems about the conscious state of preexisting souls; it raises questions similar to those posed by the Platonic idea that human souls live in another world prior to the union with their bodies.

On the other hand, to maintain that the soul of the offspring preexisted not actually but potentially within the parents' souls is to leave unanswered the question as to how the generative act alone, which is merely physical, could account for the actualization of a new form that is intellective in nature and hence transphysical. If the parents are truly the sufficient cause of their offspring, then there seems to be no way of explaining how the offspring could possess a soul that is subsistent and immaterial, for the latter could not be educed from a material principle; nor is it understandable how it could be fashioned or drawn from the parent souls.

The theory that parents are the sole cause of their offspring was first proposed in the early Christian era, and it was commonly referred to as the traducianist position, after the Latin word *traducere*, which means *to hand over to*, or *to impart*. Thus, in the traducianist view, the parents give a new, immaterial life to their children. This theory was condemned in the fifth century by the Catholic Church as incompatible with Christian teaching. Before its condemnation, however, it was commonly held by Christian thinkers and for a short while had even been tentatively held by Augustine.

The alternative way of seeking to explain the origin of the human soul is that of creationism. This theory assigns to the parents the task of forming the body; that is, of predisposing living matter to receive the human form. This form itself, however, does not arise out of a generative act but derives directly from the cooperative yet creative action of God. According to this view, the new soul does not potentially or actually preexist in the soul of the parent but is, rather, an entirely new actuality by which the matter disposed by the parents first becomes a human. Since human nature is not merely body or soul but the union of the two into one being, the individual human person cannot exist, in this view, before the consummation of this union.

Philosophically speaking, the adoption of the creationist theory is not a step that is easily taken, since it clearly involves an element of mystery regarding the origin of each human being, which the human mind is incapable of penetrating. Yet it is taken only because no other explanation can adequately account for all of the experiential factors that surround this highly complex question of human reproduction. Only if one reduces the human person to the level of the brute animal does some form of traducianism become a truly viable alternative. The creationist theory alone realistically accounts for the singular dignity of the human person, while at the same time providing the basis for a reasonable explanation of the phenomenon of religious experience common to humans of all cultures and of all ages.

The Problem of Individuation

Every human person is distinct from every other, yet at the same time all are truly human. It is clear that the same principle cannot account for both realities. One cannot be both *human* and *this human* because of the soul alone, for this would preclude the possibility of there being many human beings. The fact of each person's distinctiveness and individuality is beyond question, and this is not a matter of acquired characteristics. The problem of one's individuality is not identical with that of personality, which was studied earlier. If we differed by reason of our personality alone—by reason of the sum of habits consciously acquired during the course of our lifetime—it would follow that at one time we were all identical. While it is true that our individual personalities develop through the course of time, it cannot be true that we acquire our *individuality* through time. Rather, we are individuals from the first moment of our being human.

The assertion that there is a close correlation between the being of an individual person and that person's individuality is clearly supported by an impressive array of physiological data. Not only does every person possess his or her own distinctive consciousness but his or her own unique physical characteristics as well. Thus the timbre of the voice of every individual differs from that of every other, as do the fingerprints and footprints, and the genetic code found within the DNA molecule present in every cell of a human body. One very practical medical result of this uniqueness is found in the manner in which the human body rejects grafts and transplants from a donor not closely related to the host body.

What, then, is the principle, or source, of this individuality? What ultimately accounts for the fact that Socrates and Plato, for example, are two unique and distinct individuals? In short, what is the principle of individualization? As already indicated, this role cannot be played by the human life principle for, were the soul an individual by reason of itself, it would be impossible for us to speak in any meaningful way of *many* individual persons. That is, were the nature of every person distinct as a nature by reason of itself and not as the result of something added to its nature, each nature would constitute a species in itself. This would preclude our being able to refer to both Plato and Socrates as human. For in this view, if Plato were human, Socrates could not be, since Plato would be human by reason of being Plato. Clearly this would empty the term *human* of all specific meaning as a term applicable to two or more individuals and identical in its signification. At best human nature would then signify the genus only of all humans. Were this the case, in saying that Plato and Socrates are human we would simply mean that they share the same nature generically but not specifically. Since the human does in fact share a generic nature with the brute animal, the consequence of this would be that humans are related to each other by nature in the same manner they are related to the brute animal; but this is surely an intolerable conclusion. Indeed, it would render the phenomenon of human reproduction an utter impossibility. Under such a grotesque hypothesis, what we term offspring could bear no specifically *essential* resemblance to those parenting them, and the chimera would cease to be a mere mythological figure.

It can only be, therefore, that the individuality of the human person lies on the side of body and its material characteristics. It is through its union with body that the formal life principle becomes individualized. Thus, although the soul of Socrates is indeed singular and unique, it is so not by reason of itself but by reason of its having been united with this particular body which, through its quantitative dimensions, is *de se* individual. Expressing it another way, one might say that the soul of Socrates is individual because it has been individualized through its initial contact with body. This is why Aquinas states, "The essence of Socrates is not Socrates" (*On Being and Essence*, ch. 2). That is to say, the essence of Socrates is *to be human,* since Socrates is a human being. What, therefore, renders this human being Socrates is something other than the essence, since it lies outside essence. Thus it is that the essence of Socrates is the composite of body and soul, united to form a third thing, that is, something that is neither body nor soul. The essence, which is not individuated by reason of itself, becomes individuated through quantity or individual matter which, for Aquinas, belongs to the category of accident. This, then, permits one to say that both Plato and Socrates are fully human, sharing in the same nature, even though they differ accidentally in that each is a distinct individual. The phenomenon, then, of many individuals sharing a common nature provides the ultimate ground for those dimensions of human experience touched upon in the previous chapter; namely, those of community and social dependence on the one hand, and loneliness and solitude on the other.

Since no single individual human possesses, nor is the totality of, humanity, it is only through knowing other persons that we are able to come to a fuller understanding of who we are as human beings, for only in this way can we concretely realize the diverse ways in which humans actually can be. It explains also at a somewhat deeper level the reasons underlying human alienation and loneliness, since no individual human can be fully human.

Further, it should be emphasized that, in the creationist view, the soul of the human does not in any way exist prior to its union with body. It does not exist within the souls of the parents; it does not exist in the essence of God precisely as a created form, or essence. If it did, it could only be singular and this would straightaway rule out the possibility of there being more than one human being. Further, in this case, the union of the soul with body could not be an essential but merely an accidental union. Body would no longer be an essential component of being human but would be a mere appendage to soul. In this case, the human would be defined simply as mind or spirit.

From this it further follows that the transmigration of souls theory is fully eliminated, for the soul has its existence only from the moment it actually informs a body and becomes individualized by it at the very moment of its union. Furthermore, since individuality is ineradicably communicated to soul by this particular body, it is ordered to this body alone and thus is permanently coded to "reject" union with all other bodies.

An objection might arise with regard to the individuality of the soul and its continued existence after death. It may be asked whether, since the soul's individuation derived from its union with body, it might not be reasonable to suppose that, at the moment of separation of soul and body, the soul would lose its singular identity. This conclusion is, however, ruled out for a twofold reason. First, the immaterial nature of the soul guarantees the permanency of the individual imprint of the body upon it. Hence, upon separation from the body, the soul would continue to enjoy its singular mode of existence. Second, nothing can exist outside the mind as a universal thing. Whatever exists independently of mind must, therefore, exist as a singular thing. Were the soul to lose its individuating characteristics at the moment of death, it would then become a "universal." But this would mean that it would simply cease to exist as a thing in itself.

The Beginning of Human Life

In the previous section we discussed the problem of the individuation of the human soul. We now focus our attention on the time at which the individual human life begins. It is a question of considerable importance for, as is obvious, the contemporary social and moral issue of the rights of the unborn is diversely resolved depending on when authentic human life is thought or presumed to begin.

Since this question concerning the point at which individual human life begins is intimately related to the science of genetics, it will prove helpful to consider, in the briefest possible way, something of the history of this science as well as some of its recent developments. As is known, the science of genetics was very slow in developing. It was not, indeed, until the nineteenth century when Mendel made his discovery of the law of heredity in plants and animals that some of the more egregious and elemental errors in the theory of human genetics were overcome. To speak perhaps more accurately, genetics is really more rightly viewed as a strictly twentieth-century science. The reason for this perhaps startling fact is that little progress could be made in this area until very precise and advanced instrumentation had been developed by which the molecule could be observed and accurately studied.

As a result, it should not be surprising to learn that the predominant figure in biological studies for centuries was none other than

Aristotle, the father of biology. Of course, much of what Aristotle had to say about human reproduction was necessarily the product of very limited observation and mere conjecture. He maintained that the embryo developed in stages, advancing from lower life forms to higher ones during prenatal life. Consequently, he maintained that the human soul did not inform the body until more than a month after the time the ovum and sperm were joined. Indeed, for Aristotle, the span of time required for human ensoulment varied depending upon the sex of the embryo. The male soul was thought to be present forty days after conception, but the female soul did not appear, he felt, until the eightieth day. This teaching was generally accepted by philosophers and life scientists, not only through the entire period of the Middle Ages, but even as late as the eighteenth century. There are echoes of it in the nineteenth-century evolutionist theory.

Probably by observing animal embryos, Aristotle, noticing the various stages of their development, concluded that only gradually did the embryo assume a recognizable likeness of the animals that parented it. Hence, he concluded that the embryo underwent a series of very radical changes during the period of gestation, and he accounted for this by positing a true succession of substantial forms, one after the other. Applying this theory to humans, he then maintained that the embryo was first inhabited by a vegetative form, that this form was later replaced by a sensitive or animal form, and that this was finally succeeded by a true human form or soul. Thus a human could not be said to be present until the final form had appeared.

It was this theory of Aristotle's that Thomas Aquinas adopted with some modifications concerning the origin of the human form. As a result, philosophers have until recently invoked the authority of Aquinas to support the evolutionary theory of the development of the human embryo and fetus. However, the brilliant advances in genetics in our own era, particularly the discovery of the DNA molecule and all that it entails for the programmization of the living organism, now render such a theory obsolete.

There is today no scientific evidence that favors a theory of embryonic development similar to that of Aristotle. Rather, it has now been shown that, from the initial moment of the union of the sperm with the ovum, all the developmental elements of the mature human are already present. Thus, there exist within the full set of chromosomes of the fertilized egg the determinants of the color of the eyes and hair, the size and shape of the mouth, the height and various anatomical proportions of the body, as well, of course, as the sex. From these chromosomes the future appearance of the mature human person can be accurately predicted.

Hence modern genetics does not lend scientific credence to the strict evolutionist model of human development. On the contrary, it strongly supports the idea that human life actually begins at the moment of conception. Only if it is held that the human organizing principle is initially present at conception is the very process of embryonic development, fetal and human, rendered intelligible. The soul itself is the unifying factor of a living being, making it a living human substance. It thus provides the program of developmental stages through which the zygote, the embryo, and then the fetus will successively pass during the nine months of gestation in the mother's womb. In short, to claim that the human embryo is not a human being in the proper sense is to make a claim that finds no support from contemporary genetic theory.

The Evolutionary Theory

We now turn our attention to the last question we intend to raise in our study of the human person; namely, that of *collective origin*. The question of collective origin is considered last, not because it is viewed as among the least important but because it is both so difficult and complex, and because much of what we have already considered about the human is crucial to an assessment of its meaning.

It was only a few decades ago that the origin of humankind was thought by many to have been a comparatively recent event, occurring little more than four or five thousand years ago. Recent developments in the field of anthropology and archaeology, however, have shattered this view. New methods of dating bones and artifacts have enabled the scientists to claim that humans have inhabited this earth for approximately three million years or even longer.

Since the nineteenth century, owing in good part to the discoveries of Darwin, it has been rather generally assumed, especially by experts, that humankind evolved from lower life forms. The evolutionary model had come to provide the almost universally accepted model by which the origin of humans was accounted for. So much a part of the everyday scene had it become that it occurred to few people to view the evolutionary theory critically. Scientists simply assumed its truth and sought to interpret all "scientific facts" concerning humankind within the "light" of Darwinian evolution.

However, from a philosophical point of view, evolution offers some profound problems which simply have not faded away and which continue today to haunt the scientific theorist who is willing to take a second look at the data and the problem. The theory of evolution is a human attempt to explain all known facts concerning humankind and the universe. It is thus an umbrella explanation and, as such, is dependent on some basic philosophical presuppositions. Indeed, properly speaking, evolution is itself trans-scientific, for it is unabashedly philosophical in both scope and nature.

The term *evolution* derives from the Latin word *volvere*, meaning "to turn" or "to roll." The prefix *e* adds the notion of "out of" or "from." Thus, *evolution* means simply a turning out from, that is, an unfolding, a development. The term clearly takes its first meaning from the phenomenon of growth in the development of plants and flowers, which was observed as being a kind of outward twisting. Evolution involves a form of change. Through growth, something becomes different from what it was, yet all the while maintains its basic identity. There is always continuity in growth and hence in evolution. Things advance on an ascending scale; they become more perfectly what they once already were potentially.

It can be noted, however, that the meaning behind "evolution," when it is applied to the "ascent of species," involves considerably more than growth within a living individual organism. What the evolutionist means in applying this term to the world of creatures is a development that entails a leap from one species to another. Thus he advocates a *transformism,* whereby somehow and perhaps very gradually, one kind of being develops into another. To accomplish this transformation a macromutation is invoked, which lifts the inferior organism to a higher, more perfect form of life. Thus, in its most radical and materialist form, the evolutionary theory attempts to account for the origin of the human race by the claim that the human ascended from apes or from some primate closely related to the apes.

In this view, then, the greater proceeds from the lesser, whether strictly by chance or by some internal design in nature, and this developmental process gradually worked itself out through the lengthy passage of time, perhaps even millions of years. It is just such an assumption that encounters serious philosophical problems, for no explanation has ever been presented that enlightens us as to the manner in which such an evolution might have occurred. Always it is "time" that is called upon to effect the passage from lower to higher life forms, as though time itself were some kind of transforming agent. The more dubious the argument, the greater the length of years that is invoked to account for the evolutionary process. As long as one skirts the basic issues of the differentiation of species, the evolutionary model appears reasonable, and of course, its simplicity and universality are singularly inviting. Doubtless, many who have ascribed to this theory have never suspected that there were serious grounds for challenging its authenticity.

The grounds for the challenge derive in good part from the science of genetics, in which spectacular progress has been made during the past few decades. Much of this progress has been possible because of the development of highly sophisticated laboratory instruments, notably the electron microscope. In addition, the computer has enabled geneticists and other biologists to work with figures of enormous magnitude in a matter of seconds, thus vastly facilitating the study of microscopic life systems. What scientists have learned from the brilliant progress made in these areas, which includes the discovery of the DNA molecule, is that living organisms are enormously complex and intricate, infinitely more so than previously even the most competent biologists supposed. Moreover, their complex infrastructure is coordinated in a manner of unbelievable balance and harmony.

The newly discovered complexity of single living cells of all organisms, not to mention the complexity of the total organisms themselves, is such as to render the emergence of new life forms, if this depends upon chance mutations within the cells themselves, as all but unintelligible. Indeed this point has been emphasized by W. H. Thorpe in his book, *Animal Nature and Human Nature.* The point being that, although mutations within the genes do occur and can, through human intervention, be *arranged* to occur, these mutations cannot be said to account for the origin of the genes themselves. The latter are much too complex and, as Thorpe indicates, too unique to have arisen out of some primordial cosmic soup by the simple sheer mechanism of chance mutation. Under the constraints of such a supposition there would be nothing for natural selection to act upon (Thorpe, 1974, p. 57).

Thorpe has unerringly put his finger on the truly sensitive area of the evolutionary theory, which requires that all complex organisms derive from those that are less complex. The view that all development and progress is the result of a greater complexus of nature reductively entails the claim that living organisms spontaneously emerged from wholly inert, or nonliving matter. Such is the view advanced by Teilhard de Chardin in his well-known work, *The Phenomenon of Man*.

What is now known about the complexity of the cell renders any theory of the spontaneous emergence of life from nonlife as simply unworthy of serious credence. The contemporary biologist, through the use of the electron microscope and other ingenious techniques borrowed from physics and chemistry, knows that some cells contain as many as 200 trillion tiny groupings of atoms or molecules. Furthermore, the human cell has been found to contain as many as 100,000 different genes, which are biochemical bits of information constituting a distinct segment of the DNA strand. The genes in turn derive their code or individual program from the various combinations of nucleotides within the cell. It has recently been estimated that the number of different ways of putting together all nucleotides in a set of human chromosomes is approximately 256 followed by 2.4 billion zeros. This number is so appallingly large that, it has been calculated, a person working twelve hours a day would take ninety years to write it down.

The cell is also known to be a bustling center of activity, possessing many "factories" where amino acids are produced in addition to giant molecules or proteins, some of which are themselves composed of several hundred different amino acids. To drive and fuel this biochemical machinery, an active cell is estimated to need more than 2 million molecules of ATP (adenosine triphosphate) every second.

In the face of such incontrovertibly staggering statistics, the unbiased evolutionist has been forced to rethink his entire Darwinian tradition and to look for a more sophisticated explanation of the nature and origin of life than the formula of random selection and mutation can provide. At an international conference of paleontologists, anatomists, evolutionary geneticists, and developmental biologists held in Chicago (October 1980), the majority of the 160 members supported a new form of evolutionary theory that turns away from classical Darwinism and embraces what has been called a theory of *punctuated equilibria*. According to this view, the details of which have not yet been worked out, macromutations would replace Darwin's theory of minimutations. In short, the development of species would now be explained through a series of sudden gigantic changes analogous to a quantum leap in physics.

It was several years ago that Professor Frank B. Salisbury, a member of the Plant Science Department of Utah State University, estimated that the mutation mechanism of life-forms as presently envisaged by scientists could fall short by hundreds of orders of magnitude of producing a *single gene* over a period of more than *four billion* years. Doubtless, it was calculations such as those made by Professor Salisbury which have led the modern life-scientist to re-evaluate the applicability of classical evolutionary theory to current scientific findings and to consider as open once again questions that some time ago were felt to have been satisfactorily answered (*Nature*, vol. 224, Oct. 25, 1969).

Those contemporary scientists who would attempt to reduce all vital activities to mere physical and chemical reactions fail to confront the uniquely perplexing aspect of the phenomenon of living things. This lies not in the fact that all the structures and molecules within the cell appear to comply with the known laws of physics and chemistry, though such compliance is itself a matter of true wonderment. What most compels our attention and awakens within us a profound sense of awe with regard to life-phenomena in general is the mysterious but universally verifiable constraint that controls and harnesses these chemical and physical laws, directing them to fulfill particular and highly specialized functions, which dramatically overarch the development of the individual cells themselves. This is the phenomenon of "hierarchical structure," whereby the cells and organs within the total living thing unite in their effort to promote the overall well-being of the organism. This phenomenon has been termed by Professor Thorpe "hierarchical control," and it is his contention that such control comprises the central problem of the origin of life, for it is only through such control that diverse aggregates of matter, which previously merely obeyed the elementary physical laws, first begin to unify and direct them to enter into a new form of behavior which is at once collective and functional (Thorpe, 1974, p. 20).

It thus seems beyond controversy that one who is prepared to assess the full sweep of the most recent discoveries in molecular biology and genetics will plainly recognize that these findings seriously challenge the classic evolutionary theory regarding the very origin of organic life on this planet. As Thorpe acknowledges, these discoveries render it far less comprehensible how living things might have arisen from nonliving matter and simply rule out the possibility of their having occurred merely by chance. In fact, as he views it, science as such is presently in no position even to express an opinion on this subject (Thorpe, 1974, p. xvii).

The discovery in 1953 by Crick and Watson of the structure of the DNA molecule renders the classic evolutionary attempt to explain the origin of life and indeed the origin of "higher life forms from lower ones" by a process of randomly selective mutation hopelessly circular. The DNA molecule, which can be likened to an actual program tape within the heart of every cell, provides it with the direction needed in order to adjust favorably to its changing environment, furnishing as well the blueprint for the cell's entire replicatory system, which includes the replication of the replication program itself. The DNA molecule cannot itself be the fortuitous result of random mutation. In order for mutation initially to take place, there must first exist a program which can be mutated. There must already be, that is, a program in existence within the heart of matter (the cell) guiding and directing the mutation process, thus rendering possible the very possibility of a mutation and a subsequent "upward" change. In short, the "life from nonlife" hypothesis is wantonly lacking in scientific as well as logical rigor.

That life scientists and others should have sought to unify all science by the formulation of a single, unified theory according to which all experienced life phenomena could be meaningfully explained is, of course, perfectly understandable. The human intellect naturally seeks understanding and all understanding is but the result of the unification of a portion of the varied data of experience. Now that the deficient presuppositions of the classic Darwinian theory have surfaced, many scientists have grown considerably more sensitive to the need to assume an objectively critical stance. At last scientists are boldly raising the searching questions which they ought to have raised long ago.

Professor von Bertalanffy, in a fairly recent lecture delivered in Austria, stated with remarkable openness that he felt the explanation of why scientists who habitually accede to a theory only on the basis of hard evidence should have ascribed to a theory as vague and insufficiently verifiable as the classic evolutionary theory is to be found in sociological reasons. Selection became enthroned as the ultimate reality in his view because both society and science had become steeped in the ideas of mechanism and utilitarianism (Koestler and Smythies, 1969, p. 66). Von Bertalanffy affirms quite candidly that in his opinion there is "no scintilla of scientific proof" that evolution has anything to do with better adaptation or selective advantage or the production of more vigorous offspring.

The eminent French biologist Pierre-P. Grassé bluntly states that the evidence available forces us to "deny any evolutionary value whatever to the mutations we observe in the existing fauna and flora. . . . Nobody can be sure that evolution consists of acquiring characteristics by use or direct influence of the environment. Nobody can prove that phyla, classes, orders, and families have their origin in random mutations similar to those undergone, at all times and in all places, by living plants and animals. Nobody can assert that the organizational schemes are the work of natural selection" (Grassé, 1977, p. 202).

In his book *Algeny* Jeremy Rifkin writes that "the geologic record does not show evolutionary change, but the opposite." Although he grants that through the many generations of a species, mutations are continuously occurring, he concludes that "there is not so much as a shred of evidence to suggest that such mutations alter the species itself in any fundamental way" (Rifkin, 1983, p. 132).

Writing in a similar vein, Professor Richard Spiegel of the University of Wisconsin asks why it is that so many thoughtful people continue to abide by the traditional evolutionary theory when its premises have never been scientifically established as a coherent system. In responding to his own question, Professor Spiegel suggests that the honest reason is to be found in the enduring aesthetic attraction the notions of natural selection, random mutation, and analysis have for the human mind and human sensibility ("The Logic of Evolution," *Contemporary Philosophy*, Summer 1980, p. 9).

The Origin of Humankind

What has been said concerning the origin of life in general applies in a special sense to the important question of the origin of human life. Here one is dealing with a life-form that vastly transcends in complexity and programmatic ability any of the millions of lower life-forms, plant and animal. The ability of the human organism to reach insight; to fashion speech in its many forms; to judge, to understand, and hence, reflectively, to be aware of the very process of judging and understanding itself combined with the correlative power to determine freely the course and direction of one's behavioral program, all these are compelling indications of the unique prowess of the human as a living being. The probability quotient of such an organism's having "emerged" from a primordial but thin genetic "soup" of vastly inferior functional capability is, to be realistic, zero.

Unfortunately, many anthropologists in the past have regarded the human as simply another primate. Consequently, they have paid a disproportionate amount of attention to the anatomical similarities between the human and the primates and other animals, and they have systematically underestimated the significance of the obvious mental differences. It is regrettable that Professor T. Dobzhansky's sage observation—if zoological classification were based not on anatomical and chemical but on psychological grounds, the human would be seen to comprise at least a separate phylum and perhaps even a distinct kingdom—has not been more widely shared (Thorpe, 1974, p. 375).

Before the dramatic and highly successful space probes conducted by the Soviet Union and the United States, astronomers and other scientists quite generally assumed that life existed in some form, although not necessarily identical to what we know on earth, elsewhere in our solar system and even beyond. The results of the numerous space probes, however, including the manned voyages to the surface of the moon, have done nothing to encourage the scientists to pursue this line of theorizing. Absolutely no positive evidence has been uncovered which would support the view that life in any form actually exists presently or ever did exist in the past on Mercury, Mars, the moon, or any planet within the solar system. The sobering conclusion emerging from the immense array of data gathered through the space explorations and the recent probes by astronomers into outer space is that *life* is, as far as we know, a unique *earthly* phenomenon.

Such a conclusion has proved a profound shock to many scientists, for it is not what one would think plausible in the light of the classic evolutionary theory. If living things originally emerged from the massings of inert molecules, all of which at one time were reducible to simple hydrogen atoms, then, given the great age of the universe, life-forms would inevitably have appeared throughout the universe. Yet the present state of our knowledge provides no encouragement whatsoever to the reductionists. Indeed the only place in the explored universe where we can be certain that life exists is here on this tiny planet Earth.

The enormity of this conclusion can be brought home to us if we compare the size of the Earth to that of the Sun, whose volume is 1.3 million times as large as that of the Earth. It is as a grain of sand to the size of an orange, a simile used by renowned astronomer-physicist Robert Jastrow, founder and director of NASA's Goddard Institute (Jastrow, 1978). Furthermore, the Sun is but a small star within a single galaxy comprised of approximately 100 billion stellar bodies. Also, astronomers have observed through their gigantic modern telescopes the existence of more than two billion other galaxies, all presumably containing a number of stars comparable to those of our own galaxy, the Milky Way. It is simply overwhelming in the face of such enormous statistical odds that life is known to exist only on the planet Earth. The question that naturally arises in the wake of these findings is *why* life seems to exist only on the planet Earth, which, in relation even only to our own galaxy, is no more than a speck of dust.

Turning to the basic evidence of the beginnings of life on this planet, we find it to be sparse and singularly puzzling. The geologist plainly acknowledges that the fossil record provides no trace of the preliminary stages in the development of multicelled animals. Rather what the record does show is that suddenly, in rocks judged to be 600 million years old, there is a profusion of diverse living forms. Writing in *Science* (128, 1958, p.7) paleontologist Daniel Axelrod of the University of California states:

> One of the major unsolved problems of geology and evolution is the occurrence of diversified, multicellular marine invertebrates in Lower Cambrian rocks on all the continents and their

absences in rocks of great age . . . However when we turn to examine the Pre-Cambrian rocks for the forerunners of these Early Cambrian fossils, they are nowhere to be found.

Stephen Jay Gould of Harvard and Niles Eldredge of the American Museum of Natural History confirm this assessment by stating simply that "phyletic gradualism was never seen in the rocks." ("Punctuated Equilibria," *Paleobiology*, 3, 1977) In short, the record itself of fossil forms is not supportive of the fundamental evolutionary assumption that the lower life-forms gradually and over a period of perhaps several billion years developed randomly into unimaginably more complex life-forms.

Nor do any findings uncovered by the astronomer or scientist support the view that, in point of fact, life does exist on other planets within our own solar system or on any of the planetary bodies affixed to neighboring stars within our own galaxy, which is known to contain approximately 100 billion stars of the magnitude of our own Sun. Further, presently there is no evidence to prove that life exists in any form whatever anywhere in the other two billion galaxies.

The most recent anthropological findings regarding the origin of the human have caused many scientists to alter their estimate both of the age of the human and of the manner in which we reached our present state of development. Especially notable among these findings are those achieved by the late Doctor Louis B. Leakey, his wife, Doctor Mary Leakey, and their anthropologist son, Richard. Their spectacular diggings in the region of Lake Victoria in Tanganyika, Africa, convinced them that the dates for the origin of humankind must be pushed back much farther than anyone had previously imagined to be at all likely or even probable. Their dating for man's origin is now conservatively placed at more than one million years ago. More recent findings indicate that the actual date exceeds three million years.

Through a comparative examination of fossils and skulls unearthed near the bottom of the Olduvai Gorge in the Lake Victoria region, the senior Leakey made the claim that the human is not, as many naturalists and anthropologists had previously hypothesized, a direct descendant of existing primates. Rather, Leakey argued, the human person and the modern-day primates both have descended from a common ancestor; both phyla are traceable to an earlier period when neither humans nor *primates*, in the modern sense of that term, existed. If one were to express it in classical evolutionary terms, one would say that Doctor Leakey views the human as having *ascended* and the nonhuman primates as having *descended* from the same ancestor. In this view the nonhuman primates—the gorilla, the chimpanzee, and the orangutan—are assumed to represent a degenerate phylum that nature has led along a genetically dead-end path, owing to an unfavorable negative mutation. Since they lack the tools, which humans alone possess, of adapting their environment to suit their physical needs, these lesser primates are headed for inevitable extinction.

What is interesting in this hypothesis of Doctor Leakey's is not that he has totally abandoned the classical evolutionary view, for he does still "believe" that the human is a natural descendant of lower life-forms, but rather the fact that he has definitively broken with the traditional manner of explaining our origin. For years the popularized view that the human is a highly developed primate had gone unchallenged in evolutionary circles. Doctor Leakey's hypothesis represents a clear break with that conviction and renders possible a kind of marriage between an evolutionary and a creationary view whereby the uniquely human phylum could be explained through a special divine creative act enabling it to emerge from, and transcend, the limitations of its natural ancestry.

Even more recently, in the mid-70s, Doctor Mary D. Leakey reported a fresh discovery, which she and her associates consider to be of great significance. What she claims to have discovered are authentic human footprints pressed into a freshly laid volcanic ash in a remote region in Kenya. This find was written up and published, together with remarkable photographs, in the *National Geographic* (April 1979). The footprints were left in volcanic ash near the base of what had once been an active volcano. Having been covered over almost immediately by a continuing ashfall from the volcano, they were preserved almost intact, despite their estimated age of from 3.25 million to 3.5 million years.

These footprints were carefully examined by Doctor Louise Robbins of the University of North Carolina, an anthropologist specializing in the reading of footprints, who was brought to Kenya for an onsite inspection. To everyone's amazement the footprints were in no way different from the footprints of contemporary humans. The best preserved print plainly indicates the raised arch, the rounded heel, a pronounced ball and a forward-pointing big toe. The last is necessary for walking erect. Pressure marks along the foot also provide evidence of a striding gait. Scuff marks even appear in the toe area, and the center of the print is lined with a seam. Doctor Leakey concludes that, at least in Pliocene times, our direct ancestor walked fully upright, employing a freestriding and bipedal gait. She is unhesitating in asserting that the form and shape of that foot were exactly the same as ours today.

This truly dramatic discovery, made possible by the most fortuitous turn of events, whereby footprints, ordinarily so vulnerable to the ravages of time, were perfectly preserved in fossilized form, would indeed seem to show that for over three and one-half million years at least, the human has walked this earth. If such indeed be the case, it would seem to render any attempt to explain our human origin in terms of slow, minuscule mutations occurring randomly as scientifically unfounded. If, over such a span of time, no recognizable structural change has occurred in the human, it is altogether reasonable to suppose that such change never took place at all. For one ought not suppose that we have a time frame of unlimited proportions within which to await the random "development" of humankind. The best current estimate of astronomers is that the planet Earth was born not more than between four to four-and-one-half billion years ago.

The above line of reasoning is even further strengthened by a recent important discovery. In 1984 the anthropological world was astonished to learn that Dr. Richard Leakey and his co-workers had unearthed an almost perfectly preserved skeleton of primitive man. The skeleton, which was found nearly intact, was found to have been that of a healthy, twelve-year-old male, who lived some three-and-one-half million years ago.

What adds to the interest of this unique find is the unusually large size of the skeleton. Dr. Leakey has stated that, had the youth lived to full manhood, he would have been six feet tall and of a robust build. Prior to this discovery it was the consensus of anthropologists that primitive man was small in comparison to contemporary humans, since all the reliable data available had indicated that our early forebears were no more than five feet in stature. What this startling anthropological finding confirms, then, is that our ancestors— as far back as we have yet been able to trace them—don't appear to have been significantly different from ourselves in matters of size and physique.

Thus, merely on the basis of anthropological findings, it seems that the more we learn about the human's origin, the less plausible becomes the classical evolutionary theory. Bipedalism is absolutely essential for hominid development, and yet the human alone has mastered the art of walking erect. Surely it is not presumptuous to surmise that such a singularly spectacular achievement could not have been the result of a wholly unplanned process of natural selection and random mutation. From the purely anthropological viewpoint it appears much more plausible to conclude that the anatomical structure of the hominid, permitting him to walk erect, to think, and to use tools, was itself the result of a dynamic internal code orchestrating that anatomical structure itself.

As mentioned earlier a significant number of contemporary anthropologists have abandoned the classical Darwinian theory, replacing it with a view that some refer to as a theory of "punctuated equilibria." Perhaps the principal spokesperson for this thoroughly modified evolutionary view is Stephen Jay Gould of Harvard.

Recognizing the impossibility of reconciling Darwin's original views with the emerging paleontological and paleobiological facts, coupled with the growing realization that the lifespan of planet Earth has been too brief to accommodate a painstakingly slow development of living life forms, many reputable anthropologists are opting for the new, macromutation theory of punctuated equilibria. According to this view the advance in life-forms is explosive, sudden, and very large.

Yet, even this view, if taken in isolation and not joined with a creationary one, continues to labor under the same burden that has brought down the classical evolutionary theory of Darwin. The newly adapted theory is unable to present any explanation as to why these so-called macromutations ever occurred, and, indeed, thus far its expositors, including Gould, have made no serious attempt to do so (Gould, 1983). In the main they seem to rely solely on future findings to corroborate their theory.

We may justifiably conclude that recent developments in the areas of microbiology and anthropology are most consonant with a theistic view, which assigns the origin and development of living things to a divine, creative act whereby nonliving matter is first organized and oriented toward a higher synthesis of a dynamically functional and creative unity. The acknowledged breakdown in the logic of classical evolutionary theory and the unsupported claims of the punctuated-equilibria theorists lends further support to the view taken earlier that the human cannot arise successfully out of the ashes of nonliving forms or inferior living species which themselves manifest no convincing share in the transcendent human spirit. Rather, the complexity of the human entails, as an unavoidable condition for coming to be, a correlative creative act matching in power and perfection the stunningly complex program of human consciousness and freedom through which the human first enters into the world.

Summary

In this chapter we have discussed the question of the origin of human life. First considered was the problem of the origin of the life of the individual human. It was concluded that the parents alone cannot be considered the adequate cause of the human offspring, but that the origin of the human soul can only result from a creative, divine act.

The problem of individuation was next considered. It was first indicated how the question of individuation differs from that of personality, and it was seen that the human soul cannot be individual by reason of itself, but rather that it becomes individualized at the moment of its union with body to form a human essence, or nature.

Lastly, the inadequacy of the evolutionary theory to account for the origin of the human was considered. A brief account of the developments in the area of microbiology and anthropology was presented, and reasons why evolutionary theory is unable to explain the origin of the human were also given.

Definitions and Conclusions

1. The problem of the origin of the individual human soul is, for the moderate dualist, one of great complexity and difficulty.

2. According to the traducianist position, the parents are the total cause of the life principle of their child.

3. The creationist position assigns to the parents the role of predisposing living matter to receive the human form, but allots the origin of the soul itself to the creative action of God.

4. The singularity of living things is accounted for neither by the body nor by the soul directly, but rather by the quantitative dimensions under which both are found. Thus quantity is the principle of individuation.

5. Of itself, the soul is not singular but becomes so the moment it informs the body.

6. The essence of "Socrates" is not *to be Socrates* but *to be human*.

7. All humans are alike in that they share in the same essence.

8. The human soul does not exist prior to its union with body.

9. The process of embryonic development in the human is, in the light of recent genetic findings, rendered intelligible only if it is assumed that the human soul is present at the very beginning of new cellular life.

10. Classical evolutionary theory, advanced to explain the origin of all species of living things, claims that complex organisms have derived from others less complex through a process of natural selection and random mutation.

11. Some cells are so complex as to contain as many as 200 trillion molecules, which themselves are clusters of atoms.

12. The human cell has been found to contain as many as 100,000 different genes, which are biochemical bits of information constituting a distinct segment of the DNA strand.

13. The DNA molecule cannot itself be the fortuitous result of random mutation. For mutation initially to occur, there must first exist a program which can be mutated.

14. The probability quotient that an organism as enormously complex as the human has emerged from a "genetic soup" of vastly inferior functional capacity is, realistically speaking, simply zero.

15. In the entire universe it is on planet Earth alone where life in any form is scientifically known to exist.

16. The record of fossil forms on earth does not support the classic evolutionary assumption that lower life-forms gradually developed through natural selection and random mutation into more complex organisms.

17. Recent developments in the areas of microbiology and anthropology are most consonant with a theistic view which assigns the origin and development of living things to a divine, creative act whereby nonliving matter is first organized and oriented toward a higher synthesis of a dynamically functional and creative unity.

Epilogue

As you conclude your study of the human person, doubtless you are amazed, if not altogether overwhelmed, at the wide range and interlocking relations of the questions you have been asked to consider. You are probably poignantly aware of how much more remains to be learned; still you have made a true beginning. Your achievement, while modest by professional standards, may be assessed as significant. Your newly acquired vision of the unlimited potential of the human should have awakened within you a quiet, growing confidence in your own abilities together with an unremitting resolve to exploit them fully.

This course has underscored the autobiographical dimension of all human seeking. You have seen how intellective discovery brings in its train a fresh disclosure of the authentic self. In studying the human person, you have included yourself within the scope of your inquiry. Indirectly you have relived your own personal history and in a sense you have refashioned and rehabilitated that history. Since your story is as yet unfinished, every new chapter will effect a rewriting of the past.

Among the insights to be gained from the course of our studies, perhaps none was easier to grasp than that we humans are indefatigable questioners. As intelligent beings we are continually seeking after the *causes* of things. It is this in-depth search that sets the human apart from all other animals. As Etienne Gilson has so profoundly remarked, the human is a "metaphysical animal."

It is, then, our ability to be cause-seekers that makes it possible for us to transcend the limitations of our immediate experience and to extend our knowledge far beyond the limits of everyday utilitarian goals by directing our attention to the unity and meaning of our total experience. Being able to draw back effectively from our own direct experience and from ourselves, we are able to objectively assess both and to uncover the hidden network of ontological relations that pervade the reality we call the human person.

By distancing ourselves from the immediately given, that is, from the sensible world which environs us, we humans are uniquely equipped to move effortlessly through this vast inner network at all levels of our experience, not only to understand but to modify and refashion it. The unlimited sweep of our intellective vision provides us with a freedom and a sense of responsibility unknown to other animals. It is we who are able to devise and implement our own behavioral code, for it is we who possess the awesome power to replicate ourselves in our self-conscious activity and thus to choose the very self who chooses.

Through a lived realization of this self-choosing power, we may legitimately anticipate a growth in our confidence to assume the responsibility for our own lives and to shape the contours of our future. Additionally, it may be hoped that a deepened awareness of the meaning of being human will lead us to a profounder appreciation of the unparalleled dignity of the human person.

Yet, despite the insights which we may have gained about the meaning of the human person, it still remains profoundly true that at our deepest center of being we still remain very much strangers to ourselves and to others. The shedding of further light deep within the hidden recesses of the human soul remains for us an enduring and lifelong task.

Thus the ascent from the cave of darkness and ignorance to the outer world of light and knowledge is not one that can be accomplished in one brief climb. It is rather an ascent roughly commensurate with the life-experience itself. Helping one to learn how to manage the ascent is philosophy's prime task. It is hoped that the reflections we have shared will help to illumine the way.

❧ ❧ ❧

A sound explanation may exist for the explosive birth of our Universe; but if it does, science cannot find out what the explanation is. The scientist's pursuit of the past ends in the moment of creation.

This is an exceedingly strange development, unexpected by all but the theologians . . . . It is unexpected because science has had such extraordinary success in tracing the chain of cause and effect backward in time. . . .

Now we would like to pursue the inquiry farther back in time, but the barrier to further progress seems insurmountable. It is not a matter of another year, another decade of work, another measurement, or another theory; at this moment it seems as though science will never be able to raise the curtain on the mystery of creation. For the scientist who has lived by his faith in the power of reason, the story ends like a bad dream. He has scaled the mountains of ignorance; he is about to conquer the highest peak; as he pulls himself over the final rock, he is greeted by a band of theologians who have been sitting there for centuries.

(Robert Jastrow, *God and the Astronomers*, pp. 115-6)

Study Questions

Chapter 1: Introduction

1. What is the meaning of the word *philosophy?*
2. What are some of the popular meanings of philosophy?
3. What does philosophy mean to *you?*
4. In what sense is philosophic inquiry autobiographical?
5. What is it we intend to study in this course?
6. Are philosophers on the verge of extinction?
7. What value is there in philosophizing?

Chapter 2: The Human Phenomenon of Questioning

What Is Experience?

What is experience?

Fundamental Characteristics of Experience

What are the three fundamental characteristics of human experience?

The Phenomenon of Questioning

What does it mean to question the question?

The Anatomy of the Question

1. What is a question?
2. When do we ask questions?
3. When do we stop asking a question?
4. What is an answer?
5. When we have an answer, how do we know that we have one?
6. Will we ever stop asking questions?
7. Is a person who asks questions stupid?

The False Question

1. What is a false question?
2. Can a question have more than one answer?
3. How does a false question differ from an authentic question?
4. Does one have to know the answer in some sense in order to ask a question?
5. Can a person respond to a question about the future?

Knowing That I Know

1. How are answers related to *being*?
2. What significance do you see in the fact that, even when one has an answer, one knows that there is more to be known?

Chapter 3: The Problem of Human Knowing: A Historical Overview

Plato

1. How did Plato's position regarding knowledge differ from that of Democritus's?
2. Why does Plato deny that the material world is a cause of our ideas?
3. For Plato, does the material world play any role at all in the formation of our intellective ideas?

4. Why does Plato say that learning is always a question of remembering?

Aristotle

1. How does Aristotle's position regarding knowledge differ from that of Plato's?
2. Does Aristotle hold that the material world is merely an occasion of our knowledge? Why?
3. What does Aristotle mean by saying that the material world is potentially intelligible?

René Descartes

1. Why is René Descartes considered to be the father of Modern Philosophy?
2. What is the starting point of Descartes's philosophy?
3. What does Descartes mean by his "methodic doubt"?
4. Why does Descartes accept mathematical theorms as true and certain knowledge?
5. What is Descartes's position with regard to the existence of God?
6. Does Descartes admit to the existence of a material world? Why?

John Locke

1. Is John Locke an empiricist? Why?
2. What does Locke understand by primary qualities? By secondary qualities?
3. How, precisely, do primary qualities differ from secondary qualities?
4. What does Locke understand by substance? What is its function?
5. Is Locke to be considered a "materialist"?
6. Contrast Locke's position on knowledge with that of Descartes's.

George Berkeley

1. Does Berkeley accept Locke's distinction between primary and secondary qualities? Why?
2. What are "objects of knowledge" according to Berkeley?
3. Do material things exist for Berkeley?

4. Does Berkeley admit to the existence of a divine mind? Why?
5. Contrast Berkeley's views with those of Descartes's, Aristotle's, and Plato's.

David Hume

1. What does Hume mean by "idea"?
2. Does Hume accept the reality of universal ideas?
3. Why does Hume reject the causal principle? Explain.
4. How does Hume's position regarding knowledge differ from that of Descartes? In what sense is it similar?
5. Contrast Hume's position with that of Locke's. In your opinion is Hume's critique of Locke's position valid?
6. Contrast Hume's position with that of Berkeley's.

Immanuel Kant

1. How does Kant differentiate between synthetic and analytic judgments?
2. How does a synthetic *a posteriori* judgment differ from a synthetic *a priori* judgment?
3. Which of these two judgments is truly significant from the philosophical standpoint? Why?
4. What kind of judgments, according to Kant, are mathematical judgments? Why?
5. How does Kant feel that he has supplied a response to Hume?
6. Is Kant a defender of the validity of metaphysics? Explain.
7. For Kant, is it possible to know things as they really are, i.e., as they are in themselves?
8. What is the importance of Kant in terms of the development of philosophy?

Post-Kantian Era (1805-1985)

1. How do the German absolute idealists respond to Kant's critique of knowledge?
2. What characterizes the positivist view toward human knowledge and language?
3. How is existentialism related to idealism and positivism?
4. What is phenomenology and how is it related to the philosophy of Descartes and of Kant?
5. How does existential phenomenology differ from the phenomenology of Edmund Husserl?

6. What is hermeneutics and how is it related to phenomenology?
7. What position does the structuralist take with regard to human language and the interpretation or hermeneutic of human experience?

Chapter 4: Sensory Consciousness

Preliminary Notions Regarding Sensory Consciousness

1. Why does our investigation begin with sensory experience?
2. Is there such a thing as "purely sensory" experience?
3. Can sensory consciousness be proved? Why?

Sensory Acts Contrasted with Vegetative Acts

1. How does a sensory act differ from the vegetative act of intussusception?
2. How does an intentional union differ from a physical union?

The Diversification of Sensory Consciousness

1. What is the meaning of "object" in the sensory act?
2. How are the various sensory acts distinguished one from another?
3. What is it that is *seen* or *heard*?
4. How does the formal object differ from the total object?

Common Sensibles

1. What is a common sensible?
2. Do common sensibles help us to distinguish one kind of sensory act from another? Why?
3. How precisely does the act of seeing differ from the act of hearing?

The Role of the Sensory Image in Sensation

1. Is the sensory image that which is sensed? Explain.
2. What is a sign?
3. How does a material sign differ from a formal sign?
4. Is it possible for a sensory power to sense something other than the way it is? Explain.
5. Why is the sensory act of knowledge intrinsically relational?

Chapter 5: The Internal Senses

The Coordinating Sense

1. What is the function and value of sensation for sensing organisms?
2. Why is the coordination of sensory activities important?
3. How does the coordinating sense differ from the special senses?
4. What is the material and formal object of the coordinating sense?

The Imagination

1. What is the basic function of the imaginative sense?
2. What is the material and formal object of the imaginative sense?
3. Why is the operation of the imagination concerned wholly with the present?
4. Why is the imagination the source of fantasy and creative images?
5. What is meant by saying that the creative imaginative act is "constructionist"?
6. Why did Aristotle consider the imaginative power to be the source of error in human knowing?
7. What is a dream?

The Memory

1. How is the memorative act related to the past?
2. What does it mean to say that something is past?
3. Can I remember what never actually occurred?
4. How is remembering related to the present?
5. How is remembering related to non-being?
6. How does the memorative act differ from the act of imagining?
7. Why is the memory referred to as the temporal or "time" sense?
8. How important is the memorative act to the human?
9. Can the memorative act itself be fanciful or imaginary?
10. How does the memorative act relate us to the "real"?
11. In what sense can the memorative power be viewed as the power of self-identity and constitutive of I-consciousness?

Forgetting

1. Is forgetting identical with not knowing?
2. Can one forget what one never knew?
3. Why is forgetting said to be "partial" remembrance?
4. In what does forgetting consist? How does it differ from remembering?
5. What is the fundamental source of the phenomenon of forgetfulness?
6. Do you see any relation between questioning and forgetting?
7. In what sense might a philosopher be said to be one striving to overcome the "forgetfulness of being"?

The Evaluative Sense

1. What evidence is there that animals truly make an evaluation of what they sense?
2. What is the material object of the evaluative sense?
3. What is the formal object of the evaluative sense?
4. Why do different animals react differently to the same object sensed?
5. What value does the activity of this sensory power have for the animal?

Instinctive Knowledge

1. What is meant by instinctive knowledge?
2. Cite examples giving evidence that animals do possess an instinctive knowledge?
3. Are all animals equally dependent on instinctual knowledge? What significance do you see in this?
4. Does the evaluative process that is found in animals appear to be instinctive? Why?
5. Does instinctual knowledge appear to enhance or inhibit the freedom of the animal? Explain.

Chapter 6: From Sensation to Intellection

The Unspecialized Nature of the Human Body

1. What significance is to be found in the fact that the human body is highly unspecialized?

284 Philosophy of the Human Person

2. What significance is found in the human's lack of instinctive knowledge?
3. Does instinctive knowledge provide the animal with an advantage over the human?
4. What evidence is there of a parallel between the human body and the human intellect?

Archimedes and the Gold Crown

1. What was the problem Hiero presented to Archimedes?
2. In what sense was this problem unique?
3. To whom could Archimedes go to find the solution to his problem?
4. Does this problem meet the conditions of an authentic question?
5. What role did the baths of Syracuse play in Archimedes' obtaining his insight?
6. When Archimedes made his famous discovery in the baths of Syracuse, did he have an answer to his problem?
7. How does Hiero know that Archimedes' solution is the correct one?
8. Does the experiment performed in his laboratory afterwards "prove" the correctness of his insight? Explain.
9. Explain briefly how Archimedes knows that the crown either is or is not of pure gold.
10. By reflecting on Archimedes' dramatic discovery, what are the five corollaries we are able to derive from it?
11. Which of these corollaries seems to you to be the most significant? Why?
12. Is intellective insight a phenomenon of relatively rare occurrence?

Chapter 7: Intellection

The Moderate Realism of St. Thomas Aquinas

1. Why is Aquinas's position on knowledge properly viewed as a development of that of Aristotle's?
2. What is the role of "phantasm" in Aquinas's intellective theory?
3. What does Aquinas understand by "intelligible species"?
4. Is the intelligible species *that which* is known, according to Aquinas?

5. In what sense is the intellect said to be one with the object known?
6. Is the material thing an actual cause of the knowing act?

The Role of the Active Intellect

1. What is the role of the agent intellect in the intellect act?
2. In its illuminative act does the agent intellect change the phantasm? Explain.
3. How would the elimination of the agent intellect in one's explanation of intellective insight modify or change one's theory of knowledge?
4. How might the action of the agent intellect and the act of understanding be likened to (a) an act of illumination; (b) an x-ray; (c) the projection of a slide upon a screen?

Aquinas's Theory of Knowledge Contrasted with Those of Other Philosophers

1. Does insight into phantasm have a place in Plato's theory of knowledge?
2. Contrast Thomas's position regarding the origin of knowledge with that of Descartes's.
3. Why does Hume find no need for an illumination of phantasms?
4. Explain briefly the basic difference between Kant's theory of knowledge and that of Thomas's.

Understanding and Judging

1. What is the relationship of insight to understanding?
2. In what sense is the act of understanding relational?
3. What is truth?
4. Why is the intellect always true when it understands?
5. In the first act of understanding does the intellect realize its own truth?
6. What is judgment?
7. How is judgment related to the first act of understanding and truth?
8. What is meant by saying that the intellective act is reflective?
9. Why is the intellective act fully reflective while the sensory act is not?

Existential and Essential Judgments

1. How do existential judgments differ from essential judgments?
2. What are the logical elements of the essential judgment?
3. How are these elements defined?

The Significance of Judgment in the Human Intellective Act

1. Why do judgments necessarily follow upon the first act of understanding?
2. If the human intellect did not derive its knowledge from the sensible world, would the distinction between simple understanding and judgment exist?
3. What is the difference between an affirmative and a negative judgment?

Reasoning: The Mind's Struggle for Further Understanding

1. What is reasoning? How does it differ from simple understanding?
2. What are two senses in which reasoning can be understood?
3. In what sense does reasoning involve a synthesis?
4. What is a syllogism?
5. What is the importance of reasoning to the human?
6. Why is judgment said to be the goal of all reasoning?
7. Is the purpose of reasoning the elimination of all questions?

Thinking as Imperfect Reasoning

1. Does reasoning always result in new knowledge? Why?
2. Why is the mind said to be always engaged in a reasoning process at some level?
3. How is thinking related to reasoning?
4. What is the difference between a proposition and a judgment?
5. Why is it important to make the distinction between propositions and judgments?
6. What is the difference between a statement containing a contradiction in terms, a statement containing a probable statement, and a statement containing a judgment?

Understanding and Error

1. If all authentic judgments are true, does it follow that there is no such thing as error?
2. What follows if authentic judgments can be erroneous?
3. Why is the claim that knowledge is not of itself true, self-defeating?
4. How does the reality of the authentic question rest on the assumption that of itself knowledge cannot be erroneous?
5. How does a judgment differ from a mere proposition?
6. How can error be explained if knowledge is by nature true?
7. What is the role of will in the formation of erroneous statements?
8. If all authentic judgments are true, how is it possible for there to be an actual growth in knowledge?
9. How does a mere affirmation become an authentic judgment?

Chapter 8: Language

The Language Phenomenon

1. How often do humans employ language?
2. What do we talk about?
3. What evidence is there that humans enjoy talking?
4. What is meant by saying that the human is a universal talker?

The Nature and Structure of Language

1. What is the basic unit of language?
2. How does a word differ from a sound or mark?
3. Why is a word said to be a conventional sound?
4. What is a language?
5. What is the function of grammar within a language?
6. What is particularly remarkable about human speech?
7. Why is language said to be the inverse of insight?
8. What is so remarkable about the discovery of the alphabet?

The Philosophic Significance of Language

1. What in-depth significance does the phenomenon of language have for us humans?
2. In what way do foreign languages emphasize the difference be-

tween "simple hearing" and "understanding what was said"?
3. How does the phenomenon of language present special difficulties to both the materialist and the idealist?
4. In what sense does language represent the junction of two "worlds"?

The Ambiguity of Language

1. What is meant by saying that language is ambiguous?
2. In what sense is it unavoidably ambiguous?
3. How is the ambiguity of language related to the multiplicity of words and the fact that we talk constantly?
4. How is the ambiguity of language related to grammar?
5. What are the effects of the ambiguity of language on human communication? How is it related to the problem of misunderstanding?

The Phenomenon of the Plurality of Language

1. What does the fact of the plurality of language tell us about the nature of human languages?
2. What does this same fact tell us about ourselves as humans?
3. What are we able to learn about ourselves and our abilities when we contrast our linguistic abilities with those of the animal?
4. What special significance is to be found in the fact of the intertranslatability of human languages?

Written Language

1. What special importance is to be attached to the phenomenon of written as opposed to oral language?
2. How is written language related to human civilization?
3. How is written language related to human memory?
   In what sense might it be considered an extension of it?
4. Do you see a relation between the development of writing and philosophizing? Explain.

The Human as a Universal Speaker

1. What significance do you see in the fact that humans often talk about what does not exsit?
2. What do the many genres of human speech tell us about the intellective dimension of the human?

3. Does the human's ability to talk about everything seem to have any special philosophical significance?
4. How do animal speech patterns differ from those of humans?
5. In what sense can one say that thinking and speaking go hand-in-hand?

Art and Technology as Language

1. How is knowing related to doing?
2. What is the difference between doing and making something?
3. How is the fact that the human is intellective relate to his abilities as artist and technician?
4. In what sense can man through his activity be said to humanize the world?
5. Do you see a special relationship between human language and creative making? Might art be viewed as a form of language?
6. Why do you think the human person performs as an artist?
7. Why might the human person be called the transcendental worker and artist?
8. Does the fact that the human is curious about the nature of language have any special significance?
9. Why does the human converse philosophically?

Chapter 9: Willing and Choosing

From Understanding to Willing

1. In what sense are the knowing acts of animals functional?
2. What is an appetitive act?
3. How do sensory and volitional acts of appetition differ fundamentally?

The Problem of Volition

1. What is meant by saying that an act is free?
2. Why does the materialist reject freedom?
3. What are the consequences of the denial of freedom in the human?

Human Freedom: The Determinist View

1. What is the determinist view? What are the reasons the deter-

minist gives in support of his or her view?
2. What are the various kinds of determinism?
3. Is there a correlation between determinism and the "scientific method"?

An Anatomy of the Human Free Act

1. How does "the good" of the intellective appetite (will) differ from "the good" of the sensory appetites?
2. What is the formal object of the will?
3. Is the will free as regards the "universal good"? Explain.
4. Why is the will said to be free as regards its relation to limited goods?

Free Choice as Self-Determination

1. In what sense is the act of free choice caused?
2. Why is the act of choosing referred to as an act of self-determination?
3. What is the importance of the distinction between efficient and formal causality as regards the act of free choice? Explain.
4. Explain the significance of the fact that I can always provide a reason for the choice I have made.
5. Am I able to give a "full" explanation for my acts of free choice? Explain.

The Role of Deliberation in the Free Act

1. What is the meaning of the term *deliberation*?
2. Is deliberation an act of the intellect or of the will?
3. Does the will necessarily accept what is presented to it as "best"? Explain.
4. Why does one choose what one chooses?
5. What enables one to distinguish between various acts of free choice?
6. What is the purpose of the deliberative act?
7. Does one have to deliberate?
8. When does one stop deliberating with regard to a particular act of choice?
9. What is meant by saying that the will is always determined?
10. Explain in what sense the intellect and will are said to be mutually related as regards the act of free choice.

Love and the Will

1. What is the most basic meaning of the term *love*?
2. In what does authentic love consist?
3. Does the human will necessarily incline toward the Supreme Good? Explain.

The Indeterminist View

1. Describe briefly the indeterminist position regarding freedom.
2. How does this position differ from that of the determinist? From that of the self-determinist?
3. Indicate how some philosophers have assumed an atheistic position as a result of their indeterminism.
4. What important element of the free act does indeterminism emphasize?
5. Why is it that no act of choice is irrevocable?

Motivating Factors and Freedom

1. In what sense do past choices and one's overall outlook influence our present choices?
2. What is the difference between motivating factors and necessitating causes?

Sensory Appetites

1. What is a sensory appetite? How does it differ from will?
2. What evidence is there of the presence of sensory appetites in animals?
3. Why is the sensory appetite divided into *concupiscible* and *irascible*? How do they differ?
4. What is the effect of the human having both sensory and intellective appetitive powers?

Chapter 10: Emotions and Feelings

The Phenomenon of Emotions

1. Do you agree that emotions are an important component of human life? Why?
2. What significance do you find in the fact that the human actively seeks out emotional experience?

Toward the Definition of Emotions

1. How are emotions defined?
2. What is the role of the body in the emotional experience?
3. How important is the component of psychic awareness to the experience of emotions?
4. How are the sensory appetites related to the emotional experience?

The Significance of Emotional Experience

1. What does the emotional experience teach us about the human condition?
2. Does the phenomenon of emotions in any way reinforce previous considerations made regarding insight and language? Explain.
3. In what sense can emotion be viewed as a form of language?
4. What limitations do the emotions have as a mode of communication?

The Cultivation of Emotions

1. How does the human's experience of emotions differ markedly from that of the animal's?
2. What makes possible the human's active cultivation of emotions?
3. What do humans strive to achieve through the arts?
4. Why is the human said to be an "anxious" animal? What grounds man's anxiety?
5. Why do you think the human is drawn to tragedy and sadness in so many of their writings and songs?

Controlling the Emotions

1. What is meant by the expression *intellectualizing the emotions*? Is this synonymous with suppressing them?
2. In what ways can the emotions contribute to significant achievement? In what ways can they impede it?
3. What role do you think leisure can play in the attainment of emotional balance and control?

The Phenomenon of Humor

1. How is the human smile related to intelligence? Do you think that animals smile?

2. What is humor? What constitutes something as humorous?
3. Do you see a relation between humor and the phenomenon of the ambiguity of language which we discussed earlier?
4. Why do you think people use humor? Is its use always justifiable?
5. Why is it important that a person have a sense of humor?
6. How are emotions related to feelings and mood?

Chapter 11: Habits and Learning

Acquired Operational Structures

1. Why is the human so dependent on the acquisition of skills and abilities?
2. Why is it possible for the animal to have inborn skills, while it is *not* possible for the human?
3. In what way is the human's dependence on learning an advantage?

The Nature of Habits

1. What is a habit?
2. How are habits related to the powers in which they inhere and to the acts toward which they are ordered?
3. How does the habit contribute to the dynamism of the human person?
4. Explain what is meant by the statement that habits provide us with our own behavioral programming.

Habits and Traits

1. How do habits differ from a mere repetition of acts?
2. Can a habit be described as an "operational residue"? Explain.
3. How do habits differ from mere traits or mannerisms?

The Value of Habits

1. How important to the human is the acquisition of operational habits?
2. In what sense do habits represent a conservation of habits and learning?
3. What is the relationship between the acquisition of habits and learning?

The Division of Habits/Intellective Habits

1. What is the first and most basic division of habits?
2. What is an intellective habit? How are they related to learning?
3. How does a speculative habit differ from a practical habit?
4. What are the three speculative habits? How do they differ?
5. What are the two practical habits? How are they defined?
6. How is prudence related to the study of ethics?
7. How are art and prudence related to the deliberative act?

Appetitive Habits

1. Why is the rational appetite in need of habits?
2. What is the most fundamental habit of the will? How is it defined?
3. What is the primary function of the habit of justice?
4. How is justice related to human society?
5. How is the virtue of justice related to love?
6. Why do the sensible appetites require habits?
7. How is the habit of temperance defined?
8. How does the habit of fortitude perfect the irascible appetite?
9. Explain how the habits of temperance and fortitude perform contrary functions for the respective power in which each resides?

Habits and Education

1. How are habits related to the mature development of the individual?
2. In what sense can habits be likened to an "ontological memory"?
3. Indicate in what manner the acquisition of habits is related to one's self-liberation.
4. Why is the human said to be the world's greatest learner?
5. Who is the truly educated person?
6. In what sense is becoming educated a highly personal achievement?
7. What is the role of a school?
8. Of what importance is the curriculum within an academic institution?
9. What is the goal and function of a liberal education?
10. Who is the liberally educated person?
11. How are professional studies related to education?

Habits and Freedom

1. Does the acquisition of habits inhibit or enhance one's freedom? Explain.
2. In what sense do habits permit an accelerated creative development of the human person?

Habits and Technology

1. Distinguish between the human and the animal as "technologists."
2. In what sense can it be said that humans impose "human" structures on their world?
3. What is a tool? How is it related to the human mind?
4. What valuable function does the tool perform for man?

Chapter 12: The Human Person

The Human as an Individual

1. What is meant by the term *individual?*
2. Is the individual the same as the summation of learned habits? Explain.

The Human as a Person

1. What is the meaning of the term *person?*
2. Why is this term reserved for humans?
3. What is the meaning of *I* ?
4. Is the *I* subject to change? Explain.

Personhood and Personality

1. Is the *I* perceivable directly? Explain.
2. Do the animals have an *I* ?
3. What is the twofold signification of the word *I?*
4. How does personality differ from personhood?
5. What is the importance of this distinction?
6. In what does the human person's special dignity consist?
7. How is one's personality related to one's past?
8. Why is each personality unique?
9. In what way is personality dependent upon free choice?
10. What is meant by a "master decision"? What special relevance does it have to personality development?

296   Philosophy of the Human Person

Consequences of the Distinction between Personhood and Personality

Discuss the distinction between personality and person as it pertains to inalienable rights.

Knowing Other Persons

1. How do we know that other persons exist?
2. Is the personhood of another directly observable? Explain.

Understanding That Another Understands: A Phenomenology of "Yes"

1. What is the role of language in my coming to understand that someone else understands?
2. How is it possible for two persons to know that they understand the same thing?
3. Does the word "yes" symbolize but one act of understanding? Explain.
4. Why is it impossible for human language to be purely "private"?
5. Since it is possible for one not to speak the truth, how do I know that someone truly understands when they say they do?

Toward a Phenomenology of "No"

1. Why is the saying of *no* more than a mere denial that one has understood what has been said?
2. Why does the primary use of *yes* and *no* refer to factual statements only?
3. Can you surmise why the use of the word *no* can be a source of far-reaching conflict among individuals?

The Human Person and the Community

1. What is the meaning of love?
2. How does love ground human community?
3. In what sense is authentic love, like understanding, self-transcending?
4. In what does a contractual agreement consist? How is it related to an act of will?
5. How is *you* or *thou* related to an *I*?
6. How important for the *I* is it to recognize a *you*? Why?
7. How do two or more *I*'s become a *we*?

8. What does the reality of the *we* tell us about the nature of the human?
9. Why is the human the most authentically social of all animals?

The Human Person and Loneliness

1. Why is the phenomenon of loneliness worthy of philosophical reflection?
2. How is human loneliness related to the nature of human language and communication?
3. In what sense is one condemned to be a stranger to one's self as well as to others?
4. How does the phenomenon of forgetfulness contribute to one's experience of loneliness?
5. How does the human's relation to being as such constitute an occasion for our "cosmic" loneliness?
6. What does the phenomenon of questioning tell us about the lonely quality of the human condition?
7. How is loneliness related to self-consciousness?
8. Why is it said that we humans are a transcendental mystery to ourselves?

Self-Knowledge and Ethics

1. Why is our self-presence said to be the basis for our human sense of responsibility?
2. What is it that constitutes the human person a moral being?
3. What first awakens within the human his sense of moral consciousness?
4. What is the science of ethics?

The Human Person and Religion

1. Historically, has philosophy been able to answer all of the questions which it has raised?
2. In what sense might religion be considered complementary to philosophic inquiry?

Chapter 13: The Human as a Living Being

What Is Life?

1. Why is the question What is life? an appropriate philosophical question?

2. What is the fundamental characteristic an object must display before we can say that it lives?
3. Explain how growth is a vital process?
4. Are understanding and willing life-acts? Explain.
5. How is a living thing defined?
6. In what sense does a living thing change?

The Unity of Living Things

1. What conclusion can be drawn from the ordered structure of the living organism?
2. Why is the living thing said to be in a state of dynamic equilibrium?
3. In what sense is the living thing one?

The Soul: First Principle of Life

1. What first led Aristotle to distinguish between the matter and the form of things?
2. What does Aristotle understand by soul?
3. What is the rationale for affirming the existence of a supreme organizational principle within each living thing?
4. Is the soul observable empirically?
5. Do only humans possess a soul?

The Human Soul and Its Relation to Body

1. Why has the problem of the nature of the human soul attracted so much attention?
2. Why have many scientists in the past denied a distinction between body and soul?
3. What ultimately does the mechanist mean by the term *soul*?
4. How does spiritual monism differ from materialist monism?
5. What is the definition of monism within the context of the nature of living things?
6. How does Plato's theory of soul differ from that of Aristotle's?
7. Does Descartes's view of the human soul appear to more closely approximate Plato's or Aristotle's?
8. What did Leibniz understand by his theory of preestablished harmony? What is your comment on this view?
9. How does the moderate dualist position of Aquinas's differ from that of Descartes's; from that of Plato's?

10. In the moderate dualist view of Aquinas's (Aristotle's), what is the precise function of soul?
11. How many souls does an individual living thing possess? Why?
12. Where is the soul found in the organism of which it is the life principle?
13. How is the total living thing related to each of its parts?

The Uniqueness of Human Life: Self-Presence

1. In what sense is there a deeper interiority in the human than in other organic life forms?
2. What does the human's self-presence awareness enable him to accomplish which no mere animal is capable of?
3. How is self-programming a life act?
4. Discuss the sense in which the human "dwells" and is "at home" *within the house of being.*
5. Why is it that only the human knows *who* animals are?

The Phenomenon of Death

1. Why is death referred to as a type of change?
2. What happens to the organism when it dies?
3. What special problem faces the material monist and spiritual monist in attempting to explain the phenomenon of death?
4. How does the moderate dualist explain the phenomenon of death?
5. Why are all living organisms said to be essentially subject to death?

Human Death and Immortality

1. Why is the human said to stand closer to death than any other organism?
2. In what sense does the awareness of death pervade the human consciousness?
3. What meaning do you see in Heidegger's expression that "Man is a being toward death?"
4. What do the existence of burial grounds and funereal monuments tell us about the human's consciousness of death?
5. What other evidence is there that the human views the death of people as a special phenomenon among the world of living organisms?

6. Why is it important for man to inquire philosophically into the nature and meaning of his own death?
7. What is Aquinas's philosophy of death?
8. What does Aquinas mean by saying that the human soul is subsistent?
9. What reasons does he give to argue the subsistent nature of the human soul?
10. In support of the immortality of the human soul, does Aquinas argue that the soul has no dependency whatever on the material world? Explain.
11. Does Aquinas's argument fundamentally rest on the point that the human soul is simple and hence incorruptible? Explain.
12. What can be said philosophically, according to Aquinas, concerning the state of the separated soul?

Chapter 14: The Beginnings of Human Life

The Origin of Human Life: The Problem

1. What are the chief questions dealt with in this final chapter?
2. In what sense are the prior questions concerning the nature of the human relevant to the questions concerning our origin?
3. What is it that renders these questions difficult to respond to?

The Origin of the Human Soul

1. Why is the question of the origin of the individual human a problem only for the dualist?
2. What fundamental options are available as regards the solution to the problem of the origin of this individual human?
3. What is the traducianist solution to this problem? What are its weaknesses?
4. Explain briefly the creationist position as regards the origin of the human.
5. According to the creationist view, does the human soul preexist to its union with the body?

The Problem of Individuation

1. What is the problem discussed in this section?
2. Why cannot the soul be the source of its own individuation?

3. How does the question of individuality differ from that of personality?
4. What ultimately grounds the fact that Plato and Socrates are both human?
5. Why is Socrates' soul said to be singular but not by reason of itself?
6. Why does Aquinas state that "the essence of Socrates is not Socrates"?
7. How is the human's social nature and need for intersubjective communication related to the problem of his individualization?
8. What is meant by the statement that no individual human is fully human?

The Beginning of Human Life

1. What was Aristotle's theory regarding the origin of the individual human?
2. Why is this theory now obsolete?
3. Why is the view that human life begins at the moment of conception said to be supported by modern discoveries in genetics?

The Evolutionary Theory

1. Why is the question of the collective origin of man raised last in our study of the human person?
2. Why is the evolutionary theory regarding humankind's origin said to be trans-scientific or philosophical?
3. What is the etymology of the term *evolution*?
4. Why is the evolutionary theory said to involve "transformism"?
5. What is the point made by Thorpe and Salisbury regarding the inadequacy of the evolutionary model to explain the origin of life?
6. Why is it that Thorpe argues that recent scientific discoveries have made "it far less comprehensible how life might have arisen from non-living matter than it was before."

The Origin of Humankind

1. Why is it argued that the human life form could not have emerged from lower forms merely through random selection and chance mutation?

2. What connection do you see between the bipedalism and intellective nature of the human?
3. Do you think that recent anthropological findings in Africa support or weaken the traditional evolutionary view regarding the origin of humans.

Bibliography

General Works

Clark, Malcolm. *The Need To Question.* Englewood Cliffs, N.J.: Prentice-Hall, Inc., 1973. See especially Chapter I: "What Do Philosophers Do?"

Collins, James, *The Existentialists.* Chicago: Henry Regnery Co., 1952.

Copleston, Frederick, S.J. *Contemporary Philosophy.* Westminster, Md.: The Newman Press, 1956.

Donceel, Joseph F., S.J. *Philosophical Anthropology.* New York: Sheed, 1967.

Gilson, Étienne. *Spirit of Medieval Philosophy.* New York: Charles Scribner's Sons, 1936.

———. *A Gilson Reader.* Edited by Anton C. Pegis. Garden City, New York: Doubleday & Co., Inc., 1957.

Joad, C.E.M. *Guide to Modern Thought.* 4th ed. London: Faber & Faber, 1948.

Jones, W. T. *A History of Western Philosophy.* 4 vols. New York: Harcourt Brace, Inc., 1952.

Kelly, William, and Andrew Tallon, eds. *Readings in the Philosophy of Man.* New York: McGraw-Hill Book Co., 1967.

Langdon-Davies, John. *On the Nature of Man.* New York: Mentor, 1961.

Maritain, Jacques. *Existence and the Existent.* Translated by L. Galantière and G. B. Phelan. New York: Pantheon Books, 1949.

Royce, James E. *Man and Meaning.* New York: McGraw-Hill Book Co., 1969.

Russell, Bertrand. *What I Believe.* New York: E. P. Dutton & Co., Inc., 1926.

Sartre, Jean-Paul. *Existentialism.* Translated by B. Frechtman. New York: Philosophical Library, 1957.

Stumpf, Samuel Enoch. *Socrates to Sartre: A History of Philosophy.* 2d ed. New York: McGraw-Hill Book Co., 1975.

Titus, Harold H. *Living Issues in Philosophy.* New York: Van Nostrand Reinhold Co., 1970.

Urmson, J. O. *Philosophical Analysis.* Oxford: Oxford Univ. Press, 1956.

Wild, John. *The Challenge of Existentialism.* Bloomington, Indiana: Indiana Univ. Press, 1955.

Chapters 1 and 2

Aristotle. "Metaphysics" (Books 1 and 2) and "On the Soul." In *The Basic Works of Aristotle.* Edited by Richard McKeon. New York: Random House, Inc., 1941.

Augustine, Aurelius. *The Confessions of St. Augustine* (Books 1-10). Translated by F. J. Sheed, New York: Sheed & Ward, 1942.

Barret, William. *Irrational Man.* Garden City, N. Y.: Doubleday & Co., Inc., 1958.

Boethius. *The Consolation of Philosophy.* Translated by Richard Green. New York: Library of Liberal Arts, 1962.

Bontempo, Charles I., and Jack S. Odell, eds. *The Owl of Minerva.* New York: McGraw-Hill Book Co., 1975.

Burnet, John. *Greek Philosophy: Thales to Plato.* New York: St. Martin's Press, Inc., 1962.

Cassirer, Ernst. *An Essay on Man.* New Haven, Conn.: Yale Univ. Press, 1944.

Copleston, Frederick. *History of Philosophy.* 7 vols. Garden City, N. Y.: Doubleday & Co., Inc. 1961-65.

Coreth, Emerich, S.J. *Metaphysics.* Edited by Joseph Donceel, S.J. New York: Herder & Herder, 1968.

Danto, A. C. *What Philosophy Is.* New York: Harper & Row Publishers, Inc., 1968.

Fichte, Johann Gottlieb. *Vocation of Man.* Translated by William Smith. Chicago: Open Court Pub., Co., 1925.

Heidegger, Martin. *What Is Philosophy?* Translated by Jean T. Wilde and William Kluback. New Haven, Conn.: College and University Press, 1956.

Husserl, Edmund. *Phenomenology and the Crisis of Philosophy.* New York: Harper Torchbooks, 1965.

Jaspers, Earl. *The Way to Wisdom.* Translated by R. Manheim. New Haven, Conn.: Yale Univ. Press, 1951.

Joad, D. E. M. *Guide to Philosophy.* New York: Dover Publications, Inc., 1936.

Machan, Tibur R. *Introduction to Philosophic Inquiries.* Boston: Allyn and Bacon, Inc., 1977.

Maritain, Jacques. *An Introduction to Philosophy.* Translated by E. I. Watkin. London: Sheed & Ward, 1932.

——. *On the Use of Philosophy.* Princeton, N. J.: Princeton Univ. Press, 1961.

Mouroux, J. *The Meaning of Man.* Translated by A. H. C. Downes. New York: Sheed, 1948.

Nozick, Robert. *Philosophical Explanations.* Cambridge, Mass.: The Belknap Press of Harvard Univ. Press, 1981. See Chapter III, "Knowledge and Skepticism."

Pirsig, Robert M. *Zen and the Art of Motorcycle Maintenance.* New York: Bantam Books, Inc., 1974.

Plato. "Meno." In *Great Dialogues of Plato.* Translated by W. H. D. Rouse and edited by Erick H. Warmington and Philip G. Rouse. New York: Mentor, 1956.

Solomon, Robert C. *The Big Questions: A Short Introduction to Philosophy.* New York: Harcourt Brace Jovanovich, Inc., 1982.

Stevenson, Leslie, ed. *The Study of Human Nature.* New York: Oxford Univ. Press, Inc., 1981.

Chapter 3

Adler, Mortimer. *Aristotle for Everybody.* New York: Macmillan Publishing Co., Inc., 1978.

Aiken, Henry D., ed. *Age of Ideology: The 19th Century Philosophers.* New York: New American Library of World Literature, 1957.

Anscombe, G. E. M., and P. T. Geatch. *Three Philosophers.* Ithaca, N. Y.: Cornell Univ. Press, 1961.

Aquinas, Thomas. "Summa Theologica." I: Questions 84 and 85. In *The Basic Writings of St. Thomas Aquinas.* Edited and annotated by Anton C. Pegis. New York: Random House, Inc., 1944.

_____. *Introduction to St. Thomas Aquinas.* Edited with an introduction by Anton C. Pegis. New York: Modern Library, Inc., 1947.

_____. *Introduction to the Metaphysics of St. Thomas Aquinas.* Edited and translated by James F. Anderson. South Bend, Ind.: Regnery/Gateway Inc., 1953.

_____. *The Pocket Aquinas.* Edited with an introduction by Vernon J. Bourke. New York: Pocket Books, Inc. 1960.

Ardley, Gavin: *Berkeley's Renovation of Philosophy.* The Hague: Nijhoff, 1968.

Aristotle. "On the Soul." In *Basic Works of Aristotle.* Edited by Richard McKeon. Translated by J. A. Smith. New York: Random House, Inc., 1941.

Armstrong, David M., and C.B. Martin. *Locke and Berkeley, A Collection of Critical Essays.* Garden City, N. Y.: Doubleday & Co., Inc., 1965.

Ayer, A. J. *Philosophy in the Twentieth Century.* New York: Vintage Books, 1984.

Barrett, William, and H. D. Aiken, eds. *Philosophy in the Twentieth Century.* New York: Random House, Inc., 1962.

Beck, Lewis W. *Early German Philosophy: Kant and His Predecessors.* Cambridge, Mass.: Harvard Univ. Press, 1969.

Berkeley, George. "The Principles of Human Principles of Human Knowledge." In *The Works of George Berkeley.* Edited by A. C. Fraser. Oxford: Clarendon Press, 1901.

———. *Principles of Human Knowledge and Three Dialogues between Hylas and Philonus.* Cleveland: World Pub. Co., 1963.

———. *Principles of Human Knowledge: Text and Critical Essays.* Edited by Colin M. Turbayne. Indianapolis: Bobbs-Merrill Co., Inc. 1969.

Berlin, Isaiah, ed. *Age of Enlightenment: The Eighteenth Century Philosophers.* New York: New American Library of World Literature, 1956.

Blackham, H. J. *Six Existentialist Thinkers.* New York: Harper Torchbooks, 1959.

Bleicher, Josef. *Contemporary Hermeneutics: Hermeneutics as Method, Philosophy and Critique.* London: Routledge & Kegan Paul,1980.

Bochenski, I. M. *Contemporary European Philosophy.* Berkeley: Univ. of California Press, 1961.

Chesterton, G. K. *St. Thomas Aquinas.* Garden City, N.Y.: Doubleday & Co., 1936.

Collins, James. *A History of Modern European Philosophy.* Milwaukee: Bruce Publishing Co., 1954.

———. *Interpreting Modern Philosophy.* Princeton, N. J.: Princeton Univ. Press, 1972.

Comte, Auguste. *The Positive Philosophy of August Comte.* 2 vols. London: 1853.

Copleston, Frederick, S.J. *Aquinas.* Baltimore: Penguin Books, Inc., 1955.

——. *Contemporary Philosophy: Studies of Logical Positivism and Existentialism.* Westminster, Md.: Newman Press, 1956.

——. *A History of Philosophy.* Garden City, N.Y.: Doubleday & Co., Inc., 1966.

Cornford, F. M.: *Plato's Theory of Knowledge.* New York: Liberal Arts Press, Inc., 1957.

Derrida, Jacques. *Speech and Phenomena: and Other Essays on Husserl's Theory of Signs.* Evanston, Ill.: Northwestern Univ. Press, 1973.

Descartes, René. "Discourse on Method: Meditations." In *Essential Works of Descartes.* Edited and translated by Lowell Bair. New York: Bantam Books, Inc., 1961.

De Wulf, Maurice. *Scholastic Philosophy.* New York: Dover Publications, Inc., 1956. Originally published in 1903.

Dryer, D. P. *Kant's Solution for Verification in Metaphysics.* Toronto: Univ. of Toronto Press, 1966.

Edie, James E., ed. *What is Phenomenology?* Chicago: Quadrangle Books, Inc., 1962.

Edwards, Paul, editor in chief. *The Encyclopedia of Philosophy.* New York: Macmillan Publishing Co., Inc., 1967.

Esposito, Joseph L. *Schelling's Idealism and Philosophy of Nature.* Lewisburg: Bucknell Univ. Press, 1977.

Fabro, Cornelio. *God in Exile: Modern Atheism.* Westminster, Md.: The Newman Press, 1968.

Fremantle, Anne, ed. *The Age of Belief: The Medieval Philosophers.* New York: New American Library, 1955.

Gadamer, Hans-Georg. *Philosophical Hermeneutics.* Translated by David Linge. Berkeley: California Univ. Press, 1976.

Gilson, Étienne. *The Philosophy of Thomas Aquinas.* New York: Cambridge Univ. Press, 1937.

____. *The Unity of Philosophical Experience.* New York: Charles Scribner's Sons, 1937.

Grene, Marjorie. *Introduction to Existentialism.* Chicago: Univ. of Chicago Press, 1948.

____. *A Portrait of Aristotle.* Chicago: Univ. of Chicago Press, 1963.

Grube, G. M. A. *The Trial and Death of Socrates.* Indianapolis: Hackett Publishing Co., 1974.

Hampshire, Stuart, ed. *Age of Reason: The Seventeenth Century Philosophers.* New York: New American Library of World Literature, 1956.

Hegel, Georg W. F. *Hegel Selections.* Edited by Jacob Lowenberg. New York: Charles Scribner's Sons, 1929.

____. *The Philosophy of Hegel.* Edited by Carl J. Friedrich. New York: Modern Library, Inc. 1953.

____. *Phenomenology of Spirit.* Translated by A. V. Miller. New York: Oxford Univ. Press, Inc., 1977.

Heidegger, Martin. *Kant and the Problem of Metaphysics.* Bloomington, Ind.: Indiana Univ. Press, 1962.

____. *Being and Time.* Translated by John Macquarrie and Edward Robinson. London: S.C.M. Press, 1962.

Hume, David. A Treatise on Human Nature. Oxford: Clarendon Press, 1951.

____. *An Enquiry Concerning Human Understanding.* New York: The Library of Liberal Arts, 1955.

Husserl, Edmund. *The Crisis of European Sciences and Transcendental Phenomenology: An Introduction to Phenomenological Philosophy.* Translated by David Carr. Evanston, Ill.: Northwestern Univ. Press, 1970.

Hyman, Arthur, and James J. Walsh, eds. *Philosophy in the Middle Ages: The Christian, Jewish and Islamic Traditions.* Indianapolis: Hackett Publishing Co., 1978.

Kant, Immanuel. *Critique of Pure Reason.* Translated by Norman Kemp Smith. New York: Modern Library, Inc., 1958. Abridged ed.

Kaufmann, Walter. *Existentialism from Dostoevsky to Sartre.* New York: Meridian Books, 1956.

Kenny, Anthony. *Descartes: A Study of His Philosophy.* New York: Random House, Inc., 1968.

———. *Wittgenstein.* Harmondsworth, Middlesex: Penguin Books, Inc., 1973.

Kockelmans, Joseph J. *Phenomenology: the Philosophy of Edmund Husserl and Its Interpretation.* Garden City, N. Y.: Doubleday & Co., Inc., 1967.

Koerner, S. *Kant.* Baltimore: Penguin Books, Inc., 1955.

Lauer, Quentin J. *Phenomenology: Its Genesis and Prospect.* New York: Harper Torchbooks, 1965.

———. *Hegel's Idea of Philosophy.* New York: Fordham Univ. Press, 1971.

Lawrence, Nathaniel, and Daniel O'Connor. *Readings in Existential Phenomenology.* Englewood Cliffs, N. J.: Prentice-Hall, Inc. 1967.

Locke, John. *An Essay Concerning Human Understanding.* Edited by A. C. Fraser. Oxford: Clarendon Press, 1894.

Loewith, Karl. *From Hegel to Nietzsche: The Revolution in Nineteenth Century Thought.* Translated by David E. Green. Garden City, New York: Doubleday & Co., Inc., 1965.

Luijpen, William A. *Existential Phenomenology.* Pittsburgh: Duquesne Univ. Press, 1960.

McKeon, Richard, ed. *Medieval Philosophers.* 2 vols. New York: Charles Scribner's Sons, 1959.

Marcel, Gabriel. *The Philosophy of Existentialism.* New York: Citadel Press, 1961.

Maritain, Jacques. *The Dream of Descartes.* New York: Philosophical Library, Inc. 1944.

Merleau-Ponty, Maurice. *Phenomenology of Perception.* Translated by Colin Smith. London: Routledge and Kegan Paul Ltd., 1965.

Mure, G. R. G. *Aristotle.* Fair Lawn, N.J.: Oxford Univ. Press, Inc., 1964.

Palmer, Richard E. *Hermeneutics: Interpretation Theory in Schleiermacher, Dilthey, Heidegger and Gadamer.* Evanston, Ill.: Northwestern Univ. Press, 1969.

Pereleman, Charles. *A Historical Introduction to Philosophical Thinking.* Translated by Kenneth A. Brown. New York: Random House, Inc. 1965.

Plato. "Meno" and "Phaedo." In *Great Dialogues of Plato.* Edited by Eric H. Warmington and Philip G. Rouse. Translated by W. H. D. Rouse. New York: Mentor, 1956.

_____. *Plato's Theory of Knowledge: "The Theatetus" and "The Sophist."* Translated and commented on by Francis M. Cornford. New York: Library of Liberal Arts, 1957.

Randall, J. H., Jr. *Aristotle.* New York: Columbia Univ. Press, 1960.

Ricoeur, Paul. *The Conflict of Interpretations.* Evanston, Ill.: Northwestern Univ. Press, 1974.

Rorty, Richard. *Philosophy and the Mirror of Nature.* Princeton, N. J.: Princeton Univ. Press, 1979.

Ross, W. D. *Plato's Theory of Ideas.* Fair Lawn, N. J.: Oxford Univ. Press, 1951.

_____. *Aristotle.* New York: Meridian, 1959.

Ryle, Gilbert. *The Concept of Mind.* New York: Barnes & Noble Publications, 1949.

Sartre, Jean-Paul. *Being and Nothingness.* New York: Philosophical Library, Inc. 1956.

Scheler, Max. *On the Eternal in Man.* Translated by Bernard Noble. New York: Harper & Bros., 1960.

Seung, T. K. *Structuralism and Hermeneutics.* New York: Columbia Univ. Press, 1982.

Shorey, Paul. *What Plato Said.* Chicago: Univ. of Chicago Press, 1933.

Spiegelberg, Herbert. *Phenomenological Movement: A Historical Introduction.* 2 vols. The Hague: Martinus Nijhoff, 1965.

Stumpf, Samuel E. *Socrates to Sartre.* 2d ed. New York: McGraw-Hill Book Co., 1975.

Taylor, A. E. *Plato: The Man and His Work.* Cleveland: World Pub. Co., 1956.

Urmson, J. O. *Philosophical Analysis.* Oxford: Oxford Univ. Press, 1956.

Veitch, John, and R. H. M. Elwes. *The Rationalists: René Descartes, Benedict de Spinoza, Gottfried Wilhelm Freiherr von Leibniz.* Translated by George Montgomery. Garden City, N.Y.: Doubleday & Company, Inc., 1960.

Warner, Rex. *The Greek Philosophers.* New York: Mentor, 1958.

Warnock, G. J. *English Philosophy Since 1900.* Oxford: Oxford Univ. Press, Inc., 1958.

White, Morton, ed. *The Age of Analysis: 20th Century Philosophers.* New York: New American Library of World Literature, 1955.

Williams, Bernard. "Descartes. " In *The Encyclopedia of Philosophy.* Vol. 1. Edited by Paul Edwards. New York: Collier-Macmillan, 1967.

Wippel, John F., and Allan B. Wolter, O.F.M., eds. *Medieval Philosophy: From St. Augustine to Nicholas of Cusa.* New York: Free Press, 1969.

Wittgenstein, Ludwig. *Philosophical Investigations.* Translated by G. E. M. Anscombe. Oxford: Basil Blackwell, 1953.

Wolff, Robert Paul, ed. *Kant: A Collection of Critical Essays.* Garden City, N. Y.: Doubleday Anchor, 1967.

Chapter 4

Anscombe, G. E. M. "Intention. " In *Essays in Philosophical Psychology.* Edited by Donald F. Gustafson. Garden City, N.Y.: Doubleday & Co., Inc., 1964.

Aquinas, Thomas. "Summa Theologica." In *Basic Writings of St. Thomas Aquinas.* Edited by Anton C. Pegis. New York: Random House, Inc., 1945. See especially Questions 16, 17, and 18.

____ .*On Truth.* 3 vols. See Question 1. Translated by R. W. Mulligan,

S.J., J.V. McGlynn, S.J., and R. W. Schmidt, S.J. Chicago: Henry Regnery Co., 1952-54.

Aristotle. *De Sensu* ("Sense") and *De Memoria* ("Memory"). Text, translation, and commentary by G. R. T. Ross. Cambridge, England: Univ. of Cambridge, 1906.

———. "On the Soul." Books 1 and 2. In *The Basic Works of Aristotle*. Edited by Richard McKeon. New York: Random House, Inc., 1941.

Austin, J. L. *Sense and Sensibilia*. Oxford: Clarendon Press, 1962.

Bollnow, O. F. "Lived Space." In *Philosophy Today*. Vol. 5, 1961.

De Waehlens, Alphonse. "The Phenomenology of the Body. " In *Readings in Existential Phenomenology*. Edited by Nathaniel Lawrence and Daniel O'Connor. Englewood Cliffs, N.J.: Prentice-Hall, Inc., 1967.

Gilson, Étienne. *Being and Some Philosophers*. Toronto: Pontifical Institute of Medieval Studies, 1949.

Hamlyn, D. W. *Sensation and Perception: A History of the Philosophy of Perception*. New York: Humanities Press, Inc., 1961.

Henle, Robert J., S.J. "The Basis of Philosophical Realism." In *The New Scholasticism*. LVI:1 (1982) 1-29.

Maritain, Jacques. *Creative Intuition in Art and Poetry*. New York: Pantheon Books, 1953.

Merleau-Ponty, M. *Phenomenology of Perception*. 2d ed. New York: Humanities Press, Inc., 1963.

Piaget, Jean. *Insight and Illusions of Philosophy*. New York: New American Library, 1971.

Ricoeur, Paul. *Fallible Man*. Chicago: Henry Regnery Co., 1965.

Straus, Erwin. *The Primary World of the Senses*. New York: Free Press, 1963.

Swartz, Robert J., ed. *Perceiving, Sensing, and Knowing: A Book of Readings from Twentieth Century Sources in the Philosophy of Perception*. Garden City, New York: Doubleday & Co., Inc., 1965.

Zaner, Richard. *The Problem of Embodiment*. The Hague: Nijhoff, 1964.

Chapter 5

Albright, W. F. *From the Stone Age to Christianity.* Garden City, New York: Doubleday & Co., Inc., 1957.

Allers, Rudolf. "The *Vis Cogitativa* and Evaluation." In *The New Scholasticism.* 15 (1941): 195-221.

Aquinas, Thomas. "Disputed Question on the Soul." In *On the Soul.* Translated by J. P. Rowan. St. Louis: Herder, 1949.

Aristotle. "On Dreams." In *The Basic Works of Aristotle.* Edited by Richard McKeon. New York: Random House, Inc., 1941.

——. "On Memory and Reminiscence." In *The Basic Works of Aristotle.* Edited by Richard McKeon. New York: Random House, Inc., 1941.

——. "On the Soul." In *The Basic Works of Aristotle.* Edited by Richard McKeon. New York: Random House, Inc., 1941. See especially Book II.

Augustine, Aurelius. *Basic Writings of Saint Augustine.* Edited by Whitney J. Oates. New York: Random House, Inc., 1948.

——. *The Confessions of St. Augustine.* Translated by Rex Warner. New York: New American Library, 1963. See especially Books 10, 11, and 12.

Austin, J. L. *Sense and Sensibilia.* Oxford: Clarendon Press, 1962.

——. "Pretending." In *Essays in Philosophical Psychology.* Edited by Donald F. Gustafson. Garden City, N.Y.: Doubleday & Co., Inc., 1964.

Benjamin, B. S. "Remembering." In *Essays in Philosophical Psychology.* Edited by Donald F. Gustafson. Garden City, N.Y.: Doubleday & Co., 1964.

Berger, Gaston. "A Phenomenological Approach to the Problem of Time." In *Readings in Existential Phenomenology.* Edited by Nathaniel Lawrence and Daniel O'Connor. Englewood Cliffs, N. J.: Prentice-Hall, Inc., 1967.

Bergson, Henri. *Matter and Memory.* Translated by N. M. Paul and W. S. Palmer. New York: Macmillan Publishing Co., Inc., 1950.

Flynn, Thomas V., O.P. "The Cogitative Power. " In *The Thomist.* Vol. XVI (1953), 542-63.

Heidegger, Martin. *Being and Time.* Translated by John Macquarrie and Edward Robinson. New York: Harper & Row Publishers, Inc., 1962. See especially Division II "*Dasein* and Temporality."

Husserl, Edmund. *The Phenomenology of Internal Time-Consciousness.* Bloomington, Ind.: Indiana Univ. Press, 1964.

Klubertanz, G. *The Discursive Power: Sources and Doctrine of the "Vis Cogitativa" According to St. Thomas Aquinas.* St. Louis: Modern Schoolman, 1952.

Koestler, Arthur. *The Act of Creation: A Study of the Conscious and Unconscious in Science and Art.* New York: Dell Publishing Co., Inc., 1964. See especially Book 2, Chapter 19, "Perception and Memory."

Levi-Strauss, Claude. *The Savage Mind.* Chicago: Univ. of Chicago Press, 1966.

Lynch, William F. *Images of Hope: Imagination as Healer of the Hopeless.* New York: Mentor Omega, 1965.

Macdonald, Margaret. "Sleeping and Waking." In *Essays in Philosophical Psychology.* Edited by Donald F. Gustafson. Garden City, N.Y.: Doubleday & Co., Inc., 1964.

Malcolm, Norman. "The Concept of Dreaming." In *Essays in Philosophical Psychology.* Edited by Donald F. Gustafson. Garden City, New York: Doubleday & Co., 1964

Merleau-Ponty, M. *The Structure of Behavior.* Boston: Beacon Press, Inc. 1963.

_____ . *The Primacy of Perception.* Edited and translated by James M. Edie. Evanston, Ill.: Northwestern Univ. Press, 1964.

Minkowski, Eugene. "Imagination?" In *Readings in Existential Phenomenology.* Edited by Nathaniel Lawrence and Daniel O'Connor. Englewood Cliffs, N.J.: Prentice-Hall, Inc. 1967.

Pears, D. F.: "Dreaming." In *Essays in Philosophical Psychology.* Edited by Donald F. Gustafson. Garden City, N.Y.: Doubleday & Co., Inc., 1964.

Peghaire, Julien. "A Forgotten Sense, The Cogitative According to St. Thomas Aquinas." In *The Modern Schoolman*. Vol. XL (1943) 123-40; 210-29.

Plato. "Phaedo." In *Great Dialogues of Plato*. Translated by W. H. D. Rouse. New York: Mentor, 1956.

Sartre, Jean-Paul. *Being and Nothingness*. Paris: Gallimard, 1943.

——. *Imagination*. Ann Arbor, Mich.: Univ. of Michigan Press, 1962.

Shorter, J. M. "Imagination." In *Essays in Philosophical Psychology*. Edited by Donald F. Gustafson. Garden City, N.Y.: Doubleday & Co., 1964.

Strasser, Stephen. *The Soul in Metaphysical and Empirical Psychology*. Pittsburgh: Duquesne Univ. Press, 1962.

Straus, Erwin. "On Memory Traces." In *Readings in Existential Phenomenology*. Edited by Nathaniel Lawrence and Daniel O'Connor. Englewood Cliffs, N.J.: Prentice-Hall, Inc., 1967.

Thorpe, W. H. *Learning and Instinct in Animals*. London: Methuen, 1956.

Thorpe, W. H., and O. L. Zangwill. *Current Problems of Animal Behavior*. Cambridge: Cambridge Univ. Press, 1961.

Van Peurson, C. A. *Body, Soul, Spirit*. Translated by H. H. Hoskins. London: Oxford Univ. Press, Inc., 1966.

Chapter 6

Adler, Mortimer J. *The Difference of Man and the Difference It Makes*. New York: Holt, Rinehart & Winston, Inc., 1967.

Bergson, Henri. *The Creative Mind*. Tototna, N. J.: Adams & Co., 1965.

Cassirer, Ernst. *An Essay on Man*. New Haven: Yale Univ. Press, 1945. See especially chapter 3, "From Animal Reactions to Human Responses."

Henle, Robert J., S.J. "The Basis of Philosophical Realism Reexamined." In *The New Scholasticism*. Vol. LVI, 1. (1982) 1-29.

Koestler, Arthur. *The Act of Creation.* New York: Dell Publishing Co., Inc., 1967. See especially Book I, Part 2, "The Sage."

Lonergan, Bernard J. F., S.J. *Insight: A Study of Human Understanding.* Toronto: Longmans, Green and Co., 1957.

Loux, Michael J., ed. *Universals and Particulars: Readings in Ontology.* Garden City, New York: Doubleday & Co., Inc., 1970.

Mascall, E. L. "The Gulf in Philosophy: Is Thomism the Bridge?" In *The Thomist.* Vol. XXXVIII (Jan. 1974) 8-26.

Peccorini, Francisco L. "Knowledge of the Singular: Aquinas, Suarez, and Recent Interpreters." In *The Thomist.* Vol. XXXVIII, 1:606-55.

Plato. "The Republic." In *Great Dialogues of Plato.* Translated by W. H. D. Rouse. New York: New American Library, 1956.

Thorpe, W. H. *Learning and Instinct in Animals.* New ed. London: Methuen, 1963.

Watson, J. B. *Behaviourism.* London: Kegan Paul, 1928.

Chapter 7

Adler, Mortimer J. "Little Errors in the Beginning." In *The Thomist.* Vol. XXXVIII, 1:27-48.

Aquinas, Thomas. *Truth.* 3 vols. Translated by R. W. Mulligan, S. J., J. V. McGlynn, S. J., and R. W. Schmidt, S. J. Chicago: Henry Regnery Co., 1952-54.

Aristotle. "On the Soul." In *The Basic Writings of Aristotle.* Edited by Richard McKeon. New York: Random House, Inc., 1941.

Ayer, A. J. *The Problem of Knowledge.* London: Macmillan Publishing Co., Inc. 1958.

Chenu, M.-D., O. P. *Toward Understanding St. Thomas.* Translated by A.-M. Landry, O. P. and Dominic Hughes, O. P. Chicago: Henry Regnery Co., 1963.

Gallagher, Kenneth T. *The Philosophy of Knowledge.* New York: Sheed, 1965.

Geatch, Peter. *Mental Acts: Their Contents and Their Objects.* New York: Humanities Press, Inc., 1957.

Grabmann, Martin. *Thomas Aquinas.* New York: Longmans, Green & Co., 1928.

Grene, Marjorie. *The Knower and the Known.* New York: Basic Books, Inc., 1966.

Heidegger, Martin. "On the Essence of Truth." In *Existence and Being.* Edited by William Brock. Chicago: Henry Regnery Co., 1949.

——. *Kant and the Problem of Metaphysics.* Translated by James S. Churchill. Bloomington, Ind.: Indiana Univ. Press, 1962.

——. *Discourse on Thinking.* Translated by John M. Anderson and E. Hans Freund. New York: Harper & Row Publishers, Inc., 1966.

——. *What is Called Thinking?* New York: Harper & Row Publishers, Inc., 1968.

Hoenan, Peter, S. J. *Reality and Judgment According to St. Thomas.* Translated by H. F. Tiblier, S. J. Chicago: Henry Regnery Co., 1952.

James, William. *The Meaning of Truth.* New York: Longmans, Green & Co., 1909.

Kierkegaard, Søren. *Concluding Unscientific Postscript.* Translated by David F. Swenson. Edited by Walter Lowrie. Princeton, N. J.: Princeton Univ. Press, 1941.

Klubertanz, George P., S. J. "St. Thomas and the Knowledge of the Singular." In *The New Scholasticism.* Vol. XXVI (1952) 135-66.

——. *St. Thomas and Analogy: A Textual Analysis and Systematic Synthesis.* Chicago: Loyola Univ. Press, 1960.

Lonergan, Bernard J. F., S. J. *Insight: A Study of Human Understanding.* Toronto: Longmans, Green & Co., 1957.

——. *Collection.* St. Louis: Herder, 1967.

——. *Verbum: Word and Idea in Aquinas.* London: Darton, Longman & Todd, 1968.

Luijpen, William A. *Existential Phenomenology.* Pittsburgh: Duquesne Univ. Press, 1965.

Maritain, Jacques. *Distinguish to Unite: The Degrees of Knowledge.* New York: Charles Scribner's Sons, 1959.

Peters, John A. *Metaphysics, a Systematic Survey.* Pittsburgh: Duquesne Univ. Press, 1963.

Plato. "Phaedo," "Parmenides," "Theaetetus," and "Sophist." In *The Dialogues of Plato.* 2 vols. Translated by B. Jowett. New York: Random House, Inc., 1937.

Quine, W. V., and J. S. Ullian. *The Web of Belief.* 2d edition. New York: Random House, Inc., 1978.

Rahner, Karl, S. J. "Truth in St. Aquinas." In *Readings in the Philosophy of Man.* 2d ed. Edited by William L. Kelly S. J. and Andrew Tallon. New York: McGraw-Hill Book Co., 1972.

Russell, Bertrand. *Human Knowledge: Its Scope and Limits.* London: Allen and Unwin, 1948.

Thevanez, Pierre. "Reflection and Consciousness of Self." In *What is Phenomenology and Other Essays.* Edited with an intro. by James M. Edie. Chicago: Quadrangle Books, 1962.

Weisheipl, James A., O.P. *Friar Thomas D'Aquino: His life, Thought and Work.* Garden City, N. Y.: Doubleday & Co., 1974.

Wild, John. *The Return to Reason.* Chicago: Henry Regnery Co., 1953.

Chapter 8

Anscombe, G. E. M. *An Introduction to Wittgenstein's "Tractatus."* 2d ed. New York: Harper & Row Publishers, Inc., 1959.

Aristotle. "On Interpretation." In *The Basic Works of Aristotle.* Richard McKeon, ed. New York: Random House, Inc. 1941.

Ayer, Alfred Jules. *Language, Truth and Logic.* New York: Dover Publications, Inc., 1946.

Cassirer, Ernst. *Philosophy of Symbolic Forms.* New Haven, Conn.: Yale Univ. Press, 1953-55.

Charlesworth, Maxwell J. *Philosophy and Linguistic Analysis.* Pittsburgh: Duquesne Univ. Press, 1959.

Chomsky, Noam. *Problems of Knowledge and Freedom.* New York: Vintage Books, Inc., 1971.

Cleator, P. E. *Lost Languages.* New York: Mentor, 1962.

Deely, John N. "The Two Approaches to Language." In *The Thomist.* Vol. XXXVIII, 4:856-907.

Dufrenne, Mikel. *Language and Philosophy.* Translated by Henry B. Veatch. Bloomington, Ind.: Indiana Univ. Press, 1963.

Ellard, James W. *By the Waters of Babylon.* London: Huchinson, 1972.

Heidegger, Martin. *On the Way to Language.* Translated by Peter D. Hertz. New York: Harper & Row Publishers, Inc., 1971.

———. *Poetry, Language, Thought.* Translated by Albert Hofstadter. New York: Harper & Row Publishers, Inc., 1971.

Hjelmslev, Louis. *Language.* Translated by Francis J. Whitfield. Madison: Univ. of Wisconsin Press, 1970.

Jesperson, Otto. *Language: Its Nature, Development and Origin.* New York: W. W. Norton & Co., Inc., 1964.

Kenny, Anthony. *Wittgenstein.* Harmondsworth, England: Penguin Books, 1973.

Koestler, Arthur. *The Act of Creation: A Study of the Conscious and Unconscious in Science and Art.* New York: Dell Publishing Co., Inc., 1964. See especially Book II, Chapter 14, "Learning to Speak."

Kwant, Remy C. *The Phenomenology of Language.* Pittsburgh: Duquesne Univ. Press, 1965.

Langer, Susanne K. *Philosophy in a New Key: A Study in the Symbolism of Reason, Rite, and Art.* New York: Mentor, 1942.

———. Feeling and Form. New York: Charles Scribner's Sons, 1953.

Mascall, E. L. *Words and Images.* London: Longmans, Green, 1957.

Merleau-Ponty, M. *Phenomenology of Perception.* Translated by Colin Smith. New York: Humanities Press, Inc., 1962.

———. *Signs.* Translated by Richard C. McCleary. Evanston, Ill.: Northwestern Univ. Press, 1964. See chapter I, "Indirect Language and the Voices of Silence," and chapter II, "On the Phenomenology of Language."

____. *The Prose of the World.* Translated by John O'Neill. Evanston, Ill.: Northwestern Univ. Press, 1973.

Ogden, C. K., and I. A. Richards. *The Meaning of Meaning.* New York: Harcourt Brace Jovanovich, Inc., 1938.

Ong, Walter, S.J. *The Presence of the Word: Some Prolegomena for Cultural and Religious History.* New York: Simon and Schuster, Inc., 1964.

Pei, Mario. *The Story of Language.* New York: J. B. Lippincott Co., 1949.

Picard, Max. *Man and Language.* Translated by Stanley Goodman. Chicago: Henry Regnery Co., 1963.

Potter, Simeon. *Our Language.* London: Penguin Books, 1961.

Rahner, Karl, S. J. *Spirit in the World.* London: Sheed & Ward, 1968.

Ricoeur, Paul. "The Hermeneutics of Symbols and Philosophical Reflection." In *International Philosophical Quarterly.* Vol. II, 2, 1962.

Robinson, Ian. *The New Grammarian's Funeral: A Critique of Noam Chomsky's Linguistics.* Cambridge: Cambridge Univ. Press, 1975.

Thorpe, W. H. *Bird-Song: The Biology of Vocal Communication and Expression in Birds.* Cambridge: Cambridge Univ. Press, 1961.

____. *Human Nature and Animal Nature.* Garden City, N.Y.: Doubleday & Co., Inc. (Anchor Press), 1974.

Weaver, Richard M. "The Power of the Word." In *Ideas Have Consequences.* Chapter 8. Chicago: Phoenix Books, 1948.

Wheelwright, Philip. *Metaphor and Reality.* Bloomington, Ind.: Indiana Univ. Press, 1962.

____. *The Burning Fountain: A Study in the Language of Symbolism* Rev. ed. Bloomington, Ind.: Indiana Univ. Press, 1968.

Whorff, Benjamin Lee. *Language, Thought and Reality.* Edited by John B. Carroll. Cambridge, Mass.: MIT Press, 1956.

Wittgenstein, Ludwig. *Philosophical Investigations.* Translated by G. E. M. Anscomb. Oxford: B. Blackwell, 1953.

——. *Tractatus Logico-Philosophicus.* Translated by D. F. Pears and B. F. McGuinness. London: Routledge & Paul, 1974.

Chapter 9

Adler, Mortimer J. *The Idea of Freedom.* 2 vols. Garden City, New York: Doubleday & Co., Inc., 1961.

Berofsky, B., ed. *Free Will and Determinism.* New York: Harper & Row Publishers, Inc., 1966.

Bertocci, Peter A., and Richard M. Millard. "The Nature of Human Freedom." In *Personality and the Good.* New York: David McKay Co., Inc., 1963.

Boethius. *The Consolation of Philosophy.* Translated by Richard Green. New York: Library of Liberal Arts, 1962.

Bourke, Vernon J. *Will in Western Thought: An Historico-Critical Survey.* New York: Sheed and Ward, 1964.

Chomsky, Noam. *Problems of Knowledge and Freedom.* New York: Vintage Books, Inc., 1971.

Collins, James. *Descartes's Philosophy of Nature.* Oxford: B. Blackwell, 1971.

Fabro, Cornelio. "Freedom and Existence in Contemporary Philosophy and in St. Thomas." In *The Thomist.* Vol. XXXVIII, 3 (1974): 524-56.

Farrer, Austin. M. *The Freedom of the Will.* London: Black, 1958.

Fromm, Eric. *The Art of Loving.* New York: Harper & Row Publishers, Inc., 1956.

Hampshire, Stuart. *Freedom of the Individual.* New York: Harper & Row Publishers, Inc., 1965.

Hook, Sidney, ed. *Determinism and Freedom in the Age of Modern Science.* New York: New York Univ. Press, 1958.

James, William. *The Moral Philosophy of William James.* Edited by John K. Roth. New York: Thomas Y. Crowell Co., 1969. See especially Part I: "Consciousness and Freedom."

Kane, G. Stanley. "The Free-Will Defense Defended." In *The New Scholasticism.* Vol. L, 4 (1976) 435-46.

Kant, Immanuel. *Critique of Practical Reason.* Translated by Lewis White Beck. New York: The Library of Liberal Arts, 1956.

Lucas, J. R. *The Freedom of the Will.* Oxford: Oxford Univ. Press, 1970.

Nozick, Robert. *Philosophical Explanations.* Cambridge, Mass.: Harvard Univ. Press, 1981. See especially chapter 4, "Free Will."

O'Connor, D. J. *Free Will.* London: Macmillan Publishing Co., Inc., 1972.

Pike, N. "Divine Foreknowledge, Human Freedom, and Possible Worlds." In *Philosophical Review.* Vol. 86 (1977) 209-16.

Ricoeur, Paul. *Freedom and Nature.* Evanston, Ill.: Northwestern Univ. Press, 1966.

Sartre, Jean-Paul. *Being and Nothingness.* New York: Philosophical Library, 1956.

Skinner, B. F. *Walden Two.* New York: Macmillan Publishing Co., Inc., 1948.

——. *Beyond Freedom and Dignity.* New York: Alfred A. Knopf, Inc., 1971.

Wild, John. *Existence and the World of Freedom.* Englewood Cliffs, N. J.: Prentice-Hall, Inc., 1963.

Young, R. *Freedom, Responsibility and God.* London: Macmillan & Co., 1975.

Chapter 10

Aristotle. "Poetics." In *The Basic Works of Aristotle.* Edited by Richard McKeon. Translated by I. Bywater. New York: Random House, Inc., 1941.

Arnold, Magda B. *Emotion and Personality.* 2 vols. New York: Columbia Univ. Press, 1960.

Bedford, Errol. "Emotions." In *Essays in Philosophical Psychology.* Edited by Donald F. Gustafson. Garden City, N. Y.: Doubleday & Co., Inc., 1964.

Bergson, Henri. *Laughter: An Essay on the Meaning of the Comic.* New York: The Macmillan Publishing Co., Inc., 1917.

Bwytendijk, F. J. J. "The Phenomenological Approach to the Problem of Feelings and Emotions." In *Feelings and Emotions.* Edited by M. L. Reynert. New York: McGraw-Hill Book Co., 1950.

Darwin, Charles. *Expression of Emotion of Man and Animals.* Chicago: Univ. of Chicago Press, 1965.

Descartes, René. "The Passions of the Soul." In *The Classical Psychologists.* Edited by Benjamin Rand. Translated by Henry A. D. Torrey. Boston: Houghton Mifflin Co., 1912.

James, William. *Principles of Psychology.* 2 vols. New York: Dover Publications, Inc., 1950.

Koestler, Arthur. *The Act of Creation.* New York: Dell Pub. Co., Inc., 1967. See especially Book I, Part 1, "The Jester."

Langer, Susan K. *Feeling and Form.* New York: Charles Scribner's Sons, 1953.

Leacock, Stephen. *Humor and Humanity: An Introduction to the Study of Humor.* New York: Henry Holt, 1938.

Maritain, Jacques. *Creative Intuition in Art and Poetry.* New York: Pantheon Books, 1953.

Menninger, Karl. *The Vital Balance: The Life Process in Mental Health and Illness.* New York: The Viking Press, Inc., 1963.

Pieper, Josef. *Leisure: The Basis of Culture.* New York: Pantheon Books, 1952.

Plessner, Helmuth. *Laughing and Crying: A Study of the Limits of Human Behavior.* Translated by James Spencer Churchill and Marjorie Grene. Evanston, Ill.: Northwestern Univ. Press, 1970.

Repplier, Agnes. *In Pursuit of Laughter.* Boston: Houghton Mifflin Co., 1936.

Sartre, Jean-Paul. *The Emotions: Outline of a Theory.* Translated by Bernard Frechtman. New York: Philosophical Library, 1948.

Swabey, Marie Taylor. *Comic Laughter, A Philosophical Essay.* New Haven, Conn.: Yale Univ. Press, 1961.

Chapter 11

Adler, Mortimer J. *Art and Prudence: A Study of Practical Philosophy.* New York: Longmans, 1937.

———. *The Difference of Man and the Difference It Makes.* New York: Holt, Rinehart & Winston, Inc., 1967.

Augustine, Aurelius. *Concerning the Teacher.* Translated by George G. Leckie. New York: Appleton-Century-Croft, 1938.

Bronowski, Jacob. *The Visionary Eye: Essays in Arts, Literature and Science.* Cambridge, Mass.: MIT Press, 1978.

Brumbaugh, Robert S., and Nathaniel M. Lawrence. "Education as Growth: Piaget." In *Philosophical Themes in Modern Education.* Boston: Houghton Mifflin Co., 1973.

Buber, Martin. *Between Man and Man.* Translated by R. G. Smith. London: Kegan Paul, 1947.

Castiello, Jaimie, S.J. *A Humane Psychology of Education.* New York: Sheed & Ward, 1936.

Fromm, Erich. *The Revolution of Hope: Toward a Humanized Technology.* New York: Harper & Row Publishers, Inc., 1968.

Gilson, Étienne. *Painting and Reality.* New York: Meridian Books, 1959.

Guardini, Romano. *The End of the Modern World.* Translated by Joseph Theman and Herbert Burke. Chicago: Henry Regnery Co., 1968.

Heidegger, Martin. *The Question Concerning Technology and Other Essays.* Translated by William Lovitt. New York: Harper & Row Publishers, Inc., 1977.

Huyghe, Rene. *Art and the Spirit of Man.* New York: Abraham Artbooks, 1962.

Jaspers, Karl. *Man in the Modern Age.* Translated by Eden and Cedar Paul. Garden City, N.Y.: Doubleday & Co., Inc., 1957.

Johann, Robert. *The Meaning of Love.* Westminster, Md.: The Newman Press, 1959.

Kennick, W. E., ed. *Art and Philosophy: Readings in Aesthetics.* New York: St. Martin's Press, Inc., 1964.

Klubertanz, George P., S.J. *Habits and Virtues.* New York: Appleton-Century-Croft, 1965.

Koestler, Arthur. *The Act of Creation.* New York: Dell Pub. Co., Inc., 1967. See especially Book I, Part 3, "The Artist," and Book II, "Habit and Originality."

Lawrence, Nathaniel M., and Robert S. Brumbaugh. *Philosophers on Education: Six Essays on the Foundations of Western Thought.* Boston: Houghton Mifflin Co., 1963.

Lepp, Ignace. *The Psychology of Loving.* Baltimore: Helicon Press, 1963.

Magee, John B. *Philosophical Analysis in Education.* New York: Harper & Row Publishers, Inc., 1971.

Marcel, Gabriel. *Man Against Mass Society.* Chicago: Henry Regnery Co., 1962.

Maritain, Jacques. *Art and Scholasticism.* Translated by J. F. Scanlan. London: Sheed & Ward, 1946.

Martin, William Oliver. *Realism in Education.* New York: Harper & Row Publishers, Inc., 1969.

Mill, John Stuart. "On Education." In *John Stuart Mill: A Selection of His Works.* Edited by John N. Robson. New York: St. Martin's Press, Inc., 1966.

Park, Joe, ed. *Selected Readings in the Philosophy of Education.* New York: Macmillan Publishing Co., Inc., 1974.

Pieper, Josef. *Fortitude and Temperance.* New York: Pantheon Books, 1948.

_____. *Justice.* New York: Pantheon Books, 1955.

_____. *Prudence.* New York: Pantheon Books, 1959.

Plato. "The Republic" and "Laws." In *The Dialogues of Plato.* Translated by B. Jowett. New York: Random House, Inc., 1937.

Toffler, Alvin. *Future Shock.* New York: Bantam Books, Inc., 1971.

Van Doren, M. *Liberal Education.* New York: Holt, Rinehart & Winston, Inc., 1943.

Whitehead, Alfred North. *The Aims of Education.* New York: The New American Library, Inc., 1950.

Chapter 12

Allport, Gordon W. *The Nature of Personality.* Reading, Mass.: Addison-Wesley Pub. Co., 1950.

Augustine. *Confessions.* Translated by Rex Warner. New York: Mentor-Omega, 1963.

Ayer, A. J. *The Problem of Knowledge.* Baltimore: Penguin Books, Inc., 1956, See especially chapter 5, "Myself and Others."

_____. *The Concept of a Person.* London: Macmillan & Co., 1963.

_____. "One's Knowledge of Other Minds." In *Essays in Philosophical Psychology.* Edited by Donald F. Gustafson. Garden City, N. Y.: Doubleday & Co., Inc., 1964.

Berdyaev, Nicholas. *The Destiny of Man.* Translated by Natalie Duddington. London: Harper & Row Publishers Co., Inc., 1937.

Berne, Eric. *Games People Play: The Psychology of Human Relationships.* New York: Grove Press, Inc., 1964.

Bertocci, Peter A., and Richard M. Millard. "Gordon W. Allport: The Maturing of Personality." In *Personality and the Good.* New York: David McKay Co., Inc., 1963.

Bronowski, Jacob. *The Identity of Man.* Garden City, New York: Natural History Press, 1965.

Buber, Martin. *I and Thou.* New York: Charles Scribner's Sons, 1958.

Castell, Alburey. *The Self in Philosophy.* New York: Macmillan Publishing Co., Inc., 1965.

Chappell, V. C., ed. *The Philosophy of Mind.* Englewood Cliffs, N. J.: Prentice-Hall, Inc. 1962.

Gustafson, Donald, ed. *Essays in Philosophical Psychology.* Garden City, N.Y.: Doubleday & Co., 1964.

Heidegger, Martin. "Letter on Humanism." In *Philosophy in the Twentieth Century.* Vol. 3. Edited by William Barrett and Henry D. Aiken. New York: Random House, Inc., 1962.

Hume, David. *A Treatise of Human Nature.* Edited by L. A. Selby-Bigge. Oxford: The Clarendon Press, 1960. See "On the Idea of the Self," Book I, Part 4, Section 6.

James, William. *Psychology, Briefer Course.* New York: Henry Holt and Co., 1892. See especially chapter XII, "The Self."

Jespersen, Otto. *Mankind, Nation and Individual from a Linguistic Point of View.* London: G. Allen and Unwin, 1954.

Lewis, C. S. *The Abolition of Man.* New York: Macmillan Publishing Co., Inc., 1947.

MacMurray, John. *Persons in Relation.* London: Faber, 1961.

Malcolm, Norman. "Knowledge of Other Minds." In *Essays in Philosophical Psychology.* Edited by Donald F. Gustafson. Garden City, N. Y.: Doubleday & Co., Inc., 1964.

Marcel, Gabriel. *Being and Having.* Translated by Katherine Farrer. London: Dacre, 1949.

——. *Homo Viator.* New York: Harper & Row Publishers, Inc., 1962.

Maritain, Jacques. *Scholasticism and Politics.* New York: Macmillan Publishing Co., Inc., 1940.

——. *The Person and the Common Good.* New York: Charles Scribner's Sons, 1947.

Mill, John Stuart. *A Selection of His Works.* Edited by John M. Robson. New York: St. Martin's Press, Inc., 1966. See especially the chapter, "On Liberty."

Moustakas, Clark E. *Loneliness.* Englewood Cliffs, N.J.: Prentice-Hall, Inc., 1961.

Nedoncelle, Maurice. *Love and the Person.* Translated by Ruth Adelaide. New York: Sheed & Ward, 1966.

O'Neill, J. *Perception, Expression, and History: The Social Phenomenology of Merleau-Ponty.* Evanston, Ill.: Northwestern Univ. Press, 1970.

Reichmann, James B., S.J. "The Created Person." In *The New Scholasticism.* Vol. XXXIII, 1 and 2 (1959) 1-31; 202-30.

——. "Immanently Transcendent and Subsistent Esse: A Comparison." In *The Thomist.* Vol. XXXVIII, 2 (1974) 332-69.

Riesman, David. *The Lonely Crowd.* Garden City, N.Y.: Doubleday & Co., Inc., 1956.

Ruitenbeek, Hendrik M. *The Individual and the Crowd: A Study of Identity in America.* New York: New American Library, 1964.

Scheler, Max. *On the Nature of Sympathy.* London: Routledge and Kegan Paul, 1954.

———. *On the Eternal in Man.* New York: Harper & Row Publishers, Inc., 1960.

Schoemaker, Sydney S. "Personal Identity and Memory." In *Journal of Philosophy.* Vol. LVI. October 1959.

Schuetz, Alfred. "William James' Conception of the Stream of Thought Phenomenologically Interpreted." In *Philosophical and Phenomenological Research.* Vol. II (1941) 442-52.

———. *The Collected Papers of Alfred Schuetz.* The Hague: Martinus Nijhhoff, 1962. See especially, "The Problem of Social Reality." Vol. I. and "The Stranger: An Essay in Social Psychology." Vol. II.

———. *The Phenomenology of the Social World.* Translated by George Walsh and Frederick LeKnert. Evanston, Ill.: Northwestern Univ. Press, 1967.

Strasser, Stephen. *The Idea of Dialogal Phenomenology.* Pittsburgh: Duquesne Univ. Press, 1969.

Strawson, P. F. *Individuals.* Garden City, N. Y.: Doubleday & Co., Inc., 1963.

———. "Persons." In *Essays in Philosophical Psychology.* Edited by Donald F. Gustafson. Garden City, N.Y.: Doubleday & Co., Inc., 1964.

Williams, B. A. O. "Personal Identity and Individuation." In *Essays in Philosophical Psychology.* Edited by Donald F. Gustafson. Garden City, N. Y.: Doubleday & Co., Inc., 1964.

Wittgenstein, Ludwig. *The Blue and Brown Books.* Oxford: Blackwell, 1958.

Chapter 13

Aquinas, Thomas. *The Soul.* Translated by John P. Rowan. St. Louis: Herder, 1949.

330   Philosophy of the Human Person

___ . "On the Nature of the Soul." In *Summa Theologica.* I: Question 75.

Augustine, Aurelius. *On the Immortality of the Soul.* Translated by
George G. Lekie. New York: Appleton-Century-Croft, 1938.

Avicenna. *On the Soul.* Edited and translated by F. Rahman. London: Oxford Univ. Press, 1959.

Broad, C. D. *The Mind and Its Place in Nature.* London: Routledge and Kegan Paul, 1925.

Charon, Jacques. *Death and Western Thought.* New York: Collier Books, 1963.

Chroust, Anton-Hermann. "Aristotle on the Soul." In *The New Scholasticism.* Vol. XLII, 3 (1968) 364-73.

D'Arcy, Martin C., S.J. *Death and Life.* London: Longmans, 1942.

Delaney, C. F. "Sellars and the Contemporary Mind-Body Problem." In *The New Scholasticism.* Vol. XLV, 2 (1971) 245-68.

Ducasse, C. J. *The Belief in Life after Death.* Springfield, Ill.: Charles C. Thomas, 1961.

Flew, Anthony. "Can a Man Witness His Own Funeral?" In *Hibbert Journal* (1956) 242-50.

___ . "Immortality." In *The Encyclopedia of Philosophy.* Vol. III. Edited by Paul Edwards. New York: Macmillan Publishing Co., Inc., 1967.

___ . *Body, Mind, and Death: From Hippocrates to Gilbert Ryle on the Question "What Is Consciousness?"* New York: Macmillan Publishing Co., Inc., 1964.

Frankl, Victor E. *Man's Search for Meaning.* New York: Washington Square Press, 1963.

___ . *The Doctor and the Soul.* Translated by Richard and Clara Winston. New York: Alfred A. Knopf, Inc., 1955.

Geach, Peter. *God and the Soul.* London: Routledge and Kegan Paul, 1969.

James, William. *Human Immortality.* London: Unicorn Press, 1938.

Jaspers, Karl. *The Future of Mankind.* Translated by E. B. Ashton. Chicago: Univ. of Chicago Press, 1961.

___ . *Reason and Existenz.* Translated by William Earle. New York: Noonday Press, 1955.

Jonas, Hans. *The Phenomenon of Life: Toward a Philosophy of Biology.* New York: Harper & Row Publishers, Inc., 1966.

Jung, Karl. *Modern Man in Search of a Soul.* New York: Harcourt Brace, 1933.

Kaufmann, Walter. *Critique of Religion and Philosophy.* New York: Doubleday, Anchor Books, 1961.

Koestler, Arthur. *The Ghost in the Machine.* New York: Macmillan Publishing Co., Inc., 1968.

Kuebbler-Ross, Elizabeth. *Death: The Final Stage of Growth.* Englewood Cliffs, N.J.: Prentice-Hall, Inc., 1975.

___ . *On Death and Dying.* New York: Macmillan Publishing Co., Inc., 1969.

Lamont, Corliss. *The Illusion of Immortality.* 3d ed. New York: Philosophical Library, Inc., 1959.

McLean, George F., O.M.I., ed. "The Human Person." In *Proceedings of the American Catholic Philosophical Association.* Washington, D. C.: The Catholic Univ. of America Press, Inc., Vol. LIII, 1979.

Marcel, Gabriel. "Desire and Hope." In *Readings in Existential Phenomenology.* Edited by Nathaniel Lawrence and Daniel O'Connor. Englewood Cliffs, N.J.: Prentice-Hall, Inc., 1967.

Montagu, Ashley. *Immortality.* New York: Grove Press, Inc., 1955.

Moore, Clifford Herschel. *Ancient Beliefs in the Immortality of the Soul, with Some Account of Their Influence on Later Views.* New York: Cooper Square Pubs., Inc., 1963.

Nozick, Robert. *Philosophical Explanations.* Cambridge, Mass.: The Belknap Press of Harvard Univ. Press, 1981. See especially chapter 6, "The Meaning of Life."

Passmore, John. *Philosophical Reasoning.* New York: Basic Books, Inc., 1969.

Pegis, Anton. *St. Thomas and the Problem of the Soul in the 13th Century.* Toronto: St. Michael's College, 1934.

Perry, John. *Dialogue on Personal Identity and Immortality.* Indianapolis: Hackett Pub. Co., 1978.

Pieper, Josef. *Death and Immortality.* Translated by Richard and Clara Winston. New York: Herder & Herder, 1969.

Plato. "Phaedo." In *Great Dialogues of Plato.* Translated by W. H. D. Rouse. New York: The New American Library, Inc., 1956.

———. "Phaedo." In *The Dialogues of Plato.* 2 vols. Translated by B. Jowett. New York: Random House, Inc., 1937.

Price, H.H. "Survival and the Idea of Another World." In *Exploring Philosophy.* Edited by Peter A. French. Cambridge: Schenkman Publishing Co., Inc., 1972.

Ramsey, Ian. "Persons and Funerals." In *Hibbert Journal.* 1956:330-38.

Royce, Josiah. *The Conception of Immortality.* New York: Greenwood Press, 1968.

Scheler, Max. *Man's Place in Nature.* Translated by Hans Meyerhoff. New York: Noonday Press, 1962.

Schroedinger, E. *What is Life?* New York: Cambridge Univ. Press, 1944.

Shaffer, Jerome. "Mind-Body Problem." In *The Encyclopedia of Philosophy.* Vol. 5. Edited by Paul Edwards. New York: Macmillan Publishing Co., Inc., 1967.

Smythies, J.R., ed. *Brain and Mind.* London: Routledge and Kegan Paul, 1965.

Strasser, Stephan. *The Soul in Metaphysical and Empirical Psychology.* Pittsburgh: Duquesne Univ. Press, 1962.

Taylor, Richard. "How to Bury the Mind-Body Problem." In *American Philosophical Quarterly.* Vol. VI:2. (April 1969).

Thorpe, W. H. *Animal Nature and Human Nature.* Garden City, N. Y.: Anchor Press, 1974.

———. *Purpose in a World of Chance.* New York: Oxford Univ. Press, Inc., 1978.

Toffler, Alvin. *Future Shock.* New York: Bantam Books, Inc., 1970.

Van Kaam, Adrian. "Sex and Existence." In *Review of Existential Psychology and Psychiatry.* Vol. III:2 (1963).

Van Peurson, C. A. *Body, Soul, Spirit.* Translated by H. H. Hoskins. London: Oxford Univ. Press, 1966.

Worth, C. Brooke, and Robert K. Enders. *The Nature of Living Things.* New York: New American Library (Signet), 1955.

Zaehner, R. C. *Matter and Spirit: Their Convergence in Eastern Religions, Marx and Teilhard de Chardin.* New York: Harper & Row Publishers, Inc., 1963.

Zedler, Beatrice G. "Averroes and Immortality." In *The New Scholasticism.* Vol. XXVIII (1954) 436-53.

Chapter 14

Ardrey, Robert. *The Territorial Imperative.* New York: Atheneum Publishers, 1966.

——. *African Genesis: A Personal Investigation into the Animal Origins of Nature and Man.* New York: Orion Press, 1962.

Asimov, Isaac. *Asimov on Astronomy.* Garden City, New York: Doubleday & Co., Inc., 1974.

Ayala, F. J., and T. Dobzhansky, eds. *Studies in the Philosophy of Biology.* Berkeley: Univ. of California Press, 1974.

Bergon, Henri. *Creative Evolution.* Translated by Arthur Mitchell. New York: Henry Holt, 1911.

Bertalanffy, Ludwig von. "Chance or Law?" In *Beyond Reductionism, the Alp-Bach Symposium.* Edited by Arthur Koestler and J. R. Smythies. New York: Macmillan Publishing Co., Inc., 1969.

——. *Problems of Life: An Evaluation of Modern Biological Thought.* London: Watts, 1952.

Birch, Charles. "Chance, Necessity and Purpose." In *Studies in the Philosophy of Biology.* Edited by Francisco Jose Ayala and Theodosius Dobzhansky. Berkeley, Cal.: Univ. of California Press, 1974.

Bok, Bart J. "The Milky Way Galaxy." In *Scientific American.* Vol. 244, 3, March 1981.

Bronowski, Jacob. *The Ascent of Man.* Boston, Mass.: Little, Brown & Co., 1974.

Crick, Francis. *Life Itself: Its Origin and Nature.* New York: Simon & Schuster, 1981.

Dobzhansky, Theodosius. *Heredity and the Nature of Man.* New York: New American Library, 1964.

———. *Genetics of the Evolutionary Process.* New York: Columbia Univ. Press, 1970.

———. "Chance and Creativity in Evolution." In *Studies in the Philosophy of Biology.* Edited by Francisco Jose Ayala and Theodosius Dobzhansky. Berkeley, Cal.: Univ. of California Press, 1974.

Eccles, J. C. *Facing Reality.* London: Longmans, 1971.

Gore, Rick. "The Awesome Worlds within a Cell." In *The National Geographic.* September 1976.

Gould, Jay Stephen. *Ever Since Darwin.* New York: W. W. Norton & Co., Inc., 1977.

———. *Hen's Teeth and Horse's Toes.* New York: W. W. Norton & Co., Inc. 1983.

Grassé, Pierre-P. *Evolution of Living Organisms: Evidence for a New Theory of Transformation.* New York: Academic Press, 1977.

Grene, Marjorie. *Approaches to a Philosophy of Biology.* New York: Basic Books, Inc., 1968.

Halacy, Jr., D. J. *The Genetic Revolution.* New York: Harper & Row Publishers, Inc., 1974.

Himmelfarb, Gertrude. *Darwin and the Darwinian Revolution.* New York: W. W. Norton & Co., Inc., 1959.

Hodge, Paul W. "The Andromeda Galaxy." In *Scientific American.* Vol. 244, 1, January 1981.

Jastrow, Robert. *Red Giants and White Dwarfs.* New York: Harper & Row Publishers, Inc. 1967.

———. *God and the Astronomers.* New York: W. W. Norton & Co., Inc., 1978.

Koestler, Arthur, and F. R. Smythies, eds. *Beyond Reductionism: The Alp-Bach Symposium, 1968.* New York: Macmillan Publishing Co., Inc., 1969.

Kurten, Bjoren. *Not from the Apes.* New York: Pantheon Books, 1972.

Leakey, Louis Seymour Bazlet. *Adam's Ancestors.* New York: Longmans, Green & Co., 1935.

Leakey, Mary. "Footprints in the Ashes of Time." In *The National Georgraphy.* April 1979.

McLuhan, Herbert Marshall. *Understanding Media: The Extensions of Man.* New York: McGraw-Hill Book Co., 1964.

McMullen, Ernan. "Recent Philosophy of Science." In *The New Scholasticism.* Vol. XL (1966) 478-518.

Maddox, John. *Revolution in Biology.* New York: Macmillan Publishing Co., Inc., 1964.

Mayr, E. *Animal Species and Evolution.* Cambridge, Mass.: Harvard Univ. Press , 1963.

Monod, Jacques. *Chance and Necessity: An Essay on the Natural Philosophy of Modern Biology.* Translated by Austryn Wainhouse. New York: Vintage Books, Inc., 1972.

Nogar, Raymond. *The Wisdom of Evolution.* New York: Doubleday & Co., Inc., 1963.

Piaget, J. *Biology and Knowledge.* Chicago: Univ. of Chicago Press, 1971.

Popper, K. R. *Objective Knowledge: An Evoilutionary Approach.* Oxford: The Clarendon Press, 1972.

Rensch, B. *Biophilosophy.* New York: Columbia Univ. Press, 1971.

Rifkin, Jeremy. *Algeny.* New York: Viking Press, Inc., 1983.

Romer, Alfred. *Vertebrate Paleontology.* Chicago: Univ. of Chicago Press, 1966.

Roslansky, J. D., ed. *The Uniqueness of Man.* Amsterdam and London: North Holland Publishing Co., 1969.

Simpson, G. G. *Biology and Man.* New York: Harcourt Brace and World, 1969.

____. *This View of Life: The World of an Evolutionist.* New York: Harcourt Brace and World, 1964.

Stebbins, G. L. *The Basis of Progressive Evolution.* Chapel Hill, N. C., 1969.

Teilhard de Chardin, Pierre, S.J. *The Phenomenon of Man.* New York: Harper & Row Publishers, Inc., 1959.

Thorpe, W. H. *Learning and Instinct in Animals.* London: Methuen, 1963.

———. *Animal Nature and Human Nature.* Garden City, New York: Anchor Press, 1974.

———. *Purpose in a World of Chance.* New York: Oxford Univ. Press, Inc., 1978.

———. "Reductionism in Biology." In *Studies in the Philosophy of Biology.* Edited by Francisco Jose Ayala and Theodosius Dobzhansky. Berkeley: Univ. of California Press, 1974.

Toffler, Alvin. *The Third Wave.* New York: Morrow, 1980.

Tucker, Jonathan B., and Keith R. Porter. "The Ground Substance of the Living Cell." In *Scientific American.* Vol. 224. 3. March 1981.

Van Melsen, Andrew G. *Evolution and Philosophy.* Pittsburgh: Duquesne Univ. Press , 1965.

Whitehead, A. N. *Process and Reality.* London: Macmillan Publishing Co., Inc. 1929.

Wiener, Norbert. *The Human Use of Human Beings: Cybernetics and Society.* Boston: Houghton-Mifflin, 1954; New York: Avon Books, 1967.

Index

5, 106, 107, 111–12; known secondarily, 106–7; and language, 133, 182; and Locke, 33, 39, 110; of necessity, 38, 43; origin of, 31–32, 33, 36–37, 39–40, 48, 133; and Plato, 25, 105; and reasoning, 118; universal, 25, 31, 38, 39, 43, 47, 50, 105, 110. *See also* Essence

Idealism, 37, 46, 47, 49

Images. *See* Sensory image

Images, unattached, 74

Imagination, 43, 73–77, 79–81; in brute animals, 75; creative, 75–77

Immortality, 43, 245–47

Indeterminism: compared to determinism, 162–63; and freedom, 161–64; and Kant, 163; and Sartre, 163

Individuality, 207–8, 252–55

Individuation, problem of, 252–55

Ingestive act, 59, 60

Innate ideas, 25–26, 33, 103, 109–10

Insight, 97–100, 102, 105, 109, 110–11, 112–13, 125, 132, 142–43, 179, 182, 191. *See also* Agent intellect, Intellect, Understanding

Instincts, 86–88, 92–93

Intellect, 66, 67, 103–4, 106–7, 241; active (agent), 27, 104–11; and concept, 111–12; and deliberation, 157–61; formal object of, 94; and judgment, 112–17, 122–25; material object of, 94, 106, 107; passive, 104, 105, 107, 111, 112; and questioning, 105; and reasoning, 117–22; transcendence of, 177; and truth, 112, 113–14. *See also* Intellective act; Intellective habits; Intellective knowledge; Understanding

Intellective act, 109, 111, 112, 113–14, 116–17, 118, 143, 155, 160, 168, 217–18, 228, 244–45, 246

Intellective appetite. *See* Appetite, intellective

Intellective habits, 193–97

Intellective knowledge, 24, 68, 102–25

Intelligible species (form), 104–5, 106, 107, 111–12. *See also* Idea

Intentional union, 60, 107

Interiority (intellective), 240–41

Intersubjectivity (knowledge of others), 214–18; and love, 160

Intussusception, 59

Irascible appetite, 167

Jaspers, Karl, 48

Jastrow, Robert, 265

Judgment, 41, 43, 112–17; and abstraction, 116; affirmative and negative, 116–17; analytic, 41, 42, 43; and being, 115–16, 119–20; and error, 122–25; essential and existential, 115–17; and insight, 112–13, 125; and intellective act, 116–17; mathematical, 43. *See also* Mathematics; negative, 117; probable (proposition), 120–24; and reflection, 113–14; and syllogism, 118–19; synthetic a posteriori, 42; synthetic a priori, 40, 42, 43, 48; and truth, 113, 121; as understanding of understanding, 114

Jurisprudence, 196

Justice, habit of, 197–98

Kant, Immanuel, 29, 40–45, 48; and agent intellect, 107–8, 110; and Aquinas, 105, 106; and Descartes, 40, 43, 44, 45; and Hume, 40, 43–44, 45; and indeterminism, 163; and theory of knowledge, 40–45

Kierkegaard, Søren, 47

Kinesthetic sense (defined), 72

Knowing, philosophical, 1, 3, 20–21, 23, 29, 68, 84

Knowledge: first principle of, 193–94; innate, 34, 39; instinctive, 86–88, 93; intellective, 24, 68, 93–94, 102, 103–4, 105, 119; of others, 214–18;

and questions, 123; sensory, 24, 25, 30, 31, 32, 33–34, 37, 39, 44, 47, 58, 60, 66, 68, 106; unification of, 68, 119; universal, 45, 46–7

Knowledge, theory of: Aquinas, 102–111; Aristotle, 26; Berkeley, 35–37; Democritus, 24; Derrida, 52; Descartes, 30–33, 35, 44; Hume, 38–40, 44, 103; Kant, 40–45; Locke, 33–34, 35, 37; Plato, 24–26, 32

Language, 3, 117, 129–45; and alphabet, 138; ambiguity of, 133–35; of animals, 141–42; and being, 51, 142, 145, 222; defined, 131–33; and education, 135; emotion as, 175; as environmentalization of thought, 145; experiments with chimpanzees, 142; forms of, 129; grammar of, 131–32; hermeneutics viewpoint of, 50, 51; "house of being," 142; and humor, 180–82; intersubjectivity of, 215; intertranslatability of, 136; as inverse of insight, 132, 143; limitations of, 220; listening, form of, 130; and memory, 79; plurality of, 135–36, 142; significance of, 129–31, 133, 140–41; signs of, 131; spoken, 139–40; structure of, 131–32, 136; structuralist viewpoint, 52; tactile, 129; and technology, 143–45; and thought, 130, 133; and time, 140; visual, 129; written, 137–40

Language analysts, 47
Leakey, Louis B., 266–67
Leakey, Mary D., 266, 267–68
Leakey, Richard, 266
Learning, 92, 130; and the animal, 87; as discovery, 27; and habits, 187–204; and instincts, 87; as recollection, 25
Leibniz, Gottfried, 45, 238
Leisure, 179

Life, 226–29; in the universe, 264–66; on planet earth, 266–70
Likeness, intellective. See Intelligible species
Living things, unity of, 229–33
Locke, John, 29, 33–35; and agent intellect, 110; and Aristotle, 34; and Berkeley, 35, 36; and Descartes, 35; and Hume, 39; and ideas, 33, 39; primary and secondary qualities of, 34–35, 36
Loneliness, 220–22
Lonergan, B. J., 202
Love: community of, 218–19; and justice, 198; meaning of, 160
Lysosomes, 230

Maddox, John, (on proteins), 230
Marcel, Gabriel, 48
Material forms. See Forms, material
Materialism, 24, 151
Material object (thing), 37; of coordinating sense, 73; of evaluative sense, 85; formal cause of knowledge, 25, 27, 103–4; of imagination, 74; of memory, 79
Materialist monism, 236–37, 250
Mathematics, 29, 30, 31, 33, 35, 40, 42, 43, 44, 45
Matter: Berkeley, 37; human influence on, 143
Mechanism. See Materialist monism
Memorative act, characteristics of, 74–75, 77–78. See also Memory
Memory, 77–82; and the animal, 82; and communication, 79; and emotions, 177; and forgetting, 83; formal object of, 79; and imagination, 78; and intellect, 79; material object of, 79; and personal identity, 79, 81–82; and the real, 80; and time, 74, 79
Mendel, Gregor, 255

CPSIA information can be obtained at www.ICGtesting.com
Printed in the USA
BVOW01s1900280816

460360BV00003B/319/P